Gunsmiths of Louisiana

James Biser Whisker
and
John R. Coe

Create Space 2018

printed in the United States of America
Create Space/ Amazon

This work is most respectfully dedicated to
Kit Gorman

We never had the pleasure of meeting Ms Gorman, but we are much impressed by her research as exhibited in her
New Orleans Gunsmiths and Gun Dealers Until 1900
posthumously published as a memorial by her husband,
Phil Bazer

Introduction

It is impossible to overstate the importance of Kit Gorman whose posthumously published *New Orleans Gunsmiths and Gun Dealers* covered its subject thoroughly. It is simply time consuming to read city directories and the census starting in 1850; it is far more difficult to plough through obituaries and death records. Kate gave us dates of birth [from census usually] and death for all from whom it was possible to gain such information. She also gave us an enormous quantity of trade advertisements as well as in-depth analysis of the gunsmiths.

Apparently the earliest directory for New Orleans was dated 1805, but it contained no occupational reference. Beginning in 1811 the directories carried addresses and occupations. In my decades of research I have never encountered such frequent turnover as occurred in New Orleans. Gunsmiths regularly appear in only a single directory, here today and gone tomorrow.

The United States Census is useful beginning only in 1850, the first year in which occupations were given in most jurisdictions along with the names of all family members. I used all the available censuses of 1850, 1860, 1870, and 1880. The census taken in 1890 was destroyed. There is, to my knowledge no state census in Louisiana.

The draft records were transcribed from microfilms and Xeroxes of the original *Daily Picayune*, published between March 3 and April 22, 1865, by Colleen Fitzpatrick. Some of the print is not in optimum condition, and it is hard to read. I assume these were draftees into the Yankee Army since New Orleans had been occupied for several years at this point. Also very useful were the records of the charity hospital in Orleans Parish. These records tell us something important: of the 39 recorded tradesmen of interest to us only 3 are otherwise listed, e.g., in directories and census. There must have been quite a few gunsmiths and allied tradesmen not listed in any source available to us. *Booth's Index to Confederate Soldiers of Louisiana* yielded a few names complete with CSA service record, but little to nothing was recorded after the war.

I had developed a checklist of Louisiana gunsmiths before I became aware of Ms Gorman's book. Michael Carrick of *Gun Report* sent me Ms Gorman's information on Valentine Libeau after I had published an article on him in *Muzzle Blasts*. I had added Ms Gorman's book in two cases: first, if I did not have a name of which she was a source; second when she had substantially more information than I had. Incidentally, I should have loved to have corresponded with her on Libeau partially because I do not think her man is the same man who naturalized in Bedford County, Pennsylvania, my home area.

Ms Gorman listed quite a few hardware stores, "fancy shops," variety stores, and commission agents who handled firearms on occasion or with regularity. In previous books I never listed such shops unless there was some compelling reason to do so, e.g., the store sold guns on consignment marking them with the store's logo. My guess is that the various shops listed by Ms Gorman in no way marked the imported shotguns, muskets, pistols, etc. Frankly, Belgian and English imported arms hold absolutely no interest for me. There were two shops that drew my attention. According to Ms Gorman D. DeGoicouria was a commission agent and dealer 1859-61, New Orleans. Among arms related items he offered were Mississippi rifles (altered) so one wonders which alteration?

The second merchant that drew my attention was Duperu & Blanchard, hardware and gun dealers. 1839, 32 New Levee, New Orleans. Kit Gorman observed the business was not listed in any directory and evidently did not last long. Among the more interesting items the firm advertised were "silver mounted rifles of American manufacture." In my West Virginia gunsmiths book I cited a bill of lading from the McCamant family of Wellsburg. They shipped rifles to New Orleans by flatboat in this era. James Clark of Ohio also sold his beautifully silver-mounted rifles in the South.

One German gunsmith in New Orleans is variously described, in successive years and at the same address, as a gunsmith, machinist, smith, ironworker, and locksmith. The truth is simply that the man performed whatever tasks his talents allowed. Many others left the arms trade, becoming clerks, merchants, commission agents, and whatever else they could do to support themselves and their families.

Regarding the New Orleans street called Conti or Cande, I have no idea why the two spellings are used even in the same directory or which was correct in the early- to mid-19th century. I used whatever spelling found in the directory. Spelling of various names are also suspect at times, but again I have used what appears in the document. Circus Street became Rampart Street in 1856.

Free people of color held a number of occupations including carpenters, shoemakers, blacksmiths, gunsmiths and whigmakers, and executioners to name but a few, but most of their names have been lost. For example, in 1791 there was a Creole gunsmith in New Orleans whose name is unknown. In 1795 about half of New Orleans carpenters, joiners, silversmiths, and smiths were free blacks. The LaTour family is probably the best known group of gunsmiths who were persons of color. There were more African-American gunsmiths in Louisiana than in any other state I have researched. Moreover, they seemed not to have experienced prejudice and thus sold their products to buyers of all races. Most of the quality arms black gunsmiths made were made in Louisiana.

James B Whisker

Bibliography

Booth, Andrew. *Booth's Index to Confederate Soldiers of Louisiana*[New Orleans, 1920].
Gardner, Robert. *Small Arms Makers* [New York: Crown, 1963[
Gorman, Kit. *New Orleans Gunsmiths and Gun Dealers to 1900* [privately published, 2005]
Mills, Donna Rachal. *Biographical and Historical Memoirs of Natchitoches Parish, Louisiana* [Heritage Press].
Biographical and Historical Memoires of Northwest Louisiana. [Baton Rouge: Claitor's Publishing Division, 1975].
Noble, Jerry. *Notes on Southern Long Rifles*. 4 vols. [privately printed].

The Constitutionality of the famous law prohibiting the sale pf pistols and revolvers in the State of Arkansas has been resolved in favor of the law. A test case of a gunsmith who sold a revolver to another gunsmith resulted in both parties being arrested and fined $50 apiece. Let such a law be passed in Louisiana [*Colfax Chronicle*, Grant Parish, Louisiana, 10 December 1881].

Rev. J. H. Ingraham probably fatally wounded. . . . Rector of Christ Church, Holly Springs, met with a most painful and probably fatal accident last Saturday afternoon. . . . Some unknown persons having been seen prowling about his premises, he was persuaded to have a pistol belonging to his son loaded. It was wrapped up in a piece of paper by the gunsmith and placed in his coat pocket. Having gone to the Church for some purpose, and wishing to put the pistol in a more secure place, he took it from the pocket, when it slipped out of the paper and fell on the floor. The hammer striking first it was discharged, the ball inflicting a severe wound in the right thigh, just below the crotch, and ranging upward lodged, it is supposed, in the hip near the spinal column. . . . he has grown much worse and but little hope is entertained for his recovery [*Baton Rouge Daily Gazette*, 21 December 1860]

Biographical Entries

Abbott, Elias. gunsmith. 1917, New Orleans [*Dir.*].

Ackerman, Louis W. (1831-1891). lock- and gunsmith. 1852-91, New Orleans. Census of 1870, Louis Ackerman, locksmith, 39; Victoria, wife, 29; both born in Prussia; Bertha, 9; John, 8; Augusta, 6; Emma, 4, all born in LA. Victoria's full name is Catherine Victorie Hammer Ackermann. Census of 1880, Louis Ackerman, locksmith, 48, born Prussia; Catharine, wife, 46, born in Baden; Bertha, 19; Philip, 17; Augusta, 16; Charles, 8; Katie, 6; Victor, 1, all born in Louisiana. 1861-66, machinist at 303 Elysian Fields. 1870, locksmith, same address. 1876, locksmith, 168 St. Louis. On 5 April 1880 Ackermann married the widow Catharina Schneider [*Dirs*; Gorman].

Ackermann Obituary. On Sunday, July 12, 1891 at 1:30 o'clock .Louis W. Ackermann, aged 60 years, a native of Germany and a resident of this city for the past thirty-nine years. The friends and acquaintances of the Schneider, Beck, Hamer, Mace and Miller families also the officers and members of the Louisiana Benevolent Association are respectfully invited to attend the funeral which will take place This (Monday) Evening at 4 o'clock from the late residence of the deceased, No. 39 South Villere, near Common street. [*Daily Picayune*, 13 July 1891 He was born about 1831 in Hamburg, Germany and arrived 1849 in America

Adam, John B. (1760-1842) goldsmith. 1811-23, New Orleans [M.E. S.D.A.]. Listed as g.s., which may be goldsmith or gunsmith.

Adams, Anthony (1836-). cabinet maker, gunsmith, machinist. 1857-90, New Orleans. Census of 1890, carpenter, east side Villeré, between street Louis and Toulouse. Census of 1900, ward 5: Anthony Adam, born in Italy emigrated in 1857, 65, born in January 1836, widower; Anna Crukin, lodger, 30. [*Dirs*; Gorman].

Afinger, Bernard. gunsmith. 1872, rear 46 Villere, 2nd district, New Orleans [*Dir.*].

Aitken, James Henderson. (1832-). lock- and gunsmith, plumber. Census of 1870, 205 Gravier, New Orleans. Aitken was born in Liverpool, England, and arrived in New Orleans on 3 July 1834, with his parents. 1890, plumber and pipe fitter, 190 Camp St. The business was carried on by his sons into the 20th century. Date of death unknown, but after 1911, but he was buried at Greenwood Cemetery, New Orleans [Ancestry; *Dir.*].

Albert, Frank. gunsmith. 1875, 54 St. Anthony, New Orleans [*Dir.*].

Albert, Henry (1832--1869). gun- and locksmith. 1870, 149 Baronne, New Orleans; with Henry Birrcher. Although his name appears in the 1870 directory, Henry Albert died on 15 Jun 1869 in New Orleans [Ancestry; *Dir.*].

Alexis, Bernard. gunsmith. 1832, 124 Amour St., New Orleans [*Dir.*].

Alexis, M. cutler. 1851, St. Mary's Market, New Orleans [*Dir.*].

Allany, Robert. gunsmith. 1846, Love St., New Orleans [*Dir.*].

Allen & Hills. gunsmiths. 1842, 79 Magazine; 1855, 89 Magazine, New Orleans [*Dir.*]. Charles Hills, same address. Joseph Allen & Charles Hills. 1858, Gun makers Guns, Rifles & Pistols made to order & repaired; also all kinds of Materials for the Trade No. 89 Magazine St.

To Rifle Shooters. For Sale One of Edwin Wesson's superior target rifles with telescopic and globe sights and all the equipment in perfect order. It will be guaranteed a perfect instrument in every respect, and will be sold at a great sacrifice, the present owner having no further use for it. It can be seen at Allen & Hill's, gunsmiths, 79 Magazine street [*Daily Crescent*, 18 November 1850].

Allen, Charles. gun- and locksmith. 1842, 79 Magazine St., New Orleans [*Dir.*]. Letter at the post office for Charles Allen, gunsmith [*Times Picayune*, 23 July 1847]

Allen, Joseph (1816-1860). gunsmith. Partner in Allen & Hille. June 14, 1862: On Friday morning, 13th Inst. at 3 o'clock, died of consumption, Jos. G. Allen, aged 44 years, a native of Belfast, Ireland. June 13, 1862 [Ancestry; Gorman].

Alloway, ---. gunsmith. 1830, 99 Tchoupitoulas, New Orleans. This may be John Alloway, machinist, born about 1799, departed from Belize, arrived in New Orleans on 22 November 1830 [Ancestry; *Dir.*].

Althaus, Henry (1815--1894). jeweler and gunsmith. 1860-69, Levee near Jefferson, New Orleans. Listed only twice as a gunsmith. Henry was born in Bremen, Germany and arrived in America on 19 January 1852. Census of 1860: Henry Althaus, 40, watchmaker; Anna, 46; Henry, 16; Amelia, 14; Julius, 11; Matilda, 9, all born in Germany; and Augustus, 4, born in Texas [Ancestry; *Dir.*].

Ames, Francois (1810--1860). gunsmith. New Orleans. Ames died in November 1860 in Orleans Parish, age 50, born in France [Mortality Schedule; Ancestry].

Ancard, Joseph (c.1809-). gunsmith. 1821, apprenticed to Christophe Biot, gunsmith and cutler, New Orleans. African-American tradesman. Census of 1840, Plaquemines Parish: Joseph Ancard head of household of 3 free persons of color. Census of 1880, Joseph Ancard, farmer, mulatto, Plaquemines Parish [Ancestry; Gorman].

Anderson, Emil. lock- and gunsmith. 1865, New Orleans. Anderson was implicated in a robbery scheme [*New Orleans Times*, 24 March 1865].

Angel, Carl M. (1821-). gunsmith. New Orleans. Census of 1850, Carl M. Angel, born in Prussia, gunsmith, age 29, was admitted to the charity hospital [Ancestry].

Anet, F. gunsmith. 1851, St. Claude between Phillip and Ursulines, New Orleans [*Dir.*].

Argote, Edmond. gunsmith. 1822, 23 St. Peter; 1823, 67 St. Peter, New Orleans [*Dirs.*; Gorman].

Armstrong & Company. New Orleans, Colonel James Armstrong, proprietor. James Armstrong (1821-1891) conducted a large establishment at the corner of Erato and New Levee Sts. which produced all types of machinery. Some projectiles were cast but there is no evidence that cannon were turned out. After the war Armstrong associated himself with John Roy and continued operations at the old location [*New Orleans Times*, April 22, 1866].

Arnaud, Vincent. gunsmith. 1834, Thomas St., New Orleans, noted as a gunsmith. Census of 1830: Vincent Arnaud, slave holder with 1 female slave, 1 white male 40-49, 1 slave female, 24 to 35 [*Dir*; Gorman].

Arnault, J. black- and gunsmith. Doing business as Bolet & Arnaux, blacksmiths, 106 Custom House, New Orleans. In 1867, Jacques Bolet became partners with J. Arnaux, another Frenchman, who may have been related to Jacques Bolet. The partnership lasted only a year or so. His shop was located in the commercial district.

Arnold, Michael (1828-1913). armorer. Fort Worth. Michael Arnold was born in France and emigrated to America in 1846. He worked at the arsenal at Baton Rouge and later at Fort Worth. He was employed by the federal government in making and repairing arms for over 35 years and at his death may have been the oldest federal employee. He died at Philadelphia [*Fort Worth Star-Telegram*, 14 July 1913]

Assante, Jean. gunsmith. 1841, St. Anthony, New Orleans [*Dir.*; Gorman].

Aubert, Pierre (1664-). locksmith. 1722, New Orleans, with a wife and 7 children. Pierre Aubert age 55 settled in Louisiana in 1719 [French Census; Ancestry].

Audrain, Narcisse (1801-1841). gunsmith. 1837-41, Royal St., New Orleans. 1840, ward 1: 4 white persons, 1 slave. Gorman notes that he was the operator of a dry goods store but his death certificate listed him as a manufacturer of knives and armor. He died on 25 September 1841 in New Orleans [Gorman; Ancestry].

Auer, Xavier (1828-). gunsmith. 1850-61, New Orleans. 1857-58, 49 Girod; 1859-61, 119 Tchoupitoulas, New Orleans. On 13 March 1855 Xavier was granted American citizenship, renouncing his former allegiance to Bavaria [Ancestry; Gorman; *Dir.*].

Ausonne, Bernard (1735-). armorer. 1770, New Orleans, militia list [Gorman].

Avet, Ferdinand (1802-). gunsmith. 1850-56, St. Claude, near Ursulines, New Orleans . Census of 1850, ward 7: Ferdinand Avet, blacksmith, 48; Jeanne, wife, 61; Pierre, 15, all born in the Piedmont, Italy. Census of 1860 of Lafourche, Assumption Parish: Ferdinand Avet, 56, turner, living alone [Gorman; *Dirs.*].

Babcock, John Nelson (1830-1864). gunsmith. 1855-56, 177 Circus; 1857, 177 Rampart; 1858, 239 Rampart; 1860, Magnolia; 1861-66, 260 Rampart, New Orleans. In 1860 his apprentice John Wesson was in Babcock's household. Babcock was born in NY [*Dir.* Census; Gorman]. "Maker of the increasing twist rifle" [*Daily Creole*, 12 November 1856]. John N. Babcock died on 31 May 1864, age 34 [Ancestry]. There was a John Babcock who enlisted in the 13th Connecticut Infantry, Union Army, on 21 May 1862 so he may have been killed in action.

Bader, John (1823-), armorer. Private, Company G, 1st LA Infantry. Bader enlisted on 2 May 1861. August 4,1862, discharged under Act of 6 April 1862, being over age 40. Bader was born in Germany and also claimed exemption as a foreign national. Single. Residence New Orleans. There was a John Bader, cabinet maker, in New Orleans in the 1870s [Ancestry].

Baensiger, Ferdinand. gunsmith. 1892, 56 Perdido, New Orleans [*Dir.*].

Baezinger, Ferdinand. gunsmith. 1892, New Orleans [*Dir.*].

Bagot, Paul. gunsmith. 1834, 76 St. Claude, New Orleans [*Dir.*; Gorman].

Bailey, Edward. gunsmith. 1879, 129 Carondelet Walk, New Orleans [*Dir.*].

Bailey, John B. gunsmith. 1891-94, Gretna St., New Orleans [*Dir.*].

Bailey, John Edward (1833-1909). gunsmith. New Orleans. John was a son of gunsmith Thomas Bailey and came to American from England when John was 7. In 1861 he joined the 2nd Regiment, 2nd Brigade, Louisiana Militia in the Glorious Cause. He worked initially with his father but in 1867 he ran an ad stating that he was now "to be found at the store of H. P. Buckley, 8 Camp." 1879, gunmaker, rear 129 Carondolet, with T. Bailey. Census of 1880, Ed Bailey, son of Thomas, New Orleans, age: 46, born in England, divorced, gun maker, living with Thomas. 1887, 84 Baronne St. 1 May 1890, John Edward Bailey, born about 1834, married the widow of George Meister. He worked at various addresses until about 1900. He moved to Ponchatoula, Tangiphoa Parish, where he did a thriving business. He died there at age 76. His wife had been horribly burned and died from her injuries. She was ironing clothes when they caught fire. Her husband attempted to extinguish the fire, failed, but was terribly burned himself. Both were removed to a charity hospital when they died [*Times Picayune*, 15 October 1909; Gorman; *Dirs.*]. 1893-94, Gretna, New Orleans [*Dir.*].

Bailey, John W. gunsmith. 1874, 129 Carondelet, New Orleans [*Dir.*].

Bailey, Thomas Sr (1810-). gunsmith. 1846, 110 Chartres; 1851, 106 Chartres, New Orleans; 1861, 98 Chartres. Thomas was born in England, departed Liverpool and arrived in America on 14 November 1840. Sons Thomas, Jr. and John E. were both gunsmiths. Gorman thought Thomas, Sr., left New Orleans about 1861 although his sons remained. Census of 1880, Thomas Bailey, widower, born in England, gun maker; Ed Bailey, 46; Ida Smith, 19; Robert Smith, 27; Mary O'Donnell, 23 [*Dirs.*; Gorman].

Guns! Guns! Guns! Thomas Bailey, Gunsmith, 106 ½ Chartres street, begs leave to inform his numerous friends and customers that he has just returned from Europe, bringing with him a great variety of Guns, and Sports Men's apparatus, generally consisting in part of – fine guns made under his own supervision, in the best establishments in London. Ely's caps and ammunition. Dixon & Son's flasks and pouches . . . In addition to the above he has a number of the celebrated Enfield Rifles, which send a ball 1100 yards with effect. Customers and the public are invited to call before purchasing elsewhere [*Times Picayune*, 13 January 1858]

Bailey, Thomas, Jr. (1838-). gunsmith. 1865-84, New Orleans. 1865, 156 Basin St., in partnership with G. G. Hille, doing business as Bailey & Hille. Tom served an apprenticeship with his father; brother of John E. Bailey. The 1880 Census of Industry showed he employed only one man, himself, produced $750 worth of guns, paid $150 in wages, and used $50 in raw materials. John and Thomas Jr worked together on occasion, e.g., 1879, both at 129 Carondelet. Census of 1880, Thomas Bailey, gun smith, born in England, 42; Margaret, 34; Lilly, 16; William; 13; Edward, 9; Elizabeth, 5; Caroline, 2 [Gorman; *Dirs*.]. A presumed customer stole a pistol valued at $25 from Bailey's gunshop [*Times Picayune*, 17 June 1851]. Bailey constructed a needle-fire gun similar to Dreyse's rifle, but had several problems with it [*Ibid*., 5 August 1866]

Baiteavoc, Arthur (1843-). gunsmith. 1880, Baton Rouge, East Baton Rouge Parish. Census of 1880: Arthur Baiteavoc, 37, gunsmith, born in Louisiana; Although he was reported as a married man he lived in a huge hotel with perhaps 30 others.

Baldwin & Company. hardware dealers. Camp at Common, New Orleans. The firm began as Rogers, Sill & Slocomb. Sill died in 1822 and it became Rogers, Slocomb & Company. In 1834 it became S. B. Slocomb & Company. Samuel B. Slocomb died in the autumn of 1834 so the firm's name was changed to Slocomb, Richards & Company. In 1841 Richard Montgomery and R. Richards named the firm Richards & Montgomery. In 1854 it became Richards, Slocomb & Company, with the addition of Cuthbert H. Slocomb. In 1858 Richards withdrew so the firm became C. H. Slocomb & Company. Following the Civil War the firm again sold guns and in 1867 it became Slocomb, Baldwin & Company with the addition of Albert Baldwin. Slocomb died in 1873 so the firm became A. Baldwin & Company. Finally, it was incorporated as A. Baldwin & Company, Ltd. No wonder it could advertise in 1925 that it had offered guns and gunsmithing for over 100 years. "Our repairing and service department is conducted under the supervision of an expert gunsmith" [*Times Picayune*, 23 November 1925; Gorman].

Bandle, [Jacob] Christian (1828-). lock- and gunsmith. 1851, New Orleans. Admitted to charity hospital with "int. fever" born in Wűrtemburg, Germany on 29 June 1828. He emigrated in 1848 and had worked in Cincinnati, Ohio. He married Josephine Waltzer [Ancestry].

Barbaret, Aceton (1792-). gunsmith. 1851, New Orleans. Admitted to charity hospital with cancer of the face; born in Santa Domingo. There was a J. T. Barbaret, born about 1792, who arrived in Louisiana from Havana on 29 March 1820 [Ancestry].

Barbaret, Théon. gold- and gunsmith. 1817-40, New Orleans. 1822, 42 Toulouse; 1823-27, 114 Toulouse; 1830, 197 Common. In 1817 he ran an ad referring to his work with his un-named brother. Perhaps that man was Aceton, above. Gorman refers to the 1850 Census listing of Theo Barbaré, born in Santa Domingo, in the household of Joseph Latil. This makes it all the more probable that Aceton and Theon were brothers. 1824, Théon gun & goldsmith armurier et orfevre, 114 Toulouse [*Dirs.*; Ancestry].

Barbino, Bethelmy. cutler. 1879, New Orleans [*Dir.*].

Barefield, William (1820-1862). gunsmith. western district, Bienville Parish. Census of 1850, William Barefield, 30, born in Arkansas, gunsmith; Elizabeth C., 41, born in South Carolina; Hester, 6; James, 4; Louisa, 3; all born in Louisiana. In the same household there were six apparently unrelated laborers. William S. Barefield, private, 11th Georgia Infantry, enlisted on July 3, 1861, died of disease in a Culpeper, Virginia, hospital January 5, 1862 [Ancestry].

Barelli, Joseph Albino (1800-1858). arms merchant. 1837-58, New Orleans; doing business as Barelli & Company. Joseph emigrated from Como, Italy, to Charleston, South Carolina, in 1825 and was naturalized on 26 October 1825. Subsequently he moved to New Orleans. In 1843 he offered muskets, rifles, and pistols. Barelli died on 1 June 1858 in New Orleans [Ancestry; Gorman].

Barker, Joseph (c.1803--1880). cutler and gunsmith. Houston. Joseph was born on 13 February 1803 in England. 1851, 81 St. Charles; lives on Barrone St. 1849-72, New Orleans, Louisiana. Census of 1860, ward 11 New Orleans: Joseph Barker, born in England, 57, gunsmith; Sarah, 22, born in England; Sarah A, wife, 40. Census of 1880 in Houston, Texas: Joseph Barker, retired gunsmith, born in England; wife Sara, age 72. Joseph died on 10 October 1880 in Houston and was buried in Glenwood Cemetery [Ancestry; Kit Gorman; *Dirs.*].

Barnard, Libena (1830--1863). gunsmith. Bonham, Fannin County. Census of 1850: L. Barnard, 20, gunsmith, born in North Carolina, son of Elihu. Census of 1860 of Jackson Parish, Louisiana: Libena B Barnard, gunsmith, age 30. Libena enlisted at the beginning of the Second War for Independence and served in the Ninth Louisiana Infantry. He was killed on 4 July 1863 at the Battle of Gettysburg [Ancestry]. (His Christian name was based on the 1860 Census).

Barnes, John (1843-). locksmith. New Orleans. Barnes, born about 1844, departed Holland via Liverpool, England, arriving in New Orleans on 2 August 1850. On 12 September 1865 Barnes was mustered out of the Union Army, having enlisted as a private and rose to lieutenant. 1878, rear 270 N. Derbigny, New Orleans; works for F. Frick [Ancestry; *Dir.*].

Bassettt, W. (1840-1869). gunsmith. 1868-69, 230 Rampart, New Orleans. He died at age 29 and was a native of London [*Dirs.*; Gorman].

Bastian, J. gunsmith. after 1824, Alexandria, Rapides Parish.

In 1814 Samuel G. Bastian was born in this city [Anaconda, Montana] . . . When he was 10 years of age his father, who was a gunsmith, removed to Alexandria, in Louisiana, and today after an absence of 63 years, the son revisits his birthplace, a stalwart man of 77 years. His career has been a most eventful one. He is without doubt the only surviving American who witnessed the fall of the Alamo in the Texas revolution of 1836. . . .When J. lived at Alexandria it was a frontier town and the abiding place of many of the worst ruffians in the southwest. Prominent among those was [James] Bowie.. He devoted himself to forging land titles. . . . [William B.]Travis was a very decent man, but Bowie was in effect a bully, gambler, cut-throat, and thief, and to tell the truth one-half of the garrison [Alamo] were fugitives from justice. . . [*Anaconda Standard*, 23 October 1889].

Bastian, Michael (1827-1881). lock and gunsmith. New Orleans. 1861, 166 Girod, locksmith. 1867, 263 Rampart, hardware. 1877, blacksmith, 16 Carondelet Walk. Michael was born about 1827 and died on 8 August 1881 in New Orleans [Ancestry; *Dirs.*].

Baugnut, A. locksmith. 1865, 25 Orleans, New Orleans; drafted into the Union Army.

Baynham, William (1832-1868). watchmaker. 1853-68, New Orleans. William sold guns in his "fancy store." [Gorman; *Dirs.*]. As a skilled tradesman he might easily have repaired guns unlike most dry goods salesmen.

Beck, H. gunsmith. 1851-53, 27 St. Phillip, New Orleans [*Dir*.].

Beckett, Aaron (1794-). locksmith. 1851, New Orleans. Beckett was admitted in 1851 to the charity hospital; age 55, born in Liverpool, England.

Becquet, Jean Baptiste Nicolas. blacksmith and locksmith 1722, New Orleans. Jean was the son of a locksmith in Paris. He was married and his wife Catherine was listed on the ship's manifest as a laundress from Poitou. There is a letter from Jean Francois Nicolas Becquet at Fort de Chartres, 1722 to Francoise Masse, widow Becquet in Paris, regarding his forthcoming trip up the Mississippi River.

Bell, Lloyd C. (1834-). gunsmith. Census of 1870, Twp. 4, Pike County, Mississippi. Lloyd C Bell, gunsmith, 31; Mary J, 31; John H, 9; Anna C, 7; Lloyd C, 4, all born in Virginia; Mary J, 2; Joseph E, 7 months, both born in Mississippi. Census of 1880, Covington, Saint Tammany Parish: Lloyd Bell, born in Virginia, gun smith, 46; Delia, 36, his wife; Annie, 17; Mamie, 11; Joseph, 9; George, 8. In Pike County Bell accidentally shot a man while repairing a gun [*Memphis Avalanche*, 29 December 1868. 1887, 160 Chartres, New Orleans; 1891, 207 St. Mary's; 1892, 268 Camp [Ancestry; *Dirs*.].

Bell, Louis C. gunsmith. 1890, 207 St. Mary, New Orleans [*Dir*.].

Bellew, William M. (1808--1892). gunsmith. Catahoula Parish. William was born on 9 July 1808. Census of 1850, William M. Bellew, 44, gunsmith, born in Tennessee; Nancy A., 28, his wife, born in LA; Thomas, 10, born in Louisiana; and Samuel Swazey, 19, mechanic, born in Mississippi. William died on 21 April 1892 in Adams County, Illinois [Ancestry; Find-a-Grave].

Bello, Peter (-1824). mathematical instrument maker. 81 Charles St., New Orleans. While Bello leaned toward scientific [then called philosophical] devices, such as hydrometers and telescopes, he also sold firearms, cane guns, dirks, and cane swords. Bello was a jeweler in New York City in 1820. He may have come to New Orleans principally to foster free black emigration to Haiti [*Dir*.; Gorman].

Emigration to Hayti. Information for free people of color inclined to emigrate to Hayti. All classes and descriptions of Free People of Color, of good character, are included in the liberal invitation of President Boyer. . . . Those who go as mechanics, traders, clerks, or school masters will be assigned in their different professions, and the expenses of their passages paid on their coming under engagement to repay in 6 months. 40 colored mechanics, such as carpenters, timber sawyers, blacksmiths, caulkers, rope makers &c. capable of building and equipping small vessels are also immediately wanted, to whom liberal encouragement is offered. . . .All religious professions are tolerated and men left at full liberty to worship the Almighty Creator according to the dictates of their own consciences, and through the medium of their own forms and ceremonies, provides they do not disturb the public tranquility. All letters and communications on the subject of the emigration of free people of color to the Island of Hayti, from this quarter must be directed to Mr. Peter Bello, No. 81 Charles street, New Orleans [*Wilkinson County News*, 21 September 1824]

Bender, Conrad. gunsmith. 1865, 119 New Levee, New Orleans; drafted. Also seen as Bendré.

Bender, Jacob. locksmith. 1861, 110 Prytania, New Orleans [*Dir.*].

Bennett & Surges:. arms makers. New Orleans. This firm made a few heavy iron cannon and bronze field pieces just prior to fall of the city in April 1862. [O.R. Series I, Volume 6, page 577-6]. Examination by Major-General Lovell

Question. What was the quality of the iron offered by Messrs. Leeds & Co., Bennett & Surges, and others for casting heavy guns when you made inquiries on the subject, and what amount had they on hand that was fit for that purpose?
Answer. The best opinion I can offer as to the quality of that used by Bennett & Surges is that it was good, as a gun made by them had been tested by the military authorities and approved. Messrs. Bujac & Bennett had a large amount of Tennessee iron, part of which they tendered to us to be used by other foundries, so as to expedite the making of heavy guns in the event of such shops getting out of iron. I know nothing more as to the quantity and quality of iron to be used in making heavy guns.
Question. How many such lathes and furnaces had Bennett & Surges, and what time is necessary to cast and bore an 8-inch Columbiad?
Answer. They had no lathes completed, but one was nearly done for boring large guns. I do not know that they had more than one furnace. A lathe in the machine shop of the Jackson and Great Northern Railroad and another in the Shakespeare foundry, through the exertions of the committee, were placed at their disposal. I am a novice in such matters, but should think that thirteen days would be sufficient to cast and bore such a gun-five days and nights..."
[Chapter XVI: *Capture of New Orleans*, 577-6 Series I. Vol. 6. Serial No. 6]

Benthall, T. W. (1835--). gunsmith. 1888, McCool, Attala County, Mississippi [*Choctaw Plaindealer*]. T W Benthall was a private in Company C, Third Louisiana Cavalry (Harrison's), C. S. A. He was captured, imprisoned, and paroled at Monroe, Louisiana, on June 13, 1865. His residence then was in Caldwell Parish, Louisiana. Census of 1870 of Richland Parish, Louisiana: W T Benthall, 35, blacksmith, born in Louisiana; Jane, 34; Stephen, 7 [Ancestry].

Berger, Marcus Isaac. (1842-1929). merchant gunsmith. 1877-78, St. Francisville [Bayou Sara], West Feliciana Parish. Marcus I. Berger was born in 1842 and died 10 May 1929, aged 88 yrs. He is buried in the Jewish Cemetery in Pineville, LA. He was born in Savannah, Georgia on a large plantation owned by his father. As the story goes the plantation was large enough to have many slaves. His father was wealthy enough to send his 3 sons away to Boarding School and then to college. However, as the story was told to his granddaughter Marion Berger Marcus, Marcus did not like attending school and finally left home to make his own way in life. He tried to enlist in the Civil War but was too young at 13, but he was allowed to engineer a train for soldiers. He met and married Johanna Stern. As a young widow whose husband Jacob W. Davis had died of Yellow Fever in New Orleans within a year of their marriage. They were married in Woodville, Mississippi where their 7 children were born. Marcus moved all of his family to Alexandria, LA., traveling by boat down the Red River. Marcus was a gunsmith by trade and was well known through central LA

Shoulder Arms—and march direct to M. I. Berger's establishment and have them put in tip top order and repair. We are gratified to be able to inform throughout this and the parishes of East Feliciana and Pointe Coupee that we have in our midst the desideratum for which our people have been wishing for many a long day—a first class gunsmith. Mr. Berger is a No. 1 workman, brings the very best testimonials with him and guarantees satisfaction to all who may favor him with their patronage. By reference to his advertisement, it will be seen that he does general repairing also including that of sewing machines, edge tools &c. &c. Send in your guns and pistols. In time of peace prepare for war. [*Feliciana Sentinel*, 1 December 1877]

M. I. Berger, Gun-Smith, adjoining B. Farrelly's Store, Principal street, Bayou Sara, LA. Firearms of all descriptions put in first class order. Gun stocks made or repaired, all kinds of small tools sharpened. All at reasonable rates of charge. [22 December 1877]

M. I. Berger, gunsmiths, requests we notify those who have guns or other work in his hands, to call for them by the 6th of March next as he is leaving here on that day. All persons interested should bear this in mind and act accordingly. It is with great regret that we make this announcement for it portends a loss to the community to be deprived of a workman of Mr. Berger's skill [*Feliciana Sentinel*, 23 February 1878].

Notice. I have opened my shop for the purpose of repairing guns, pistols, locks, keys, sewing machines, and filing gin saws; brushes filled, fine guns stocked, broken stocks repaired, at prices to suit the times. All work done at short notice. My shop is on the levee at John Roth's shoe shop. All work guaranteed. M. I. Berger, gunsmith & machinist [*Feliciana Sentinel*, 20 July 1878; this ad continued through 31 August]

Bessard, Louis (1845-). gun- and blacksmith. Young County. Census of 1870, Bonnet Carre, ward 5, St. John the Baptist Parish, Louisiana: Louis Bessard, blacksmith, single, 27, living alone. 1875, Louis Bessard, gunsmith, Graham, Young County, Texas [*Dir.*]. On 2 January 1878 Louis Bossard naturalized in Arizona Territory, thus becoming an American citizen. Census of 1880, Luttrell, Pima County, Arizona: Louis Bessard, blacksmith, born in Switzerland 35; Louis Pourand, miner, 31. Not located after 1880. Hirsch also listed Urban Bessard, not located.

Besuchet, Francois (--1849). gunsmith. 1838-46, New Orleans; 1838, 6 Ursulines; thereafter on Dauphine St. Francois arrived in 1849 from LeHavre, France; noted in Ward 1 in 1840. Francois died in 1849 and his will was entered in September 1849 Name also seen as Pesuchet [Ancestry; *Dirs.*].

Beuhler, Alexandre. gunsmith. 1866, 83 St. James St., New Orleans [*Dir.*]. See Buhler.

Bevol, Jean B. See Revol. Noted as Bevol in 1868 and 1876.

Bezy, Prosper (1798--1874). locksmith. 1861, 127 Ursulines, New Orleans. Census of 1860: Prosper Bezy, 59, lock smith, born in Frances; living with two unrelated Spaniards. 1866, 275 Dauphine. Bezy arrived in New Orleans from Sweden on 1 November 1838 on the ship *Morengo* [Ancestry; *Dir.*]. New Orleans death records gave his birth year as 1798 and death on 12 November 1874 [Ancestry].

Bickart, ---. locksmith. 1869, 45 Main St, New Orleans [*Dir.*]

Bienaimé, Antoine P. gunsmith. 1822-32, St. Ann below Levee, New Orleans. 1832, Dorion & Bienaime, 10 St. Ann; with Bernard Dorion [*Dir.*]. In 1880 there was a cigar maker named Antoine Bienaime, born about 1826 in LA.

Biggs, William (1811--). locksmith, hardware, gun dealer. 1851-53, 124 Circus, New Orleans [*Dir.*]. Census of 1850: William Biggs, locksmith, 39; Biggs and his wife and 6 children, ages 3 to 14, were all born in England.

Bille, Theophile (1824-). locksmith. Baton Rouge. Census of 1850: Theophile Bille, 26; apparently in the army; born in Germany. Bille enlisted on 16 June 1847 and again on 1 August 1849.

Biot, Christopher. gunsmith and cutler. 1821, Orleans Parish [Gorman; *Dir.*]. Census of 1820: Christopher Biot, free black, living alone.

Birnstein, August (1823--). locksmith, dealer. 1864-74, New Orleans. 1864, St. Joseph St., blacksmith. 1867, 264 Tchoupitoulas, New Orleans [*Dir.*]. Census of 1860: Auguste Bernstein, 37, merchant, born in Prussia; Mary, 34, born in Hanover; Otto, 7; Charles, 2, both born in Louisiana.

Birnstein, Charles August (1859-1891). locksmith. 1890, 269 Tchoupltoulas, New Orleans [*Dir.*]. On 6 August 1889 Charles A Birnstein married Sidonia Groll. Charles died on 12 February 1891.

Birnstein, L. locksmith. 1870, 261 Tchoupitoulas, New Orleans [*Dir.*].

Birnstein, Henry Otto (1853-1885). locksmith. 1872, Tchoupitoulas, New Orleans [*Dir.*]. On 2 August 1877 Henry Otto Birnstein married Catherine Christine Mathilde Exsterstein in New Orleans. Otto died on 8 December 1885, age 32 [Ancestry].

Birrcher, Henry (1833-1916). gun-, black-, and locksmith. 1867-1900, New Orleans; 1870, 149 Baronne, in association with with Henry Albert. On 20 January 1855 Henry Birrcher married Lucinda Jaeger in Madison County, Illinois. Census of 1870, ward 3: Henry Birrcher, born in Switzerland, 40, proprietor of blacksmith shop, value $500; Susan, wife, 21, born in Louisiana; Emma, 11; Louisa, 5; Lena H, 3, all born in Missouri. Census of 1880, Henry Birrcher, born in Germany, 47, lock smith; Susan, wife, 32; Emma, 22; Louisa, 16; Lena, 13. Census of 1900, ward 2: Zeno H Birrcher, 34, wood & coal dealer; Mary, wife, 31; Joseph, 4; Frances, 2 months; Henry Birrcher, born in Switzerland, 65, locksmith; Susan, 45. Birrcher died on 1 January 1816 [Ancestry; *Dirs.*].

Bissett, William (1815-). gunsmith. no township noted, Pointe Coupee Parish. Noted in the 1850 slave schedule. Census of 1870, ward 4, Pointe Coupee: William Bissett, machinist, 50, born in Scotland; Jane, wife, 27; William, 1, both born in Louisiana. Census of 1880, 3rd Ward, Pointe Coupee Parish: William Bissett, widower, born in Scotland.

Blackie, William (1821-). gunsmith and machinist. Blackie secured a liberal education in Edinborough, Scotland, and when a boy his parents moved to Glasgow, Scotland, where he learned to be a machinist. In 1849 he came to the United States, first located at New Orleans, but afterward moved to Baton Rouge, where he was in the foundry business until 1887. Census of 1870, ward 2: William Blackie, founder, 42, born in Scotland; Emily, wife, 32, born in Louisiana; Zelia, daughter, 12, born in Missouri. Census of 1880, William Blackie, iron founder, 54, born in Scotland; Emily, wife, 41, born in Louisiana. He then came to Plaquemine, and here he has continued up to the present. He was a Democrat in politics, and a member of the Masonic fraternity. During the war he was in the ordnance department making war materials for the Glorious Cause. Census of 1900, ward 1: William Blackie, 78, born in October 1821; Mary, 62, married 40 years [Census; *Biographical and Historical Memoires of Louisiana*, 2: 294]

Blache, Belisaire. gunsmith. 1846, 163 Marginy, New Orleans [Gorman; *Dir.*].

Blackman, E. S. (1787-). gunsmith. St. Helena Parish. Census of 1850, E. Blackman, age 63, born in New York, gunsmith; Octavia, his wife, 40; Charles, 16; Z. [male], 8; M. C., [male], 5; all born in Louisiana. Census of 1860 of Little River, Catahoula Parish: E S Blackman, 73, blacksmith, born in Connecticut; Octavia, 51; Zachariah, 18; and Marion, 15. Census of 1870 of Catahoula Parish: E S Blackman, 80, born in Connecticut; Octavia, 60; living with M. C. and M. J. Blackman.

Blair, Daniel. silversmith. 1821, New Orleans [M.E.S.D.A.]

Blanchard, B. gunsmith. 1867, 105 Conti, New Orleans [*Dir.*].

Blanchard, Frederick (1805-). gunsmith. 1866-67, old stand near the Catholic Church; 1869, corner of S. Boulevard and Ferdinand, New Orleans. Gunsmith and general repairer, all sorts of arms repaired on the shortest notice and at the lowest prices. Census of 1880, East Baton Rouge; Frederick Blanchard, 75, gunsmith, born in New Hampshire; Elizabeth, 68, born in Massachusetts [*Daily Advocate*, 2 March 1866; Census; *Times Picayune*, 14 June 1869; *Dirs.*].

Blanchemin, Pierre Casimir (c.1810--1874). gunsmith. 1841-44, 176 Conti, New Orleans [*Dir.*]. Pierre died on 24 August 1874 and was buried in Saint Louis Cemetery number 2, New Orleans. 1895 directory Adeline, widow of Pierre Blanchemin.

Blankenbach, John L. locksmith. 1878, Patterson below Lavergne, New

Orleans. 1861-67, plumber, Patterson St. 1868, plumber & iron worker. He arrived in U.S.A. in 1850. On 25 September 1868 Blankenbach naturalized, having formerly been a Prussian citizen. 1877, gas pipe fitter. Not located in any census [Ancestry; *Dir.*].

Bleuler, Jean Jacques (1814-). locksmith. Jean Jacques arrived in Louisiana on 22 January 1848 from Havre, France. 1851, New Orleans; admitted to charity hospital with phthisis pulmonalis; born in Basel, Switzerland. Some man named J. Bleuler enlisted in Eulers Company 3rd Regiment, European Brigade (*Garde Francaise*) in the Louisiana Militia. On Roll dated New Orleans, Louisiana, April 2nd, 1862 [Ancestry].

Boas, A. C. (1834—1918). gunsmith. 1893, Gainesville, Cooke County, Texas [*Dir.*]. On tax record of precinct 2, Cooke County of 1893. Boas died on 1 June 1918, age 84 years, in Iberia Parish, Louisiana [Ancestry].

Boirel, P. gunsmith. 1832, 29 St. Peter, New Orleans [*Dir.*].

Boisdoré, Louis Chevalier (1810-). gunsmith. 1842, 30 Conti St.; 1849-52, 18 Conti, free African-American tradesman. 1832, Villere near Ursulines, New Orleans. Census of 1850, Louis Boisdoré, mulatto, gunsmith, real estate valued at $4000 [Ancestry; *Dir.*]. Also seen as Bloisdoré.

Boissecq, Jules (1793-). gunsmith. 1841-42, 122 Bourbon St., New Orleans [*Dir.*]. Jules was a Walloon.

Boixel, Pierre Marie. (1793-1833). gunsmith. 1822, 107 Tchoupitoulas; 1824, 24 St. Ann; 1832, 107 Tchoupitoulas, New Orleans. Pierre was a native of Nantes, France [Gorman; *Dirs.*].

Bolet, Jacques (1824-1877). machinist, black-, gun-, and locksmith. Jacques was born in Laroche, Savoie, France, a son of Joseph and Charlotte (Roque) Bolet. 1866-77, New Orleans. On 11 January 1862 he married Marguerite Conroy at St. Mary's Church, New Orleans. Jacques was 38 and Marguerite was 21 when they were married. He and Marguerite lived in several places in the French Quarter close to his shop: at 60 Dauphine, 69 Dauphine, 130 Chartres, 93 Burgundy, and 119 St. Louis. Jacques is listed in the New Orleans City Directories from 1867 to 1877. 1867, Bolet & Arnaux, blacksmiths, 106 Custom House. 1869, 119 St. Louis, locksmith. 1872, blacksmith. 1875, locksmith & machinist at 104 Custom House. Bolet died on 2 August 1877. On 24 October 1868 Bolet naturalized, having arrived in U.S.A. in 1854. No military records have been found for Jacques, so it is not known if he took part in the Civil War. He owned and operated a gunsmith and locksmith shop in the French Quarter. In 1866, he took a partner, L. Frederic, but that partnership only lasted a year. In 1867, he became partners with J. Arnaux, another Frenchman. His shop was located at 106 Customhouse in the commercial district. He died in New Orleans on 2 August 1877. Jacques changed business partners again. In 1877, he became ill and died at the age of 53. His new partner, Gustave Martinet, refused to allow Marguerite into the shop, or to give her any money to pay the medical and funeral bills. She asked the court to step in, and Gustave was served with a summons to force him to divide the shop assets with her. The court ordered that he should, so a Sheriff's sale was held, and all the contents were sold for a total of $265.00, giving Marguerite $132.50 for her share of the estate. She was left to raise 4 children on her own [Ancestry; *Dirs.*].

Bomen, Louis (1863-). gunsmith. New Orleans. Census of 1880: Louis Bomen, 17, gunsmith, son of Philip.

Bomen, Philip (1835-). gunsmith. New Orleans. Census of 1880: Philip Bomen, 45, gunsmith, born in France; wife Louise, 39, born in Mississippi; Louis Bomen, gunsmith, 17; Rosa, 15; Lucie, 11; Henrietta, 9; August, 4, all born in Louisiana. Clearly Bomen had been in Louisiana at least since 1863 based on ages of his children, but he was not located in any census.

Bon, Jean. gunsmith. 1699-1706, Mobile, French colony of Louisiana. Jean Praux was a carpenter from Saint Jean d'Angély, France who migrated in 1706 aboard the ship, *Aigle* with his wife and four daughters. In 1706 he was 48 and his wife was 43. He died shortly after his arrival and his widow married Jean Bon, a gunsmith from LaRochelle, France who had arrived in the colony in 1699 [Ancestry].

Bonce, Joseph. gunsmith. 1865, 2nd district, New Orleans; home 354 Conti St. He was drafted into the Union Army.

Boone, Isaac W. gunsmith. 1901, 223 N. Broad St., New Orleans [*Dir.*].

Boone, Isaiah (1772-). gunsmith. Isiah was born on 17 November 1772 at the forks of the Yadkin River, near Salisbury North Carolina, a son of Squire Boone, Jr. (1744-1815) and his wife Jane van Cleeve (1749-1829). Isaiah fought in Amerindian battles as a boy and was with his parents at the siege of Boonesboro. He went with his father to New Orleans and stayed as a gunsmith for at least three years. In 1794 he went on Wayne's Command in Bland Ballard's Company as a lieutenant. His marriage and name of his wife, if any, and death are not known [Spraker, *The Boone Family*].

Bosier, S. H. (1827-). gunsmith. Sabine Parish. Census of 1860, S H Bosier, 33, gun smith, $100 property, $400 personal value; Cora, 30, wife; Clara, 14; Virginia, 12; Mary, 10; James, 7; Amelia, 4; Sylvester, 1. Not located after 1860; not in Find-a-Grave.

Bossier, S D (1820-1862). gunsmith. Sabine parish. Census of 1860: S. D. Bossier, gunsmith, 40; Narcissus, wife, 35; Indiana, 14; Elizabeth, 12; Albert S, 10; Robert, 8; Newton, 2; Jasper, 4 months, all born in Louisiana. While there are similarities to the S.H. Bosier, below, the wife's and children's names differ. S. D. Bosier served in the 28th Louisiana Infantry, C.S.A, rank of sergeant. He enlisted on 29 March 1862 at New Orleans. Roll for May and June, 1862, "Died at private house near Camp at Vicksburg, June 26th, 1862; cause of death, measles." [Ancestry].

Bouchoux, Joseph. locksmith. 1861, 117 Toulouse, New Orleans [*Dir.*].

Bouffleur, L. locksmith. 1861, 217 Julia, New Orleans [*Dir.*].

Bouju, Joseph. silversmith. 1821, New Orleans. Bouju purchased at least 2 slaves in 1808 [Ancestry; M.E.S.D.A.].

Boulet, Paul J. gunsmith. 1873, 165 Liberty St., New Orleans [*Dir.*
Bourquin & Bouron. watchmakers and gunsmiths. Thibodaux [*Thibodaux Sentinel,* 14 April 1877].

Bouron, Auguste. gunsmith. 1868-69, New Orleans; at Philip Bouron's gunshop [*Dir.*]. 1885, Thibodeaux, Lafourche Parish. Census of 1880: A Buron, 43, gunsmith, born in Bordeaux, France; arrived in America in 1847 [Ancestry; Census]. See Auguste Bouron.

A. Bouron, Watchmaker and Gunsmith, corner of Main and St. Philip Streets, constantly keeps on hand a large and complete assortment of fine jewelry, watches and clocks. In connection with the above a great variety of Guns, Pistols, Powder, Cartridges, Hunting Material. The celebrated Elgin Watches constantly on hand. Also the new American Sewing Machine and Lot of Accordeons. Watches, Clocks, Jewelry, Sewing Machines, Firearms, carefully repaired and guaranteed [*Thibodeaux Sentinel*, 31 January 1885]

Bouron, Auguste Albert. (1875-1925). gun- and blacksmith. New Orleans. Auguste was a son of Philip and brother of George and Louis, born on 19 September 1875. [*Dirs.*; Gorman; Census; *Times Picayune*, 26 November 1886]. Bouron, aged 45 years, committed suicide in Audubon Park and his body was found by a watchman. He had put a revolver to his head and pulled the trigger. Louis L. and George T. Bouron, brothers of the deceased, identified the body. He was a native of Biloxi, Mississippi. Although he was a gunsmith by training he had been an employee of National Enameling and Stamping Company. In his pockets were letters and other items identifying him [*Times Picayune*, 11 November 1925]

Bouron, Eugene Pierre (1841--1880). gunsmith. Orleans Parish, Louisiana; Eugene, born in France in 1841, was a brother of Phlippe Bourbon. Census of 1870 of ward 5, New Orleans: Philipp Bouron, 34, gunsmith, born in France, value $1000; Louisa, 28, born in Mississippi; George, 9; Louise, 6; Rosa, 5; and Lucy, 1; and Eugene Boroun, 29, gunsmith, all born in Louisiana. Eugene died on 27 March 1880 and was buried in St. Joseph Cemetery, Thibodaux, LaFourche Parish, Louisiana [Find-a-Grave].

Bouron, George (1861--1925). gunsmith. 1900, Biloxi, Harrison County. Census of 1900: George Bouron, 39, gunsmith, born in October 1861, son of Philippe Bourbon; Philipp Bouron, head of family, gun store, born May 1825 in France; Louis Bouron, born in May 1863, gun smith; Lucy, 28; Harriet, 25; and August, 24, druggist. George died on 2 January 1825 and was buried in Metaire Cemetery, New Orleans [Find-a-Grave; Ancestry].

Bouron, Louis Leonard (1863-1943). gunsmith. Biloxi, Harrison County. Census of 1900: Louis Bouron, born on 5 May 1863, gun smith, son of Philippe Bourbon. Louis married Louise P. Cuevas. Louis died on 21 January 1943 and was buried in the Biloxi City Cemetery [Family; Ancestry].

Bouron, Philippe (1825-1905). gunsmith. Census of 1870, Orleans Parish, Louisiana. Philippe, 34 [?] years of age, gunsmith, born in France; Louisia, 28, born in Mississippi; George, 9; Louis, 6; Rosa, 5; Lucy, 1; all born in Louisiana; Eugene Bourbon, 29, gunsmith. born in Louisiana; Census of 1900, Biloxi, Harrison County, Mississippi. Philippe, owns gun store, born May 1825 [?], George, born October 1861, gunsmith; Louis, born May 1863, gunsmith; Lucy, born January 1872; Harriet, born December 1874; August Bourbon, born September 1875, druggist. Philippe was born on May 1, 1835, in France, and died on September 1905 in Biloxi; buried at the Old French Cemetery, Biloxi [Census; family genealogy].

Biloxi, Miss. Sept. 30. Philip Bouron, aged 70 years, a native of France, and 40 years a summer resident of this city, died this morning at 6:30 o'clock at his home on the Beach, corner of Thomas street. Mr. Bouron was a gunsmith and dealer in firearms, and conducted a place of business in New Orleans, at 534 Chartres street. He leaves three sons and three *daughters. [Times Picayune*, 1 October 1905]

Bouron, Philippe George (1861-1929). gunsmith. New Orleans. P. G. was born on 15 April 1861, a son of Philippe Bouron. In 1907 Philip was noted at 534 Chartres, at P. Bouron & Sons, gunsmiths. 1900, Philip, 37, single, living with his father. 1902, 534 Chartres. He may have been active in his father's shop all along although he is elusive in public records [Ancestry; *Dirs*.].

Bouron, William. gunsmith. 1866-75, New Orleans [*Dirs*.]. William was not located in censuses and apparently unrelated to the other Bouron gunsmiths.

Bower, George. locksmith. 1861-66, St. Andrew St., near Howard St., New Orleans [*Dir*.]. There was also a George Bower, pocketbook manufacturer at same time. Neither man was located in censuses.

Boyer, Rene. gunsmith. 1706, East Carroll Parish. Boyer, his wife, and child 3; in the pay of the French king [French Census].

Bradford, Samuel. gun- and tinsmith. 1841-42, 131 Rampart, New Orleans [*Dirs*.]. Not located.

Brantan, Francois. gunsmith. 1778, St. Louis St., New Orleans [French Census; Gorman].

Brantan, Nicholas. gunsmith. 1726-33, New Orleans. Brantan was born before 1710 in France. Noted in several period documents and French Census. Gunner for the colony [Gorman; Ancestry].

Brawley, Samuel Sidney (1814--1873). gunsmith. Fannin County. Samuel S was born on 25 September 1814. 1846-57, Marion Twp., Ouachita County, Arkansas. Census of 1860, Garnett's Bluff, Fannin County, Texas: S. S. Braley, blacksmith, 45; C. L. Brawley, 40; Harrison, 19; Sarah, all born in North Carolina; Samuel, 12, born in MS; Ella, 9, born in Arkansas. During the Second War for Independence, Sam served in the 22nd Texas Cavalry, also known as the First Texas Indian Regiment. This unit was formed during the spring of 1862 with 873 men. Eventually it was dismounted and saw action in Arkansas and Louisiana. At the surrender in March, 1865, it contained a mere 14 officers and 167 enlisted men. Samuel Sidney Brawley is the man's correct name. S S died on 13 January 1873 [Ancestry; *Dir.;* Elias]

Breffheil, Jean Marie (1790-1838). engraver and gunsmith. 1831-38, Condé St., New Orleans. Jean died on 3 February 1838 in New Orleans, age

48. At the time of his death he was living at 38 Condé, address of L. T. Leduc [*Dirs*.; Gorman; Ancestry]. He was associated with gunmaker Louis Theodore Leduc.

Breffheil, Widow. gunsmith. 1842, 34 Conde St., New Orleans. It appears as though she was the widow of Jean Marie Breffhil, but may also have been a gunsmith, rather just "widow of." [*Dir*.]. She may have run the shop with the aid of slaves.

Bretch, ---. gunsmith. c.1858-63, New Orleans. Reportedly, Bretch was from Lancaster, Pennsylvania, and was a staunch Unionist. He was trapped in the Confederacy during the Civil War. Initially, he was made to assist in making and refurbishing guns for the C.S. army. In 1863 he was drafted into the C.S. cavalry. Somehow he made his way back to Lancaster and never returned to New Orleans [*Times Picayune*, 22 July 1909]. Some of the story, of course, makes no sense since the Union had long since captured New Orleans. Neither can I locate any information on a gunsmith whose name is approximately Bretch in Lancaster or in New Orleans.

Brian, Hardy, Sr. (1755-1813). frontiersman, farmer, gunsmith. Hardy was born on 20 May 1755 in Darlington County, South Carolina. He died on 31 July 1813 in Jackson, East Feliciana Parish, Louisiana. He was buried on 1 August 1813 in Brian-White Cemetery, Clinton, Louisiana [Ancestry].

Briault, Francois (1795-1850). cutler and edged tool maker; gun dealer. Vermillion Parish. Francois also offered a variety of firearms for sale. Francois died on 25 November 1850 [Ancestry].

Brinson, Haywood Nelson (1831--1904). gunsmith. 3rd ward, Bienville Parish. Haywood was born on 15 September 1831. Census of 1850: Haywood Brinson, 18, son of Philip and Mariah Haywood. Census of 1880, Haywood N Brinson, born in Louisiana, gun smith, 48; Olivia, 30, his wife; Alec, 19; Mollie, 14; Emma, 8. Census of 1900, 3rd ward: Haywood N Brinson, 68; Olivia, 55; Augustus W, 26, no occupation listed. In 1900 both Haywood and Olivia are listed as black, but their son Augustus is listed as white. On 1 June 1860 Haywood purchased 80 acres of land. Haywood died in May 1904 and was buried in Providence Cemetery, Bienville [Ancestry]. I cannot find Haywood in the censuses of 1860 and 1870.

Broadwell, Lewis Wells. inventor. 1865-68, New Orleans. Lewis W Broadwell was born in Cincinnati, Ohio, on 18 July 1820. Patent for a breech-loading firearm number 49,583, of 22 August 1865; patent assigned to C. M. Clay; patent number 55,761 of 19 June 1866 for a rifle projectile; and

55,762 of the same date for breech-loading ordnance. Reportedly, he received additional U.S. patents while residing in Russia and Austria [Gardner, *Small Arms Makers*, 25].

Brockaway, S. M. (1805-). gunsmith. 1840-50, West Feliciana Parish. Census of 1840, S. M. Brockaway, head of household, 4 white persons in household. Census of 1850, S. M. Brockaway, age 46, gun smith, born in Ohio; Amanda, his wife, 26, born in Mississippi; M. [female], 4; M. J. [male]. both born in LA. Slave holder [Ancestry]. Not located after 1850.

Bronaugh, William N. arms supplier. In 1838 William supplied Texas with three fine rifles @ $40 each. There is no proof that he manufactured these arms [Hirsch, 25]. He was probably the William N. Bronaugh noted at Ft. Scott in Georgia, in 1818-19; and in command at Ft. Smith, Red River, Louisiana in 1822. He was an officer although records are unclear as to rank. 1821-31, 7th Infantry, U. S. Army [Ancestry].

Brooks, B. armorer. Private. Company A. 2nd LA Infantry. Brooks enlisted on May 11, 1861, in New Orleans. Noted on muster rolls April to June, 1862. Detailed as gunsmith at Richmond. Discharged on July 29th, 1862, under Act entitled Conscription Act [*Booth's Index*].

Brooks, Burt (1825-). gunsmith. Natchitoches Parish. Census of 1850 of Tuscakiisa County, Alabama: Burt Brooks, 24, son of Daniel and Rhoda Brooks. Census of 1860 of Natchitoches Parish: Burt Brooks, 30, gunsmith, single, $500 each real estate and personal value. Census of 1870: B. Burt Brooks, gun smith, born in Alabama, single living alone. Census of 1880, Natchitoches, Natchitoches Parish: Burt, 55 Brooks, born in Alabama, gun smith; Evelina, 56, his wife; L. M. Gatlin, 27. Not found after 1880.

Brooks, George (1831-1869). copper- and gunsmith, metal worker. 1850-66, New Orleans; listed as a gunsmith only in 1858. Brooks died on 30 May 1869 [Ancestry; *Dirs*.].

Brown, H. M. gunsmith. 1843, 2 Notre Dame St near New Levee, New Orleans. Kit Gorman noted that Brown was known solely through one newspaper advertisement. There was a Henry M. Brown (1814-), gunsmith, in St. Louis in Census of 1850.

Bruff, Brother & Seaver. hardware merchants, gun dealers. 1861, New Orleans. This was a New York business which opened a branch in New Orleans, claiming to manufacture guns and derringers. After the war it reopened in a different form [Gorman].

Brunet, E. locksmith. 1861, 239 Johnson, door 2, New Orleans. Census of 1860, E. Brunet, 39; L, wife, 31; L, 4; C, 2, all born in Texas [Ancestry; *Dir*.]. Census illegible.

Buckley, H. P. (1822-1903). watchmaker, jeweler, gun dealer. 1853-1903, New Orleans. Buckley employed John Edward Bailey to superintend his gun business. Buckley initially worked for Nelson A. Young and eventually purchased his store from the widow after Young's death. Census of 1850, H P Buckley, jeweler, 27; C, wife, 24, both born in England; C B, 2, born in Texas [Gorman; *Dirs*.].

H. P. Buckley, No. 8 Camp street, New Orleans, Watchmaker, and dealer in fine watches, jewelry, silver ware, and spectacles; also Guns and Pistols and everything in the hunting line. Special Attention to watch repairing and jewelry work. Mr. Bailey for many years Gun Maker of Chartres street, offers his services in every branch of Gun and Pistol repairing. [*Flake's Bulletin*, 19 December 1866]

Buffle, Paul (1812-1860). lock- and gunsmith. 1854-60, New Orleans. 1858, 79 Custom House [Ancestry; *Dirs*.].

Buhler, Alexander. gunsmith. 1865-67, New Orleans. drafted; 1865, 223 St. Charles; 1866, 1867, 83 St. James; 70 Girod, [*Dirs*.]. See Beuhler.

Buron, Auguste. (1837--). gunsmith. 1868-69, New Orleans; at Philip Bouron's gunshop [*Dir*.]. A Buron, 43, gunsmith, born in Bordeaux, France; arrived in America in 1847. 1885, Thibodeaux, Lafourche Parish. Census of 1880: A Buron, 43, gunsmith, born in Bordeaux, France; arrived in America in 1847 [Ancestry; Census]. See Auguste Bouron.

A. Bouron, Watchmaker and Gunsmith, corner of Main and St. Philip Streets, constantly keeps on hand a large and complete assortment of fine jewelry, watches and clocks. In connection with the above a great variety of Guns, Pistols, Powder, Cartridges, Hunting Material. The celebrated Elgin Watches constantly on hand. Also the new American Sewing Machine and Lot of Accordeons. Watches, Clocks, Jewelry, Sewing Machines, Firearms, carefully repaired and guaranteed [*Thibodeaux Sentinel*, 31 January 1885]

Burrows, Jacob (1829-). gunsmith. New Orleans. Census of 1860: Jacob Burrows, teamster, 31, born in France, had four children born in Louisiana so he was in the state for a decade or so, but is not listed in city directories [Gorman; Census]. It is very likely he worked in another man's shop.

Busch, Frederick (1850-1914). gun- and locksmith. 1871-1914, New Orleans. 1871-76, with Michael Malone; married Malone's daughter. 1877-97, had his own shop; then got involved in the real estate business [Gorman; *Dirs*].

F Busch, 18½ Commercial Place, New Orleans. Bell Hanging and general house work attended to at short notice and at reasonable prices. Also vaults, locks, and copying presses repaired, duplicate keys of all descriptions made. Safe repairing a specialty [*New Orleans Bulletin*, 8 March 1876].

Byrac, ---. founder. New Orleans. Contracted with the Confederate Navy Department for twenty 32-pounder rifle cannons. [O.N.R., Series 1, XVII, 163]. There is no evidence that any were cast.

Cady, Perry G. (1798-). locksmith. 1851, New Orleans; admitted to charity hospital with diarrhea; born in London, England. Sole reference.

Cailler, Albert Marie (1806--1876). gunsmith. Thibodeau, Lafourche Parish. Albert was born on 2 July 1806. Census of 1850, Albert Callier, 46, born in St. James Parish; Virginia, 34, born in St. John Baptiste Parish; Ferdoussi [male], 16; Elisha [female], 12; Josephine, 9; Amelia, 8; Honorine, 6; Sostaine [male], 2, all born in Thibodeaux. Census of 1870, ward 5 New Orleans: Albert Caillier, 62; Mary V, wife, 54; Honorine, 21; Modeste, 18; Aimee, 13; James, 16, all born in Louisiana. Albert was keeping a boarding house so the Census also showed a large number of boarders. 1871, manager Strangers' Hotel. Albert died on 14 November 1876 and was buried in St. Louis Cemetery number 3 [Find-a-Grave].

Fire at Thibodeauxville. The dwelling house and gunsmith shop of Mr. Callier, at Thibodeauxville, were destroyed by fire on Thursday last about 1 o'clock P.M., together with his furniture, tools, and provisions. Mr. C. is said to be a highly respectable citizen, and by his industry had acquired a little property, all of which was thus in a moment swept away. We are happy to learn that his fellow citizens rendered him immediate assistance, and have set about repairing his losses [*Times Picayune*, 4 May 1841]

Callier, Pierre (1835-1903). gunsmith. 1859, 123 Chartres, New Orleans. Callier was related to Auguste Tigniere, gunsmith, at whose address he was located. Tigniere's wife's maiden name was Callier. Pierre died on 17 March 1903. It is unclear if Pierre was a gunsmith or clerk in the shop [*Dir.*; Gorman; Ancestry].

Canale, J. gun dealer, dry goods. 1866-69, New Orleans. Canale was noted on tax assessment lists in New Orleans from 1861 through 1865. It is certain that he made no firearms and probably repaired few [Ancestry; Gorman].

Cantin, Auguste (1822-). gunsmith.1866-80, St. Bernard Parish. Noted on tax assessment list in 1866-67. Census of 1870, Auguste Cantin, gunsmith, 47, born in Switzerland; Clemence, wife, 40; Oscar, 13; Marie, 10; Julie, 7; Gustave 2, all born in Louisiana. Census of 1880, 3rd ward, St. Bernard: Auguste Cantin, 58, gunsmith, born in Switzerland; wife Emma, 42; Marie, 18; Julie, 16; Gustave, 12; and Clement, 8. Not located after 1880.

Cardona & Cook. gun dealers. 1882-84, New Orleans. Antonio Cardona, Jr. & Louis Cook. The directory listings and Civil War draft registrations are for one Antonio Cardona (1835-1899), music professor. He or some other man by this name arrived in New Orleans on 26 December 1853 from Barcelona [Ancestry; *Dirs*.; Gorman].

Carmouche, Jean Baptiste (c.1692-c.1753). locksmith. Carmouche was born about 1692, ancestor of the Avoyelles Carmouche family, was a native of St. Laurent de Pont-de-Mousson, France.. Carmouche migrated as a locksmith from the port of Lorient, on the ship *Gironde* in 1720 to Mobile where he married and his son, Joseph Carmouche was born about 1742. Jean Baptiste died before 1753, at which time his estate included a plantation outside the city and a house and lot on Bourbon Street in New Orleans. 1746, he served as a witness in Mobile. 1746; Jean Carmouche *dit* Lorain, locksmith [Ancestry; http://www.avoyelles.com/]

Carroll, W. H. (1840-1872). gunsmith. 5 South St., New Orleans. Carroll worked for Mudge the gunsmith. Carroll committed suicide by cutting his throat with a razor [*Galveston Tri-Weekly News*, 24 May 1872]

A well-known gunsmith named W. H. Carroll, formerly in the employ of Emerson Mudge, No. 75 Magazine street, committed suicide in his room, No. 223 Julia street, about 6:30 o'clock last evening by cutting his throat with a razor. The deceased was at Mr. Mudge's place of business during the day, in search of a job, and upon remarking that he wished he could find something to do, the proprietor of the establishment suggested that he could go to work and make a lot of decoy ducks while business was dull and they would come into play when the season opened. The suggestion seemed to strike Carroll favorably and, we are informed, about 4 o'clock in the afternoon the deceased appeared to be perfectly sober and in full possession of his faculties. On Monday night, however, he was carried to the First Police Station for safe keeping, where it was stated that he had been laboring under the influence. No indication that he was suffering from any mental aberration appeared to the office in charge. Carroll remarked that "my mind is a little damaged, but I am all right now." The sergeant thought it well enough to take care of him, and for that purpose provided as comfortable quarters for him as the station house afforded until morning. Shortly after leaving Mr. Mudge's as related in a preceding paragraph, Carroll told a friend that he would go to his room and lie down, and the two parted company. About the hour mentioned in the beginning he was found lying on the floor of his room with his throat cut from ear to ear, and the instrument of death at his side. . . . Carroll was about 32 years of age, and had been married but he and his wife separated some time ago, by mutual agreement [*Times Picayune*, 22 May 1872]

Carver, Ned. gun- and blacksmith. 1863, Livingston Parish [*Dir.*].

Casimir, P. locksmith. 1861, 203 Dauphine, New Orleans [*Dir.*].

Cassels, Elias M. (1821--1890). gunsmith. Goliad, Texas. Cassels was born on 27 May 1821 in Marion County, Mississippi. 1858-70, Goliad, Goliad County, Texas: Census of 1870, Elias N Cassels, gunsmith, 49, value $2248; Lucinda, wife, 48, both born in Mississippi; William, 23, stock grower; Joseph, 18; Susan; 1 [?]; Jacob, 14, all born in Louisiana; Minnie, 12; John, 10; Francis, 7; Sarah, 5, all born in Texas. Census of 1880, precinct 1 Goliad County, Texas: E. N. Cassels, blacksmith, 59; L. E., wife, 57; Susan, 23; Winnie C., 20; Fannie V., 15; Sarah A., 13. Elias died on 9 October 1890 and was buried at Live Oak Cemetery, Fannin, Goliad County, Texas [Ancestry; *Dirs.*; Find-a-Grave]. Not located in Louisiana; presence based on birth of children in Louisiana.

Cattana, Albert (1859-1937). gunsmith. 1883-1900, New Orleans. 1900-25, gunsmith, 1153 Decatur St. Census of 1900, Albert Catania, 40, gunsmith; Philomena, wife, 30, both born in Italy; Mary, 10; Annie, 8; Stella, 7; Natzia [?], 4; Lena, 1; Nicholas, 8 months, all born in Louisiana. Census of 1910, ward 6: Albert Cattana, gunsmith, 49; Philomena, wife, 40, both born in Italy; Anna, 17; Stella, 15; Synalieass [?], 14; Lena, 11; Nick, 9; Rose, 7, all born in LA. Cattana came to America from Italy in 1886. Census of 1920, ward 6: Albert Cattana, gunsmith, 57, owned his home; Philomena, 48; Stella, 25; Earnest, 23, gunsmith; Lena, 21; Nicholas, 19; Rosie, 16; Francis, 14; John, 12. In 1920 Albert was listed as a widower although his wife was shown and the census noted he could neither read nor write. He was born on 5 December 1859 in Gibellina, Italy, and died in May 1937 in New Orleans [Ancestry; *Dirs.*].

Cattana, Earnest Ignatius (1896-1945). gunsmith. 1913, 1231 Decatur, gunsmith. Census of 1920, ward 6 New Orleans. Earnest was a son of Albert and Philomena Cattana and their only child listed with an occupation in 1920. Earnest was born on 26 January 1896 and died in October 1945 [Ancestry; Census].

Cavalier, Léon. gunsmith. 1835, 184 Chartres, New Orleans [*Dir.*].

Ceressol, Edouard J. (-c.1843). gunsmith. 1822-42, New Orleans. 1822, 142 Francois; 1827, 97 St. Peter; 1832, Bourbon St.; 1834, Armour & Unions St. See Serresol. Both spellings are used in the 1822 and 1832 directories. His estate was valued at just slightly less than $2000 [*Dirs.;* Gorman; New Orleans Estates].

Chailes, A. K. gunsmith. 1874, 199 Chartres, New Orleans [*Dir.*].

Champireaux, August. gunsmith. 1841-42, 67 Conde St., New Orleans [*Dirs.*].

Chantegrel, Joseph. locksmith. 1861, 93 Royal, New Orleans [*Dir.*].

Charleville, Francis (1825-1880). gunsmith. 1872-75, 55 St. Charles, New Orleans; purchased the store front owned by Louis Gerteis. 1874, lives rear Carondelet, between Valence & Bordeaux. 1875, Francis sold the business to Richard Rhodes. "quick sales & small profits." Noted in directories later as a clerk [Gorman; *Dirs.*].

[Results at the Agricultural Fair]We were pleased to note blue ribbons on several articles presented by Mr Charleville, the well-known gunsmith at 55 St. Charles street. His enterprise and excellent judgment entitle him to the four diplomas awarded him [*New Orleans Republican*, 29 April 1873].

Charne, M. D. cutler. 1822, 14 Ste. Ann below Conde, New Orleans [*Dir.*].

Chatel, Victor gun- and locksmith. 1846, Bayou Rd, New Orleans [*Dir.*].

Chaufel, Charles. armorer, lock-, black- & gunsmith. Census of 1840, ward 1, 4 free white persons. 1841-61, New Orleans. Also seen as Chauffeux. 1841-43, Bourbon St.; 1857, 215 Bayou Rd.; 1861, 80 Bayou Rd. [*Dirs.*].

Chenet, Vincent Alexander Tenchenet dit (1679--1724). gunsmith. 1699-1708, Biloxi. Vincent was born on 6 October 1679. Chenet married Marie Preaux. He died on 18 September 1724. The family name originally was Tichenet, Techenay or Techenet. With the use of 'dit' names in New France it is easily seen how the name became dit Chenet. Vincent went to the South with D'Iberville expedition in 1699. Vincent's father was a Carignan soldier who married a 'filles du roi'. [J. Higgenbotham, *Old Mobile: Fort Louis de Louisiana, 1702-1711*, 345; Ancestry].

On the first day of August 1806 La Salle completed a census on which he had been working since the arrival of the Aigle in accordance with instructions sent to him by Pontchartrain. This census, as recorded by La Salle showed twenty-four families, including thirty-four children, in Mobile. The total of eight-five persons . . . was not much different than it had been the year before. The few new people were barely sufficient to replace the ones who had died since the previous summer. Among the recently deceased was a forty-eight-year-old carpenter named Jean Preau from Saint Jean d'Angély near Rochefort. Preau had attempted to immigrate to Louisiana previously, but was turned down because both Bienville and Iberville felt that his five young daughters (of which only Elisabeth and Marguerite were near maturity) were too much of a liability. In the three years since his first application was turned down, however, two of his other daughters, Jeanne and Marie, had reached marriageable ages. Moreover, the colony was still in need of skilled craftsmen. He was finally allowed to take passage with his wife, Anne Prévost, whom he married in Saint Jean d'Angély in 1685, his four daughters (the fifth had died) and his brother, Antoine. Soon after his arrivl on the Aigle, however, Jean Preau had died, leaving his forty-three-year-old widow to care for the daughters, one of whom, Marie, shortly thereafter was married to Vincent Alexandre in the summer of 1706."

Chevalier, ---. armurier. 1811, 1 Levee, New Orleans [*Dir.*]

Chew & Relf. gun dealers. 1804-11, New Orleans [Gorman; *Dirs.*].

Churchill, Charles H. (-1868). gun dealer. See Taylor & Churchill. In 1861 Charles took over Taylor's interests. After Charles died in 1868 his brothers Wiley and Sylvester took over the firm.

Clarke, John. founder. New Orleans. Reportedly, early in the Civil War his firm manufactured a few bronze weapons.

Clay, John L. hardware, dealer. 1842, 96 Camp, New Orleans; offered imported arms for sale [Gorman; *Dir.*].

Clérmont, Surgy. gunsmith. 1841-42, 53 St. Louis St., New Orleans; 1845, 463 Camp St. [*Dirs.*]. Also seen as Clément.

Clérmont, Julian. gunsmith. 1846, 473 Camp, New Orleans [*Dir.*].

Closon, Charles (1805-). gunsmith. Baton Rouge. Census of 1850, Charles

Closon, gunsmith, age 45; Mary, 35, his wife, both born in Pennsylvania; I. F. Sargeant, 29, no occupation, born in Ohio; Martha Sargeant, 18, born in Pennsylvania; Mary Rodruigez, 3, born in Louisiana..

Clouatre, Pierre. armurier. Pierre Clouatre married Margurite LeBlanc and they had 11 children born between 1724 and 1746. Pierre worked at Natchez and then Point Coupee. The British deported Pierre Cloistre *dit* Clouâtre, his wife Marguerite LeBlanc, and the rest of his family to Maryland in 1755. For over a dozen years, they endured life among British colonists who, despite their Catholic roots, did not integrate with their French co-religionists who had been thrust upon them. In July 1763, British authorities counted Marguerite LeBlanc, now a widow, at Port Tobacco, Maryland. With her were sons Louis, Pierre-Sylvain, and Joseph, and daughters Anne and Marthe-Marie. Son Georges, who had married Cécile, daughter of fellow Acadian Antoine Breau, in Maryland, their children Joseph *le jeune* and Madeleine, and orphan Joseph Breau, also were counted at Port Tobacco that month. Georges died in Maryland sometime between July 1763 and December 1767. Louis may have married fellow Acadian Marguerite Landry in Maryland after July 1763. When word reached the Acadians in Maryland that they would be welcome in Louisiana, where many of their relatives already had gone, they pooled their meager resources to charter ships that would take them to New Orleans.

Pierre Cloistre *dit* Clouâtre, a gunsmith, reached Acadia from France by 1722, the year he married Marguerite, daughter of André LeBlanc, one of the pioneers of the Minas settlement. Pierre and Marguerite settled at Grand-Pré and had at least a dozen children, including five sons, all born at Minas: Louis in August 1724, Georges in November 1727, Dominique in May 1729, Pierre-Sylvain in c1740, and Joseph in c1750. Their daughter Marie-Josèphe was born in April 1723, Anne in March 1744, and Marthe-Marie July 1746. Only one of Pierre and Marguerite's sons seems to have married before *Le Grand Dérangement*: Third son Dominique married Françoise, daughter of probably Claude Boudrot, at Minas in c1752. Oldest daughter Marie-Josèphe married Pierre, son of Augustin Hébert, at Grand-Pré in October 1747 [*Acadians Who Found Refuge in Louisiana*].

Cockburn, L. E. gunsmith. 1841-42, 93 Conti St., New Orleans [*Dir.*].

Colberguer, Jean. gunsmith. 1843, 39 Perdido, New Orleans [*Dir.*].

Collins, James T. (1855-). gunsmith. Morgan City, Saint Mary Parish. Census of 1880, James Collins, 25, born in Louisiana, gun smith; Alice, 17. Census of 1900, James T Collins, born in LA, 43, jeweler; Alice, wife, 36;

James A, 19, all born in Louisiana. Census of 1930, James Collins, retired, 73. In spring 1896 a fire broke out and destroyed several buildings including the gunsmith shop of J T Collins which was a total loss [St. Joseph *Tensas Gazette*, 17 April 1896].

Conklin, Levi W (1830-). lock- and gunsmith. New Orleans. 1867-69, 276 Terpsichore. 1870-74, 372 Carondelet. Census of 1880, Levi Conklin, born in New Jersey, 50, mechanic; Lucinda, wife, 49, born in Illinois. In the July 1863 draft registration Levi was listed as confectioner, born in Morris County, New Jersey about 1827 [Gorman; *Dirs*.].

Cook & Brother. arms manufacturers. New Orleans. Ferdinand William Charles Cook & Francis L. Cook. By February 1862 the firm had almost 400 employees making Enfield Pattern 1853 rifles of various lengths. When the Yankees occupied New Orleans the Cook Brothers moved the machinery to Athens, Georgia. Ferdinand died in 1864 at age 45 in Georgia. This was the best armory after the old Virginia Manufactory at Richmond. See appendix for fuller treatment.

Cook, Auguste (1845-). gunsmith. 1886, New Orleans; working for Richard Rhodes [*Dir*.].

Cook, Gustave (1858-). gunsmith & truss maker. New Orleans. Census of 1870: Gustave Cook, 11, son of Lewis and Sophia Cook. Census of 1880: Sophia Cook, mother, 50; Louis Cook, 27, gunsmith; Gustave Cook, locksmith; 22; Sophia, wife, 25; Amelia, 13; Joe, 10; William, 24; Louisa, 25. 1886, gunsmith, 298 Annunciation St. 1891, 153 Camp St. Brother of Louis Cook; worked for Richard Rhodes. 1891, home at 137 Julia St., manufacturer of artificial limbs and iron trusses. 1900-02, 307 St. Charles St., truss maker [Gorman; *Dirs*.].

Cook, Louis (1853-1920). gunsmith. 1877-1906, New Orleans. Census of 1880: Louis Cook, born in Louisiana; wife Sophia. 1872-76, 76 St. Thomas; 1878, 135 Constance; 1879, 135 Constance [*Dirs*.; New Orleans *Daily Democrat*, 3 July 1879]. Louis was a son of Louis Kock, a cutler. Louis was a brother of Gustave. Kit Gorman wondered if he was strictly a repair man or whether he might have made some guns.

Cook, Robert (1843-). gunsmith. Shreveport. Census of 1870, ward 4 Shreveport: W T Watts, born in Georgia, 33, gunsmith; Martha, wife, 23, born in Illinois; W T, 4; Robert, 2, both born in Louisiana; Robert Cook, born in Illinois, 27, gunsmith. Census of 1880, Robert Cook, gun smith, born in Illinois, 37; Anna, 36; Robert, 8 Stella. 6; Walter, 1.

Mr. R. Cook, gunsmith on Market street, while doing some work or repairs on a pistol in his shop, accidentally caused the pistol to discharge in his hands and the ball passed through the lower fleshy part of the hand, causing a severe and ugly wound. Mr Cook said he did not know that the pistol was loaded, and thinks it was loaded by someone since he had received it in his shop. Familiarity will induce apparent carelessness, and even persons who are accustomed to handling firearms will occasionally receive a warning. We hope his injury may nopt prove serious [*New Orleans Daily Democrat,* 10 January 1880].

Cook, William D. (1855-1911). gunsmith. Plaquemine, Iberville Parish. African American tradesman. Report of 1911: William D Cook, male, Negro, married, born in South Carolina, aged 56 years, gunsmith. Mother: Alma Cook; born South Carolina. Died August 2, 1911, cause of death, insanity. No physician present. Buried at Seymourville, Louisiana, August 7, 1911, by E. W. Dickerson, undertaker, of Plaquemine. Informant: Daniel Cook of Plaquemine [Mortality Report].

Cormick John (1834-). gunsmith East Baton Rouge. Census of 1860: John Cormick, 26, gunsmith; Jailed in 1858 for horse stealing, born in England.

Cox, Elijah (1834-1898). gunsmith. Many, Sabine Parish. Census of 1860. Elijah Cox, 24, gunsmith, in home of James H. Cox, farmer, value $4000 real estate, $1200 personal value; Dorothy, 58, wife; and several siblings. Census of 1880, Elijah Cox, gunsmith, 47, born in Indiana; Anna, wife, 29; Charles, 9; Arrabella, 7, all born in Louisiana. On 1 March 1876 Cox purchased 40 acres of land in Sabine Parish. Elijah was born on 1 August 1834 and died on 11 June 1898 and was buried at Robeline, Natchitoches Parish [Ancestry; Find-a-Grave].

Creecier, ---. gunsmith. 1838, 24 Conde, New Orleans [*Dir.*].

Crenny, John. city armorer. 1851, New Orleans [*Times Picayune*, 25 June 1851].

Cross, Isham F. (1835-). gunsmith. Randolph County. Census of 1850: Isham, 15, son of Joshua and Lucinda Cross. Census of 1860 of Big Bend, Mountain Twp., Polk County, Arkansas: Isham Cross, carpenter; 24 Polly A, wife, 25, both born in Tennessee; Rebecca, 6; Elizabeth, 3; Sarah J, 1 month, all born in Arkansas. Census of 1880, 6th Ward, Livingston Parish: Isham Cross, born in Tennessee, gun smith, 45; Mary E., his wife, 26; Kate E., 3; John Weaver, 53; James Wilson, 28; Grace Wilson 8 months. There were several other men by this name in Louisiana, and at least one was born about 1840 in Tennessee.

Cullen, Thomas (1830-c.1885). gunsmith and inventor. 1852-55, New Orleans; 1860-85, San Francisco, California. Cullen held patent 72,982 of January 7, 1868 for small arms cartridges. On 13 April 1869 he received patent number 88,853 for a magazine rifle. On 29 December 1885 Patrick Kerrin received patent number 333,307 for a magazine rifle for T. Cullen, deceased [Gardner, *Small Arms Makers*, 46; Gorman].

Curtis, Bernard. gunsmith. 1832, 192 Bagatelle, New Orleans [*Dir.*].

Cushing, W. L. arms merchant. 1861, 57 Chartres St., New Orleans. Like many others Cushing was selling firearms on the eve of secession.

Cyr, Pierre. armurier. 1668-70, Louisiana. [*Acadian Families Who Settled in Louisiana*]. Also seen as Sire.

Daigle, Marcellis (1839--1915). gunsmith. Houma, Terrebonne Parish. Marcellus was born on 24 February 1839 in Thibodaux, Lafourche Parish. Census of 1860, Marcel Daigle, cooper, 26; Lavinia, wife, 20; Wiley, 4; Camilla, 2; Infant, 6 months, all born in Louisiana. Census of 1880, Marcellis Daigle, 41, born in Louisiana, gun smith; Ed---, 30, his wife; Lavinia, 12; Felina, 11; Desire, 9; Urbain, 7; Helena, 3; Giles, 2; and A. A.,1. Marcellus died on 13 January 1915 and was buried in St. Francis de Sales Cemetery in Terrebonne [Find-a-Grave; Ancestry].

Daltry, Charles. armorer. 1861, Confederate States Zouave Battalion. Daltry enlisted on May 29 1861 at New Orleans. He served as a regimental armorer. [*Booth's Index*].

Dangen, Anthony. silversmith. 1821, New Orleans [M.E.S.D.A.].

Daniels, Philander (1834-). gunsmith. St. Martin Parish. Philander was a son of Amassa and Ann Daniels. Census of 1870 of Midland County, Mississippi: Philander Daniels, born in New York, 35; Mary L, wife, 43; Druzilla, 17; Philander, 8, all born in Mississippi. Census of 1880, 2nd Ward, Saint Martin Parish, Louisiana: Philander Daniels, 46, gun smith, born in New York; wife Margaret, 36. Census of 1910 of Calcasieu Parish: Philander Daniels, 76, farmer, born in New York; Annie, 66, married 33 years.

Dansac, John (1799-). cutler. 1822, Conti near Levee, New Orleans. Dansac was born in Hanover, Germany [*Dir.*].

Darling, E. C. inventor. 1846, New Orleans. Darling apparently did not patent his invention, a repeating rifle, but did submit a sample to Ordnance [Sellers, 88]. In the 1868 New Orleans directory C. Darling was noted at 197 Terpsichore, no occupation given.

Darod, Isidore (1798-). gunsmith. 1840-50, Bayou Lafourche, Lafourche Parish. Census of 1840: Isidor Darod head of a household of , 5 white persons. Census of 1850, Isadore Darod, born in France; value $3000; Celestine, 38, his wife, born in Louisiana; slave holder. Not located after 1850.

Dart, Benjamin F. (1820-1867). gunsmith. New Orleans. 1865, 55 St. Charles; 1866-67, 375 St. Andrew. Successors to Kittredge & Folsom. Dart died of yellow fever on 20 September 1867 and the store front was sold to J. H. Lyon. Under the first two owners this was a substantial store importing many types of firearms and accouterments [Ancestry; Gorman; *Dirs*.].

Dart & Watkinson. major firearms store. 1865-67, 55 St,. Charles, New Orleans; successors to Kittredge & Folsom [Gorman]. E. J. Watkinson & Benjamin Dart. Major arms dealers and importers; U.S. arms manufacturers' representatives.

Dauphine, Richard A. gunsmith. 1811, New Orleans [*Dir*.].

David, H. L. cutler. 1832, 68 Ste. Ann, New Orleans [*Dir*.].

Davis, E. J. gunsmith and crook. Monroe, Ouachita Parish.

W F Watson, a gunsmith, and E J Davis, who worked for him, both living in Monroe, LA, have come to grief and are both now in the Monroe jail. They are two noted burglars who have been plying their nefarious trade of safe cracking in all the principal towns of north and middle Louisiana. They had a regular picnic of it. Watson fixed up the safes and Davis did the rest. This last one, when arrested, saved himself from being lynched by making a full confession of his deeds [*Meridional,* 18 June 1898].

Davis, Thomas (1854-). gunsmith. Covington, St. Tammany Parish; Census of 1880: Thomas Davis, 26, gunsmith, single, living with his brother.

Davoine, J. M. locksmith. 1861, 96 Conti, New Orleans [*Dir*.].

D'Avy, Solomon (1813--1877). gunsmith. Bellevue St., Opelousas, St. Landry Parish. Solomon was born on 23 January 1813. Census of 1850: Solomon D'Avy, 32, gunsmith, value $500; Clarissa, 32; Aurore, 16;

Josephine, 8; Joasine, 5; Virginia, 3; and Athalie, infant. Census of 1860 of Grand Coteau, St. Landry Parish: Solomon D'Avy, 47, armorer, $1500 real estate, apparently widower; Marie, 10; and Virginia, 10. Census of 1870: Solomon D'Avy, 57, gunsmith, living alone. Solomon died on 8 August 1877 and was buried in St. Landry Parish. George Moriarity advertised in 1880 that he was successor to the late Sol D'Avy [*Opelousas Courier*, 27 November 1880; see also *Opelousas Journal,* 1 February 1868].

Notice. The Public is hereby informed that all arms left with me to be repaired will remain at the risk of the owners. I shall exercise the strictest guard upon them but desire it to known that I will not be responsible if my shop is entered by burglars. Solomon D'Avy, Opelousas [*Courier*, 8 February 1868].

Public Sale. Estate of Solomon D'Avy, deceased. By virtue of an order of the honorable Parish Court, of the Parish of St. Landry, there will be sold at public auction to the highest bidder . . . at the last residence of the deceased in the town of Opelousas . . . September 15, 1877, all the movable property belonging to the said estate . . . 4 milch cows and calves, 5 head of horned cattle, one Creole horse, 1 American work horse, 1 buggy and harness, 1 old hack, ploughs and harrows, a sett of blacksmith and gunsmith tools, . . . a large number of guns, pistols, revolvers, &c. [*Opelousas Journal,* 25 August 1877].

Estate of Solomon D'Avy, To Whom It May Concern. Any person having Guns, Pistols, or other effects in possession of the above estate are requested to call on the undersigned at his residence in the town of Opelousas, make proof of their property, pay what may be due thereon, and redeem the same; otherwise everything in the possession of the estate will be sold at public auction. . . . Michel Lavergne [*Opelousas Journal,* 25 August 1877].

DeBarbieris, Henry (1844-1904). gun- and locksmith. 1860-1900, New Orleans. 1880; born in Marseilles, France; wife Catharine. Census of 1870, Henry Debarbieris, locksmith, 26, born in France; Catharine, born in Ireland, 24, wife; Henry, 4; Mary L, 3; Mary M, 11 months. Census of Manufactures of 1880: Henry made guns valued at $600 from $50 worth of raw materials and a $100 capital investment. He worked full time at gun making only 4 months a year. Census of 1900 ward 5: Henry Debarbieris, born in France, 54, gunsmith, widower; Louise, born in Louisiana; 22 Marie, born in Texas, 23. Henry died on 4 January 1904 [*Dirs*.; Ancestry].

DeBarbieris, Henry Joseph (1865-1928). gunsmith. Henry J. was born on 7 October 1865. 1885-87, 221 Chartres, New Orleans. 1902, 935 Chartres. Listed in other unrelated professions thereafter. Son of Henry. Census of 1920, ward 7: Henry, 52, cashier, living with his brother Charles. Henry died on 5 December 1828 [Ancestry; *Dirs*.].

Deck, ---. In 1822 the gunsmith, Deck, settled in Webster Parish. In 1822, Deck the gunsmith, blessed with an interesting family, built a house in Claiborne Parish [Smith, *History of Claiborne Parish*, 51].

Dejoux, Fred (1840-). gunsmith. 4th ward, Caldwell Parish. Census of 1880; Fred Dejoux, 40, gunsmith, born in France, living in a rooming house.

Delambre, Amedée Constant (1821-). planter and gunsmith. East Feliciana Parish. Amedée Delambre was a son of Philip Constant Delambre and was born on France. He worked as a gunsmith, and also worked with copper and tin ware, in Jackson before 1857, after which he switched to agriculture. Census of 1860: A. Delambre, 38, overseer, born in France, value $2000; A., 27, wife. Census of 1870: A Delombre, 49, farmer, real estate $8000, widower, Born in France; son L, 22. On 3 March 1870 Delambre married Lovey A Knox [Ancestry].

Delassize, Laurent. gunsmith and merchant. 1762, New Orleans [Catholic Church records; Gorman].

Delassize, Louis T. (1818-). gunsmith and inventor. African-American tradesman. 65 Orleans, New Orleans. Residence 68 Orleans. On 20 July 1869 he received patent number 92,799 for a breech-loading firearm. He also received a patent for non-arms related device, a brick making machine, pursuant to his pre-Civil War business. 1870, Louis T Delassize, mulatto, 52; Sophie, wife, 42; Mary, 5. In 1870 he was noted as superintendent of the city's waterworks. He had real estate valued at $20,000 and $500 in personal value [Census; Gorman].

Delaton, A. (1834-). gunsmith. Graver St., New Orleans. Census of 1880; A Delaton, 46, gunsmith, born in Cuba; wife Fecilie, 52. Not found after 1880.

DellaTorre, A. M. variety store. 1838-43, 99 Chartres, New Orleans. He sold firearms among other items [Gorman; *Dirs*.].

DellaTorre, Antonio. gunsmith. 1877-79, 49 Bourbon St., New Orleans; boards rear 64 Dauphine. He abandoned the gunsmith's trade and entered other professions [*Dirs.;* Gorman].

Delrieu, Jules Pierre. gun- and locksmith. 1858-66, New Orleans. 1858, doing business as Barthelemy & Delrieu. Captain, Third company, 3rd regiment, French Regiment, C.S.A, physically 5' 8" tall, 158 pounds. 1869, 67 Marais, 1861-66, 243 Burgundy [*Dirs*.; Gorman]. Not found after 1869.

Demoustier, Joseph. gunsmith. 1841-42, 176 Bienville St., New Orleans [*Dirs.*]

Dempsey, James W. (1828-). 1854-72, New Orleans. 1857, doing business as Gerteis & Dempsey, 113 St. Charles. Artificer in Companies 1st, 2nd and 3rd Battalion Washington Artillery. Physically, 5' 6", 158 pounds. He enlisted on May 26th, 1861 at New Orleans. He was transferred to 2nd Company on June 24th, 1861. Present on all muster rolls through April 1862. Also present for muster roll for May and June 1862. Transferred from 2nd Company to 3rd Company on June 10th, 1862. Present on muster rolls from July 1862, to February 1863. Present on muster rolls from March 1863 to August 1863. Absent from muster roll for September and October 1863. Absent since September 4th, 1863, at Staunton, VA, undergoing sentence of G. C. M., four months' pay forfeit by G. C. M. [General Court Martial], General Order No. 62, Army of Northern Virginia, May 12th, 1863. Present on muster rolls1863. Returned to Company on November 27th, 1863, after undergoing sentence of G. C. M. Present on muster rolls from January 1864 to February 1865. He was born in New York, occupation gunsmith, Residence New Orleans, age when enlisted 33, single. Census of 1870, successor to W. Basset, gunmaker, 230 Rampart St.; 1876, gunsmith for Henrietta, widow of J. F. Dittrich, 75 Chartres [Dirs.; Gorman; *Booth's Index*]. Artificer and armorer to Washington Artillery, 1875 [*Times Picayune*, 30 July 1875]. Not located after 1875.

Dempsey, Nelson. gunsmith. 1854, 176 Circus, New Orleans [*Dir.*].

Derepa, V. (1804-). lock- and gunsmith. 1842-50, 87-89 Conti, New Orleans. Derepa was born in Ireland and came to New Orleans via Havre, arriving on 18 November 1837 [*Dir.*]. Also seen as Derepas. Possibly Vivant Derepa. Not located in any census.

Desangles, Francois (1815-1880). black-, lock-, and gunsmith. 1868-80, New Orleans. Noted as a gunsmith only 1879-80, 947 Chippewa, between Toledano & Louisiana Ave. Desangles died on 29 January 1880 in New Orleans [*Dirs.*; Gorman].

Deuraugh, F. locksmith. 1861, Chippewa near Louisiana, New Orleans. 1866, blacksmith, Chippewa below Louisiana [*Dir.*].

Deville, Victor (1815-). gunsmith. Victor Deville, 22, gunsmith, arrived from Havre on 28 January 1827 on the Crescent.

Dickerson, Lewis (1805--1861). gunsmith Lewis was born in Mississippi on 29 October 1805. He had a brother named Newton and they settled in Natchez. Lewis was a gunsmith and married Lucinda Miley Hobbs and had 12 children. Census of 1850 of Jackson County, Louisiana: Lewis Dickerson, 45, born in Mississippi; Milley, 33; Lucinda, 10; Jesse, 8; Almina, 6; and Presley, 4, all born in Louisiana. Census of 1860 of Vernon, Jackson County, Louisiana: Lewis Dickerson, farmer born in 1805 in Kentucky; Millie, 43; 4 children, ages 4 to 17, all born in Louisiana. Lewis died on 15 August 1861 [Ouachita Parish Archives; Family]. The 1850 Census places his birth in Mississippi, but 1860 places it in Kentucky as does family tradition.

Dietzler, Simon (1813-). locksmith. 1853, New Orleans. Simon was a patient in the charity hospital with a fever; born in Coblentz, Prussia.

Dils, J. H. (1841-). gunsmith. Helena, Phillips County, Arkansas. Census of 1860: J W H Dils, 20, born in Louisiana, son of S H Dils [mother]. Census of 1880: J. H. Dils, born in Kentucky, 39, gunsmith; Mary T., wife, 34, born in Mississippi; Josephine, 9, born in Louisiana; Lewis, 6, born in Mississippi; Wm, 5, born in Texas [Census]. Not located after 1880. Despite differences in state of birth I believe the two censuses are of the same man.

Dittrich, John Frantz (1826-1875). gunmaker, importer and manufacturer. 1850-59, 96 S. 2nd, St. Louis, Missouri; 1861-68, Mobile, Alabama; 1868-75, New Orleans. Census of 1860, ward 3 Mobile: John F Dittrich, born in Saxony, 34, gunsmith; Henrietta, wife, 26, born in Prussia; Antonio, 4, born in Missouri. 1868, 199 Canal St. In 1867, John opened a variety store. He advertised that he was agent for Bismarck double needle guns. This is the only time I have seen an American advertisement for a needle-fire gun of any sort. This arm appeared in several subsequent advertisements. 1869-75, 82 Chartres St. dealer in, importer of, guns, pistols, cutlery, gun materials, and ammunition; repairing done with neatness and dispatch and warranted. Census of 1870, ward 4 New Orleans: J. F. Dittrich, gunsmith shop, 46, born in Saxony; Henrietta, wife, 36; Antonia, 14. John died on 24 July 1875. His wife Henrietta took over his shop and ran it for nearly 20 more years. [*Dirs*; Gorman; Ancestry; Noble].

To His Excellency Governor William P Kellogg: I have just be waited on by Mr J F Dittrich, Gunsmith, No. 82 Chartres street, and learn of him that he is apprehensive that his store will be broken into and his stock of arms seized by parties to him unknown. I informed him that the police force of this city was not in any manner under my control that I could render him no protection whatever. . . .
Louis A Wiltz, Mayor

To Honorable Louis A Wiltz, mayor of New Orleans: I hasten to reply to your communication of this day stating that you have information of a proposed attack upon the store of Mr J F Dittrich, a gunsmith at No. 82 Chartres street in this city. I have directed the detail of a sufficient police force to prevent the apprehended attack. I am not surprised at the fears of Mr Dittrich since the proceedings of last night. These riots and tumults though now ostentatiously disavowed in the public prints by some of the very persons whom the public judgment will hold in a great measure responsible for them, are, but the natural results of the course of a considerable body of our citizens, who, I regret to say, have been engaged in advising resistance to land and open rebellion against all order and government . . . . William P Kellogg, Governor [New Orleans *Republican,* 8 May 1873].

Dittrich, Henrietta (1834-1900). gunsmith. 1875-92, 75 Chartres, New Orleans. Henrietta was the widow of John Dittrich. She ran his gunshop for nearly 20 years after John's death. On 8 April 1876 she remarried to Herman Wehrmann. Henrietta died on 15 October 1900 [Ancestry; Gorman].

Doclar, Edward (1841-1873). gun- and locksmith. 1860-73, New Orleans. Census of 1860, Edward Doclar was apprenticed to Louis Juzan, living in Juzan's household. 1869, 123 6th St. Census of 1870, Edward Doclar, 114 Prytania St. He died on 3 January 1873 [Ancestry; *Dirs.*]. See also Duclére.

Doranthy, William G. locksmith. 1861, Magazine near St. Andrew, New Orleans [*Dir.*].

Dorian, Charles (1848-1942). gunsmith. 1870-80, Shreveport, Caddo Parish. Census of 1870, John Dorian, carpenter, 61; Catharine, wife, 62; Peter, 20; Charles Dorian, 23. Census of 1880, Charles Dorian, born in France, gun smith, 32; Alma, his wife, 22; Charles, 3; Lena, 2; Albert, 11 months.. Although born in France Dorian departed from Hamburg, Germany, and arrived in America on 31 March 1869 [Ancestry].

Dorion, Pierre. gunsmith. 1822-32, New Orleans; doing business as Dorion & Bienaime 1822, doing business as Dorion & Bienaimé, 10 St. Ann. 1826, 26 St. Ann; 1832, 10 St. Ann [*Dirs.*].

Doyle, William H. Jr. (1866-1901). gunsmith. New Orleans. Doyle was just 35 when he died of heart failure, leaving a wife and several children. He was a son of W. H. Doyle and his wife née Stott. Doyle was married to a daughter of gunsmith Hector Latil, suggesting the possibility that he apprenticed with Latil. He was a member of the Silver Coronet Band and a musician in Fourrier's orchestra [*Daily Advocate*, 1 September 1901].

Drapeaux, Sieur Nicholas. gunsmith. 1740, New Orleans. Sieur Nicholas was gunsmith to the French king and acted as a guarantor for his widowed sister-in-law, Marie Jeanne Drapeuax, in her forthcoming second marriage [Ancestry].

Dreier, Wilhelm (1828-). gunsmith. 1851, New Orleans; noted for admission to charity hospital. Dreier was born in Prussia.

Drew, Newitt (1772-1842). gunsmith. Drew first moved to the area that is Webster Parish c. 1822. He was born 26 February. 1772, a son of Jeremiah Drew and Mary "Polly" Parker.. He married Sarah A. Maxwell on 7 July 1799 probably in Wilson County, Tennessee. Newitt Drew was a farmer, gunsmith, and sawmill owner, a Baptist, and was supposed to have founded the town of Overton. Newitt Drew was from Southampton County, Virginia, moving from there to Wilson County, Tennessee, in 1797 or 1798. He settled at Overton, which was a place on Dorcheat Bayou approximately 2 1/2 to 3 miles south the present side of Minden, Louisiana, between 1815 and 1817. He was a gunsmith and had a gristmill there. Claiborne Parish. In 1821 Drew settled on Black Bayou, near Driskill and was a gunsmith by trade. Newitt died pn 26 May 1842

One morning he sent Jack, his servant, to drive up his horses. That morning Jack found a bear turning over a log in search of bugs, and thinking himself a good bear hunter, picked up a pine knot and made for the bear. Slipping close up he let go at the bear, and to his astonishment the bear wheeled around to see what the trouble was. Seeing Jack, the bear laid his ears back and went for him, but Jack, fled like a scared rabbit. He escaped from the bear, but when he finally stopped he was lost, and wandered around for three or four days when he was found in Dorcheat Swamp, about twenty miles from home. Jack quit the bear business. Drew afterward moved down on the Dorcheat, established the lower landing and got under way the town of Overton. He also built the first saw and grist mill in the parish. It was on the Cooly and ran by water power [Smith, *History of Claiborne Parish*].

Dubuc, Michel. [*Serruier*] locksmith. 1718 sent from France to Louisiana.

Duchemin, Victor (1832-). locksmith. 1851, New Orleans; admitted to charity hospital with "int fever"; born in Pau, Bearn, France. Victor, born about 1832, departed from Bordeaux, arriving in New Orleans on 16 October 1849 [Ancestry].

DuClére, Edward. locksmith. 1861, 248 Orleans, New Orleans; 1870, rear

114 Prytania [*Dir.*]. See Doclar.

Dufilbo, A. H. cutler. 1861, 21 Royal, New Orleans [*Dir.*].

Dugas, Abraham (1616-1698). armurier.Dugas was probably born in Chouppes, Poiters, France, and may have had Jewish ancestors. In 1640 the first Acadian families settled in Louisiana, included Abraham, a skilled gunsmith. Dugas was from Chouppes, Poitiers, France. Another reference suggested he was from Topulouse and was a gunsmith to the king, in Louisiana before 1636. He married Marguerite, daughter of Claude Petitpas, at Port-Royal, c.1677. In October 1687, Abraham "made his mark on an attestation in favour of Governor d'Aulnay's accomplishments," which attests to his early presence in the colony. Abraham also was more than a gunsmith at Port-Royal. According to a high French official, Abraham Dugas "carried out the functions of general representative of the King [in civil and criminal matters]," so he probably came from an influential family in France. He operated from Port Royal, Acadia, Nova Scotia, Canada. The first Dugas in Louisiana arrived in 1765. Several of these first families settled the region known as the Acadian Coast along the Mississippi River above New Orleans. How much time Dugas spent in Louisiana is open to discussion. Abraham's oldest son Claude, born c. 1649, was also a gunsmith, primarily at Port Royal [Ancestry].

duHamel, C. (1817--1871). mathematical and philosophical instrument maker. New Orleans. There is a refractor telescope of about 4 inches aperture, on an unusual lightweight equatorial mount, signed either on tube or mount *Wm. Shawk / Maker / St. Louis & Carondelet MO*. Also signed on the drawtube: *duHamel / New Orleans*. It is without an objective lens. Census of 1860, ward 4: C Duhamel, optician, 43, value $10,000; P, wife, 40, both born in France. Census of 1870: C. DuHamel, optician, born in France about 1818, living alone. He died on 24 June 1871 and was buried in St. Louis Cemetery No. 2. There was also a S. duHamel, female, born in France, living alone, optician, about 1820 in 1880 [Ancestry; Find-a-Grave].

Duhart, Louis Adolph (1810--?). gunsmith. 1827-60, New Orleans. African American tradesman. Louis Adolph Duhart married Francoise Palmire Brouard (1810-?), both born in Santa Domingo. [Find-a-Grave says he was born in Cuba]. 1851, gun- and blacksmith and lightning rod maker, 1827-31, 22 Toulouse; 1841, 146 Chartres; 1841-55, 99 Elysian Fields. Census of 1850, ward 1: A Duhart, mulatto, born in Havana, 40, gunsmith; P Duhart, 36, born in Santa Domingo; Adolphe Duhart, 20, mason; Adeline, 18; Ernest, carpenter, 17; Telcide, 16; Armand, 12; Maria, 10; Aristide, 8; Felicia, 3, all born in Louisiana [*Dirs.*]. Dates of death and burial and location of cemetery are unknown. Not located after 1850.

Dumont, L. Julien. gunsmith and locksmith. Baton Rouge. Not located in any census. There was a Julien Dumont, cooper, in St. John the Baptist Parish in 1880 and 1900.

Gunsmith, Locksmith and Machine Repairer. Mr L. Julien Dumont has just opened on Third street, opposite Pike's Hall, Baton Rouge, a shop where he will attend to repairing Guns, Pistols, Locks, Keys, and Sewing Machines. He has a forge where he also can repair vehicles and shoe horses. He will be found constantly at his shop , ready to perform all manner of work as above, besides overhauling and mending umbrellas and parasols [Baton Rouge *Tri-weekly Gazette*, 29 March 1866]

Gunsmithing and Repairing by L. Julien Dumont north of Third street Theater. Mr Dumont having received a full and complete set of gunsmithing articles from one of the largest importing houses in New York respectfully informs his friends and the public generally that he is now better prepared than ever to execute work in his line. He is amply provided with gunstocks of various kinds, Gun-locks, Mainsprings, and every other variety of mechanical apparatus and appliance necessary to the construction and reparation of Guns and Pistols. As he is determined to attend to all orders for work in a prompt and thoroughly efficient manner, he solicits a liberal share of the patronage from those requiring services with which he has had great experience and familiarity [Batron Rouge *Tri-weekly Gazette*, 17 January 1867].

Dupas, Mathurin (1807-). gun- and locksmith. 1838-50, New Orleans. 1838, 19 Ursulines; 1842, 10 St. Louis St. Census of 1840, M. Dupas head of household of 7 free white persons, one male age 15-19, one male age 30-39, one engaged in manufacture. Census of 1850, M Dupas, 43, blacksmith; ---, wife, 27, both born in France; Andrew, 7, born in Texas; Octavius, 5; Matthew, infant, both born in Louisiana; William Barnes, 24, blacksmith. Mathurin. son of Jean DuPas, married Marie LeRoux near Paris [Census; Gorman; *Dir.*]. Not located after 1850.

DuPont, Joseph (1821--). gunsmith. 1850, ward 2, New Orleans. African American tradesman. Census of 1850: Rachel Nelson, mulatto, 49, born in South Carolina; Joseph Dupont, gunsmith, 29, born in France; Martin Monahne, 30, weighs cotton. DuPont appears in no other source [Ancestry].

DuPuy, Bernard (--1848). gunsmith. 1822-32, New Orleans. 1822, 80 Bourbon; 1823-27, 132 Bourbon; 1830-32, 149 Main St. Census of 1840: Bernard DuPuy, head of household of three persons, two slaves and Bernard, age 30-39, who was engaged in a commerce [*Dirs.*]

DuPuy, Bienaime (1800-). apprentice gunsmith. 1814 apprenticed to Jean B. LeGrand. DuPuy was born in Santa Domingo [Gorman].

Duty, Asa S. (1798-1874). gunsmith. Western District, Bienville Parish. Census of 1850: Asa Duty, carpenter, 52, born in North Carolina; John W Duty, carpenter, 29; Littleton A Duty, farmer, 25, both born in Louisiana; Permilia, wife, 21, born in Arkansas; Littleton S, infant, born in Louisiana. Census of 1860, Plaquemine, Iberville Parish: Asa Duty, living alone, widower, mechanic. Census of 1870, ward 4, Union Parish; born in North Carolina; $10 real estate, $50 personal value [Ancestry].

Eberhardt, A. armorer. 1861, Hall of Orleans Fire Company No. 21, New Orleans [*Times Picayune,* 7 February 1861]

Edberg, A. locksmith. 1861, 96 Conti, New Orleans [*Dir.*].

Eddings, Abraham (1809-). gunsmith. East Feliciana Parish. Census of 1850, Abraham Eddings, gunsmith, 41, born in North Carolina; Sarah, 34; W.S.B. [male], 6; Mary, 3, all born in Louisiana. Not found after 1850.

Effinger, Bernard (1826-1883). gunsmith. 1871-83, New Orleans. 1871, employed by Julien Saget; 1875-76, Rampart St.; 1877-78, Royal St.; 1882-83, Rampart St. Census of 1870, ward 4: Bernard Effinger, born in Germany, 44, gunsmith; Lucia, wife, 33, born in France. 1871, armorer, Customhouse. He died on 28 May 1883 in New Orleans [*Dirs*.; Gorman].

Erries, François. gunsmith. 1846-61, New Orleans. 1846, 161 Old Levee; 1848-49, Jefferson; 1851, 8 Toulouse; 1852, 291 Bayou Rd; 1853, 175 Ursulines; 1859, 178 Old Levee; 1861, 309 Old Levee [Gorman; *Dirs*.]. Not located in any census.

Ertle, Clemence (1837-1892). gunsmith. New Orleans.

Clemence Ertle, a gunsmith, age 55, who has been missing from his home on Angelrodt street since July 1 was found floating in the river yesterday at the foot of Buchanan street by David Robecker. The body was removed to the morgue. The deceased had a wife and child living at 1563 Tchoupitoulas street, New Orleans. He lived on a flatboat, and it is supposed committed suicide, as he had been suffering from despondency [*St. Louis Republic*, 4 August 1892]

Estranspes, Luis Adofo. gunsmith. 1870, Dryades St., New Orleans [*New Orleans Times*, 25 January 1870]. He became a physician by 1886 [*Dir.*].

Not found in any census.

Eternod & Piaget. dry goods, gun dealers. 1860-61, 40 Chartres, New Orleans. Offered Monte Christo rifles and pistols, and 4 and 6 shot pistols [Gorman; *Dirs*.].

Fannier, Louis (1860-). apprentice gunsmith. New Orleans. Census of 1880: Louis Fannier, 20, apprentice gunsmith, in home of J. B. Revol, 81, gunsmith; Joseph L. Revol, 49; Henrietta, 52, Joseph's wife; Josephine, 12; Amelia Revol, 28; Eugene Gerard, 18; Louis Fannier, 20, apprentice.

Farish, Claude M. locksmith. 1876-1910, 616 Magazine, New Orleans [*Dir*.].

Farish, George R. (1834-). lock- and gunsmith, bell hanger. 1868-1908, New Orleans; 1868, below Josephine & Jackson; 1883, 616 Magazine; 1908, 2039 Magazine [*Dirs*.]. Census of 1880, George R Farish, 46, gun smith, born at Jackson, Mississippi; E.V., his wife, 32; Emma V., 13; R.L., 9; Florence, 6; George, 5 [*Dirs*.].

Faulhaber, Oswald. armorer. 1883, Crescent Regiment; rear 185 Canal, New Orleans [*Dir*.].

Faust, C. L. (1819--). gunsmith. Washington, St. Laundry Parish. Census of 1870: C L Faust, retired merchant, 51,. $600 real estate, $300 personal value; Margaret, 55, both born in France. Census of 1880: C Faust, 61, grocer, widower. Not located after 1880.

For Sale by the Undersigned on account of departure the following property: a HOUSE and LOT an old and well-established business stand in Washington a Gunsmith shop including Guns, Stock, Arms, etc. a stock of Dry Goods, Groceries, etc. The whole will be sold together or separately at a great sacrifice. The merchandise will be at 20% below cost for cash. All or any of said property can be purchased at private sale until the 19th of November next when all not disposed of will be sold at public auction. C. L. Faust opposite the Old Urban Store, Washington, LA [*Opelousas Courier*, 18 July 1874].

Favre, Justin. watchmaker, jeweler, gunsmith. 1842-60, Chartres, New Orleans [Dirs.; Gorman]. Noted as a gunsmith in 1846 only.

Fayn, ---. gun- and locksmith. 1841-42, 91 Conti St., New Orleans [Gorman; *Dir*.]. Not located in any source.

Febiger, Henry Boyce (1852-1927). gunsmith & inventor. 1882-1927, New Orleans. 1885, doing business as Febiger & Company, with Foster Olroyd. 15 August 1905, patent number 797,420 for a firearm, issued to him at Philadelphia. 5 January 1908, patent number 908,553, issued to him at Philadelphia. 14 December 1908, patent number 943,344, for a movement for a firearm, issued to Febiger at New Orleans. He also was an agent for Western Cartridge Company. 1887, 168 Gravier, Febiger & Company. Febiger died in New Orleans [Gardner, *Small Arms Makers*, 63]. Reportedly, his brother John was also an inventor.

Febiger, John C., Jr. inventor. New Orleans. Kit Gorman reported that John, a brother of Henry Febiger, was an inventor whose patents included a combination slide action and semi-automatic .22 rifle which he sold to Savage. He also reportedly invented a semi-automatic infantry rifle about 1917. Interestingly Ms Gorman supplies no patent dates or numbers and there is no entry for John in Colonel *Gardner's Small Arms Makers*, source of virtually all firearms patent information, including mindlessly copied by Sellers.

Feiman. See Fieman.

Felix, ---. cutler [*coutelier*]. 1811, 8 St. Phillippe, New Orleans [*Dir.*; M.E.S.D.A.].

Fellen, Matthew, Sr (1797--1878). gun- and locksmith. New Orleans. Census of 1840: M. Fellen, only person in household, white male age 20-49. Census of 1850: M. Fellon, 53, gunsmith, born in Germany. Fellen apparently worked for another since he appears only in 1853 and 1867 at 6 Perdido St. His son Matthew Jr was born in New Orleans in 1850. Matthew died on 19 April 1878 in New Orleans [Gorman; *Dirs.*].

Fellen, Matthew, Jr (1850-). gunsmith. New Orleans. Census of 1870; Matthew Fellen, 20, born in Louisiana, apprentice gunsmith, noted in his father's household [Gorman]. Not located after 1870.

Fenroot, Christian (1811-). gunsmith. New Orleans. Census of 1860; Christian Fenroot, 49, gunsmith, in household of J. Ribriou, gunsmith. Not found before or after 1860.

Ferguson & Hall. hardware store, gun dealers. 1838, Old Levee, New Orleans; sold Colt rifles [Gorman; *Dir.*].

Ferree, Isaac (1786-1821). gunpowder maker & gunsmith. Isaac was a son of Jacob and Alice Powell Ferree. He married Hannah Wall. He made gunpowder with his half-brother, Colonel Joel Ferree before 1810 when he moved to Pittsburgh, PA. Had a gun shop there until 1812. He then enlisted in the army and assigned to the 1st Regular U. S. Infantry as armorer. He owned land in both Arkansas and Missouri. In 1822 while working as an armorer he contracted a fever and died in Baton Rouge. [http://www.ferreereunion.com/gunsmiths.htm].

Ferrier, Joseph (1826--). mechanic. Donaldsonville, Ascension Parish. Joseph Icard was in partnership with Joseph Ferrier. Notice in the *Louisianais* of 6 October 1877 that the partnership was dissolved. The multi-functional firm performed services in the following fields: blacksmithing, wheelwright, locksmith, coach maker and gunsmith. Ferrier continued the businesses. [*Thibodaux Sentinel*, 14 April 1877; *La Louisianials*, 6 December 1879; *Donaldsonville Chief*, 13 December 1879]. Census of 1880: Joseph Ferrier, 54, blacksmith, born in France; Eugenie, 27, wife; Henry, 6; and an infant [Ancestry]. Date of death, place of burial not found.

Feurché, Edward. locksmith. 1865, 105 Conti, New Orleans. Edward was drafted by the Union Army [Ancestry].

Fick, George A. (1873-1944). lock- and gunsmith. after 1900, 1009 Tulane St., New Orleans [*Dirs*.; Gorman]. Sellers listed one George A. Fick in 1869 in New Orleans, citing some directory.

Fiebick, Robert (1817-). locksmith. 1847, New Orleans; confined to lunatic asylum for past 2 months; born in Silesia, Germany.

Fieman, Patrick. gunsmith. 1865, 111 Burgundy, New Orleans; drafted [*Times Picayune,* 19 April 18665].

Fink, Andrew, Sr. (1820-). gunsmith. Baton Rouge. On 3 August 1847 Andreas Fink arrived in America from Harve, France on the *Viola*. Census of 1860, Andrew Fink, age 40, born in France, gunsmith, value $500; Agatha, his wife, 39, born in France; Emily, 9; Andrew, 8; Agath, 6, all born in Louisiana. Census of 1870: Andrew Finke, 50, gunsmith, born in France, $600 value; Agatha, 48, born in France; Andrew, 18, works on ferry; Louis, 6, both born in Louisiana. Not found after 1870.

Mr. Andrew Finck narrowly escaped being killed on Tuesday morning. . . . a colored man was in Mr. Finck's gunshop, on Main street, and was handling a loaded pistol in a careless manner. In attempting to cock the weapon the hammer slipped from his thumb, discharging the pistol. The ball cut the skin above Mr. Finck's right eye, near the temple. Had the ball ranged a fraction farther to the left Mr. Finck would have been instantly killed. [*Daily Advocate*, 23 December 1885]

Fink, Andrew Jr. (1851--1930). gunsmith. Baton Rouge. Census of 1880, Andrew Fink, gun smith, born in Louisiana, 27; Mary, 23; Ada F., 4; Louis Fink, his brother, 16 [Census]. *The Louisiana Capitolian* of 3 November 1881 referred to him as "the young gunsmith who is an ordnance department within himself". Andrew died on 7 April 1930.

On Wednesday Aaron Johnson, alias Pound Cake, was jerked up before the Mayor's Court. . . . There was a long file of witnesses of both sexes whom Pound Cake had hit with sticks and skillets, after which occurrences he had dusted from police who were never able to catch him until the other night when they cornered him by chance . He started to run away from the Chief and an assistant but unsuspectantly ran into the outstretched arms of Andrew Finck the young gunsmith who is an ordnance department in himself, who happened to be acting as an officer [*Louisiana Capitolian*, 3 November 1881]

Finley, William Oscar (1830--1861). gunsmith. Orleans Parish. Census of 1860; born in Alabama. William Oscar Finley died in early 1861 [German].

Fisher, Louis (1826--1899). gunsmith. 1860-66, New Orleans. Census of 1860; Louis Fisher, gunsmith, born in Germany. 1861, 145 Main; 1866, 70 Girod. He died on 4 February 1899 [*Dir.*]. Also seen as Fischer.

Fitz, Hense J. P. gun- and locksmith. 1843, Dryades near Edward, New Orleans [*Dir.*].

Fitzgerald, Michael. armorer. 1865, home at 195 Calliope, New Orleans, home. In 1865 the Union Army drafted Michael Fitzgerald [*New Orleans Times,* 17 March 1865]

Fitzpatrick, Reese (1808-1868). gunsmith. 1829-38, Baton Rouge, Louisiana; 1839-68, Union, between Main and State Sts., Natchez, Adams County. 1840-43, in partnership with Stephen O'Dell. Reese was born in Ohio. He made percussion rifles and Bowie knives. In 1860 he employed 3 men [Noble 1: 48]. Frost in his *History of the Bowie Knife* refers to "Captain Reese Fitzpatrick, famous Natchez gunsmith." He employed 3 to 5 men [Adams County Historical Society]. Census of 1850, Natchez South. R. Fitzpatrick, age 55, gunmaker, value $400, born in Ohio; Ruth, 38, born in Alabama; L.W., 12 [female], born in Louisiana; Charles H., 10; J. H., 8 [male]; Jno., 6; Margaret, 7; George, 4; Frederick, 2; infant male, 1, all born in Mississippi. In the next household was J. Dellahunt, 35, gunsmith. Reese then moved to Natchez, Mississippi. Fitzpatrick is considered one of the South's greatest weapons artisans and was an expert craftsman in working silver and gold. The *Natchez Free Trader* reported on May 17, 1861, that Reese Fitzpatrick, gunsmith of Natchez, made fine Bowie knives when he was in Louisiana.

Mr. Fitzpatrick . . . has just shown us one of the richest and most splendid rifles we ever saw, which he has completed for General Felix Houston of the Army of Texas. It is of surpassing finish and differs in its armament from any rifle we ever before have seen. It is of the usual length of Tennessee and Kentucky rifles, the barrel being inlaid with gold and silver. The mountings are of massive silver, the pan inlaid with gold; a back-action flint-lock, with a beautiful Star of Texas inlaid on one side of the breech, with alternate rays of gold and silver. The most remarkable feature of the armament is the bayonet which is truly a terrific weapon. It is two and one-half feet in length, as wide as a Bowie knife of the largest size, strait, two-edged, with a handle fitted to a socket by the side of the barrel and is carried in a sheath like a sword at the side, except when attached to the rifle for a bayonet charge. It may be used either as a hand dagger or bayonet. Such is the beauty and finish of the workmanship of this splendid firearm that it is impossible to detect a fault. Besides the improvement of the sword bayonet there is an important invention to facilitate loading: it is the cartridge case made of brass about an inch and a half in length in the cavity of which the powder and ball are placed. The cases are taken from the cartridge box in loading, and placed in the muzzle of the rifle, where it rests on an inner moulding and the contents are rammed through it into the barrel and the case replaced in the cartridge box to be filled again. By this means the rifle can be loaded and discharged four or five times a minute. As a piece of curious workmanship, Natchez has reason to be proud of it, and we shall be much mistaken if Mr. Fitzpatrick does nothave as many orders for such pieces as he can fill. The cost of General Huston's rifle was $300. [*Telegraph and Texas Register*, 4 September 1839 from *Natchez Free Trader*].

Gunsmithing. Main street, Natchez, nearly opposite the Masonic Hall. The Subscriber still continues his shop at the old stand, nearly opposite the Masonic Hall, where he is prepared to make or repair anything appertaining to the Gunsmithing business, on terms 25% cheaper than any other establishment in the city. Mathematical Instruments repaired; Seals cut and Presses furnished; Seel Type and Stamp cutting; and Canes mounted, in a superior manner. Rees Fitzpatrick [*Free Trader*, 21 January 1845]

A Hopeful Lad – We understand that he Gunsmith shop of Mr. Fitzpatrick of this city was entered on Sunday night last and several guns, pistols, &c. were extracted there from. The burglary has been traced to a promising youth of about 12 summers [*Free Trader*, 7 March 1849]

Florent, Huss. gunsmith. 1846-53, New Orleans. 1851, Levee & Jackson [*Dir.*]. Not in any census or Ancestry.

Fluck, Adam (1853--1906). gunsmith. Alexandria, Rapides Parish. Census of 1880; Adam Fluck, 27, gunsmith, born in Bavaria; single, living in a boarding house. Census of 1900: Adam Fluck, born in August 1847 in Germany, gunsmith, 52, naturalized in Pennsylvania; Dora, 40; Edwin, 16; Francis, 14; Lenora, 13; Sadie, 10; Dora, 8; Felix, 5; and George, 1, all born in Louisiana. Adam died in 1906 and was buried in Rapides Cemetery, Pineville [Find-a-Grave; Ancestry].

Flus, Louis Antoine. locksmith. 1851-53, New Orleans. 1851, 205 Gravier; 1853, Phillippa near Poydas Market [*Dirs.*].

Flynn, James. gunsmith. 1865, home at 63 Erato, New Orleans. The Union Army drafted James Flynn in 1865.

Folsom & Sanborn. arms dealers and importers. 1861, 55 St. Charles, New Orleans. George Folsom had earlier been in business with Benjamin Kittredge. The latter left at the onset of the Civil War and G. B. Sanford took his place. Yankee occupation ended all arms sales [Gorman].

Folsom Brothers. gun store. 1868-88, Old Levee, also known as 9 Decatur St., New Orleans. This was a major branch of the Folsom Brothers store in New York. In May 1873 rioters broke into the store cleaning out its inventory. Folsom represented Winchester and other domestic brands as well as better European arms. George, Henry and David Folsom [Gorman; Gardner, 65].

Folsom, George (1831-1890). arms dealer. 1851-55, St. Louis, working for H. E. Dimick; 1856, New Orleans, working for B. Kittredge, doing business, 1858-61, as Kittredge & Folsom. 1861, Folsom & Sanborn. 1868-90, New Orleans, doing business as Folsom Brothers. The firm eventually became H. & D. Folsom, 188-99 [Gorman].

Folsom, Henry & Company. gun merchants. 1865, 3 Old Levee, New Orleans. David Folsom ran this store. Folsom eventually became sole agent for Remington arms in Louisiana. In 1868 the name changed to Folsom Brothers [Gorman].

Fortier, Francois (1697-1733). gunsmith. 1720-29, New Orleans, "master gunsmith." Francois Fortier was born in 1697 in St. Malo, France. He sailed aboard the *St. Andre*, arriving in Louisiana on August 24, 1720. He married

Gabrielle Moreau who came from Provence, France but had traveled to LA with her parents. Francois and Gabrielle Moreau Fortier were the parents of two sons and one daughter. The 1732 Census lists Francois registered in New Orleans with "one man carrying arms, his wife and three children, and one Negress slave." They lived on Royal Street where he was by profession a gunsmith and manufactured and sold arms in New Orleans. He was given the title of *L'Armurier du Roi a*nd trained his son Michel in the business. He died in New Orleans [Ancestry].

Fortier, Michael (1725-1785). gunsmith. 1755-59, New Orleans "royal gunsmith." Michel Fortier was born in New Orleans in 1725 the son of Francois and Gabrielle Moreau Fortier. He was an apprentice to his father's gunsmith business and later would succeed his father as "Armurier du Roi," manufacturing and selling arms and ammunition. The success of this business enabled him to purchase land to raise crops as well as an interest in several sailing vessels which carried cargoes to and from Europe. In January 1750 Michel married Perrine Langlois, an heiress with substantial land holdings in both Louisiana and the Illinois territories. Michel became the administrator of this estate for his wife, her brothers and several minor children of her deceased sister. Michel and Perrine Langlois Fortier were the parents of twelve children: seven sons and five daughters. Michel and two of his sons, Michel II and Jacques fought against the British during the Revolutionary War. Michel was a colonel with Galvez, supplying arms, ammunition, ships and money against the British. His will was executed before a notary on September 17,1785. In it he lists his wife and eleven children; his property including 35 slaves; 35 head of cattle, 6 horses and 10 sheep. He left his plantation in St. John the Baptist Parish to his wife. Michael died on September 24, 1785 Ancestry].

Fortier, Michael Jr. (1750-1819). gunsmith. New Orleans. The inscription on his tombstone indicates that Michael fought with the Spanish to destroy the British. It also indicates that he was a gunsmith. Kit Gorman thought that Michael Jr was confused with his father and was not a gunsmith.

Founier, Louis. gunsmith. 1860, Orleans Parish. Census of 1860: Louis Fournier was J. P. Revol's apprentice. Not located after 1860.

Fouquet, Edward (1829-). gun- and locksmith. 1851-61, 124 Bienville, New Orleans [*Dir.*]. In 1851 Fouquet, a locksmith, was admitted to the charity hospital with "int. fever." He had been born in Moselle, France [Ancestry; *Dirs.*].

Fox, John Nicholas. gunsmith. 1834, 183 Bayou Rd, New Orleans [*Dir.*].

Frahlich, Heinrich (1822-). locksmith. 1850, New Orleans; patient in charity hospital.; born in Germany, age 28. Also seen as Trahlich.

Franz, Peter (1824-1870). lock- and gunsmith. Peter was born in Bavaria and emigrated to New Orleans, arriving on the Juilius on 2 January 1858. He soon moved to Texas where he was noted in Robertson County. Census of 1860: Peter France, 36, blacksmith, $100 property, $300 personal value; Barbara, 33; Anna, 7, all born in Bavaria. Franz, died in Sterling, Texas, in June 1870 of dysentery at age 47, noted as a gunsmith [Mortality Schedule].

Frederic, L. gun- and blacksmith. Commercial District, New Orleans. In 1866, Jacques Bolet took a partner, L. Frederic, but that partnership only lasted a year. In 1867, he became partners with J. Arnaux, another Frenchman who appears to be related [Gorman; *Dirs*.].

Frombino, Frank. gunsmith. 1904, 504 St. Philip, New Orleans [*Dir*.].

Frugelaar, Casper (1827-). gunsmith. Trinity, Catahoula Parish. Census of 1880: Casper Frugelaar, gunsmith, born in Norway; Laura, 34, wife, Laura, born in Mississippi; Thomas H., 17; Vainey [?], 12; Enoza [?], 10, all born in Louisiana. Not located before or after 1880.

Bring Your Guns! Now prepared for carrying on the Gunsmith business. Prompt attention will be paid to all work sent to my shop. C. Fugelaar. Trinity, LA [*Harrisonburg Independent*, 11 July 1860].

Fuselier, Narcisse. gunsmith. 1832, 286 Bagatelle St., New Orleans [*Dir*.]

Gabrel, Louis (1805-). gunsmith. 1850, New Orleans. Census of 1850; Louis Gabrel, 45, gunsmith, born in Switzerland [Census]. Gabrel is not found in directories or other sources so he may have been employed by some firm or gunshop.

Gaetano, E. & M. gunsmiths. 1915-23, 737 Barracks, New Orleans [*Dirs*.].

Garcia, Adolphe Desire E. (1822--1879). armorer. 1851-61, keeper of the state arsenal, 214 Dauphine, New Orleans [*Dirs*.]. Census of 1850: Adolphe Garcia, 28, arsenal; Maria, 22; Maria, 2; Adolphe, 2. Census of 1860: Adolphe Garcia, 38, engraver, born in New Orleans; Mariette, 25, born in France; Marie, 13; Cecelia, 8; Emile, 6; Eugene, 4; and an infant, all born in New Orleans. Garcia died on 25 January 1879 [Ancestry].

Garcia, Louis. gunsmith and bell hanger. 1868, 139 Carondelet, New Orleans [*Dir.*]. Not located, single entry.

Garnier, Gustave (1823-). gunsmith. New Orleans. Census of 1850; Gustave Garnier, 27, gunsmith, born in France; in household of L. T. Leduc.

Gartese, J. gunsmith. 1873, Laurel, corner of 3rd, New Orleans [*Dir.*].

Gauchey, Etienne. locksmith. 1861, 117 St. Louis, New Orleans [*Dir.*].

Gaudion, Charles. lock- and blacksmith. 1851, 95 & 80 Rampart, New Orleans [*Dir.*].

Gautier, E. cutler [coutelier]. 1811, Conde & Ste. Anne, New Orleans [*Dir.*].

Geissler, Conrad. armorer. 1881, armorer, German Battalion; lived at 13 Dryades [*Dir.*].

Gelbke, F. gunsmith. 1855, 180 Circus, New Orleans [*Dir.*].

Gelday, E. J. (1851-). gunsmith. 3rd ward, Iberville Parish. Census of 1880; E J Gelday, 29, gunsmith, born in Louisiana; wife Carmelite, 30; Thomas, 4.

Geneste, Louis (1879-1943). gunsmith. New Orleans. 1872, 523 Annunciation; 1902, 117 Decatur [Gorman; *Dir.*]

Geneste, William (1852-1916). gunsmith. New Orleans. Census of 1880, William Geneste, 28, born in Louisiana, gun smith; Lizzie, 23, his wife; William, 2; Lewis, 6 months; Lizzie, 45, his mother; David, brother, 10. According to Kit Gorman, Geneste apprenticed with Alexis Hebert. In 1877 he went to work with Folsom Brothers. In 1896, William started own shop at 117 Decatur St. [Gorman]. A local news editor remarked on the quality of the calendar Geneste was distributing, showing a pointer dog. At the time Geneste was a gunsmith with the Henry M. Martin Company [*Times Picayune*, 2 January 1909]

William Geneste practical gun maker and locksmith. No. 84 Carondolet street near Poydras. Special attention given to country work at low rates and satisfaction guaranteed [*New Orleans Times*, 11 February 1876]

Where to Have Your Guns Repaired. William Geneste is a modest man, and he is the proprietor of a very quiet little establishment, No. 70 Gravier street. But as a gunsmith, knowing all about shooting irons, William G. is immense. Artemas Ward said that every man of intellect had his forte, and Geneste's forte is repairing, cleaning, and reconstructing guns, pistols, and fishing rods. The latter he manufactures, and no man in the country can turn out anything neater, more tasty, or cheaper than he. Geneste is the right sort of man for our amateur sportsmen and nimrods to know. He is prompt, reliable, and cheap [*New Orleans Times*, 16 December 1877]

Genois, Jean (1840-). gunsmith. ward 5, New Orleans. Census of 1860; Jean Genois, 20, gunsmith, born in Germany; living in a large hotel. Census of 1880: Jean Genois, 43, tinsmith, Royal St., born in France, single.

Genolin, John (1815-1875). gunsmith. New Orleans. Genolin was born in 1815 in Marseilles, Cher, Centre, France [Ancestry].

Gerard, Eugene (1862-). apprentice gunsmith. 1868-90, New Orleans. 1880, in home of J. B. Revol, 81, gunsmith; Joseph L. Revol, 49; Henrietta, 52, Joseph's wife; Josephine, 12; Amelia Revol, 28; Eugene Gerard, 18; Louis Fannier, 20, apprentice. He later clerked for Revol. Apparently he left gunsmithing [Census; Gorman].

Geren, John (1813-1862). gunsmith. Claiborne Parish. Census of 1860, ward 4 Claiborne: John Geren, born in Arkansas; Rachel Ann, born in Tennessee, 49, wife; children ages 10 to 14, all born in Louisiana [Ancestry].

John Geren

Gerkis, Louis (1831-). gunsmith. New Orleans. Census of 1880: Louis Gerkis, 49, gunsmith; wife Mary, 45, both born in Bavaria; Louis Gerkis, 21, gunsmith; Rosalie, 17; Matilda, 10; Louisa, 7; Marie, 3, all born in Louisiana. Not located before or after 1880.

Gerkis, Louis (1859-). gunsmith. 1880, New Orleans. Census of 1880; Louis Gerkis, son of Louis and Mary Gerkis; born in Louisiana.

Gerteis & Dempsey. gun manufacturers. 1856-58, 113 St. Charles, New Orleans [*Dirs*.].

Gerteis, Louis (1830-1899). gunsmith. 1847-99, New Orleans; born and apprenticed in Germany. 1887, 162 Poydras. 1858-59, doing business as Gerteis & Dempsey. He was robbed and barely escaped with his life [*Times Picayune*, 23 April 1897; Gorman; Dirs.]. Kit Gorman thought him to be a superior workman whose reputation was fully deserved. At the beginning of the Civil War Gerteis offered a new sword bayonet, invented by Colonel A, Trudeau, to be used with double barrel guns. Reportedly, it was the only bayonet the French army used on its double barrel guns [*Times Picayune*, 14 September 1861].

Louis Gerteis rifle

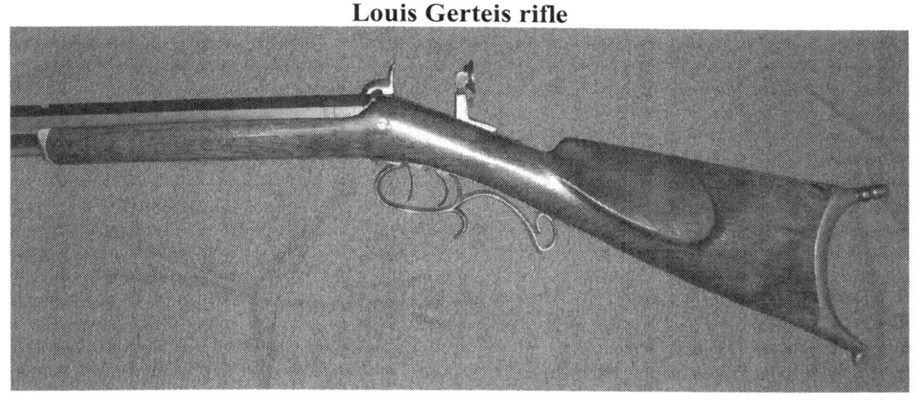

L. Gerteis Gun Maker 18 ½ Commercial Alley, New Orleans. Target Rifles made to order. Muzzle-loaders changed to breech-loaders, and repairing done neatly [*New Orleans Bulletin*, 8 March 1876].

The Veteran Gunsmith Passes Away in Peace. On Sunday morning there passed away one of the old German residents of this city, who was identified with the progress of New Orleans over half a century. Louis Gerteis was one of the old fashioned gunsmiths, and plied his trade here for many years in various workshops of his own. At one time he had become quite successful, but the advent of the new ideas and methods forced him to the rear, and with his advancing years his business correspondingly felt the pinch of time. Mr. Gerteis was born in Baden-Baden, Germany, 68 years ago, and migrated to this country when a lad of 17. He came to New Orleans and settled, opening a gunsmith shop. He was in business all his life, having learnt the trade over in the old country. At one time he had stores on Magazine, near Poydras, and on St. Charles street. For a number of years before his death he had a workshop on Baronne street near Poydras . . . He left a wife and four children to mourn his loss. [Times Picayune, 1 August 1899].

Gerteis, Louis, Jr. (1858-1925). gunsmith. New Orleans. Initially he worked for his father and then at local armories and back again to his father. He took over his father's shop upon the elder man's death [*Dirs*.; Census; Gorman]. He was the center of a test case brought by animal rights advocates against live pigeon shooting. Gerteis was charged with shooting a pigeon in flight. Henceforth, there will be no live pigeon shoots within the city limits of New Orleans [*Times Picayune*, 25 January 1905].

LGerteis Practical Gunsmith, dealer and jobber if guns, pistols, breech-loaders, ammunition and fishing tackle. No. 55 St. Charles street, New Orleans. Arms made to order and repaired by experienced and thorough workmen. Models neatly made from drawings with secrecy and dispatch. Mr Gerteis expects in a few days a large assortment of newly invented arms. He has on hand now every article necessary for a sportsman, and also a great variety of loaded and unloaded cartridges. A good gunsmith wanted [*New Orleans Republican*, 11 Oct 1871]

The many old friends and customers of that accomplished gunsmith, Mr L. Gerteis will doubtless be pleased to learn that he has again opened an establishment in his old line. He present place is at 130 Common street where he designs keeping the best kind of stock of Guns and Rifles, sporting and fishing tackle, and, in fact, everything in his old line. He will also devote attention to altering muzzle loading fowling pieces into breech-loaders, and parties entrusting work to him can rely upon its being done in the most workmanlike and perfect manner. His reappearance in his old trade will be doubtless hailed with joy by many a veteran sportsman who had bewailed his absence [*New Orleans Republican*, 26 January 1873].

Gery, Alfred (1835-). cutler. New Orleans. Census of 1880; Alfred Gery, 45, cutler, born in France.

Giertese, J. See Gartese.

Gilfaux, --- . gunsmith. New Orleans. Gilfaux's gunshop was ransacked. He put in a claim for loss property including brass knuckles. The newspaper expressed disgust that "such heathenish weapons be called property" [New Orleans *Republican*, 25 March 1873]. See Grilfoure.

Gilmore, Jerome Bonaparte (1827--1900). gunsmith. Shreveport. Census of 1850, J. B. Gilmore, age 23, born in Kentucky, gunsmith; living with David Probst, 29, gunsmith, and also two carriage makers. Fire threatened Gilmore's gunshop, but was stopped by a brick wall. Contents of the building were removed with some loss [*Daily Advocate*, 14 January 1859]. Census of 1860: J B Gilmore, 33, gunsmith, $4400 real estate, personal value

$4000; Emma, 26; Emma, 2. J B was a colonel in the Third Louisiana Infantry, fighting for the Glorious Cause. Census of 1870: J B Gilmore, mayor, 43, real estate $9000, personal value $1000; Emma, 28; Emma, 12; W F F, 9; and Henry, 1. J B died on 7 May 1900 and was buried in Greenwood Cemetery, Shreveport [Find-a-Grave; Ancestry].

Jerome Bonaparte Gilmore

Ginder, A. locksmith. 1861, 263 Chartres, New Orleans [*Dir.*]

Glandiere, Auguste. locksmith. 1895, 59 St. Anthony, New Orleans [*Dir.*].

Gloie, John. locksmith. 1861, 220 St., Mary, New Orleans [*Dir.*].

Gordy, John C. gunsmith. 1846, Franklin, Parish St. Mary. The sole man by this name was a physician, born in 1809 in Maryland.

Wanted – a Gunsmith and Blacksmith who can do work in the best style. The Subscriber will remain in the city two days only, and may be addressed during that time, at No. 55 Tchoupitoulas street, or can be addressed at his residence, Franklin, Parish St. Mary, Reasonable wages will be given, or an interest in each establishment, as the terms may be agreed upon. John C Gordy [*Times Picayune*, 22 May 1846]

Gorsch, Louis (1828-). gunsmith. 1866-73, New Orleans; 1870, 260 Rampart; 1872, 200 Rampart; 1873, 244 Rampart. Census of 1870: Louis Gorsch, 42, gun repairer [*Dirs.*; Gorman]. Having shot at the shooting gallery of H. Paland, Louis carelessly placed a loaded gun where his own youngster Otto could get to it. The Smith & Wesson rifle accidentally fired, killing the lad [*Times Picayune*, 13 September 1870; see also New Orleans *Republican*, 13 September 1870]. Not located in censuses.

Graci, Biagio. gunsmith. 1910, 341 Bourbon St., New Orleans; 1912, electrician [*Dir.*].

Graci, Gaetano. gunsmith. 1912-20, 406 Chartres; home 1604 Ursuline, New Orleans [*Dir.*]. Also seen as Groci.

Graves, Charlie (1860--1930). gunsmith. 6th ward, DeSoto Parish. Charlie was born on 26 April 1860. Census of 1880;Charlie Graves, 20, gunsmith, single, living alone, born in Louisiana. Charlie died on 10 April 1930 and was buried in Evergreen Cemetery, Kingston, DeSoto Parish [Ancestry].

Grellette, Myrie C. (1856-1891). gunsmith. Boyce, Rapides Parish.

Myrie C. Grellete, aged 35 years, shot himself 4 times this morning at 9 o'clock at his home in Boyce, with suicidal intent. He was in the house with his wife and 5 children when he went into a back room of the house and with a .44 caliber double action pistol attempted the rash act. He was still lingering at 5 P.M. but no hopes were entertained of his recovery by his attending physicians, and his end was considered a matter of a very short time. Mr. Grellette was a good citizen and a fine gunsmith and no one can account for this suicide. [*Times Picayune*, 8 August 1891]

Grilfoure & Lee. gunshop. New Orleans. J. Grilfoure and L. E. Lee. Grilfoure and Lee sued the city of New Orleans for loss of guns and accouterments incurred when on 6 March a mob broke into their gunshop. [New Orleans *Republican*, 25 March 1873].

Griffin, D. P. (1829-). gunsmith. Abbeville, Vermillion Parish. Census of 1860 or Choctaw County, Alabama: D P Griffin, 32, planter, $1600 real estate, $3500 personal value; S C, 27, wife; T, 9; C, 7; James, 5; and infant Census of 1880, D. P. Griffin, 51, born in Alabama, gun smith, widower; Beulah, 13; Effeginia, 11. Not located after 1880.

Griffille, Louis (1780-). gunsmith. St. Landry Parish. Census of 1820 of St. Landry Parish: L. Griffill, living alone, age 26 to 44. On 13 July 1821 Louis Griffille married Divine Bordelon in St. Landry. Census of 1830: Louis Griffil, head of household of seven persons, one free black, six whites; one white male 40 to 49. Census of 1850, Louis Griffille, age 70, born in France, gun smith, value $300; Devine, 48, his wife; Adolphe, 23; Louise, 20; Louis, 19, laborer; all born in Louisiana.

Griswold, Arthur B. (1829-1877). jeweler, gunsmith, manufacturer and importer. 1845-70, New Orleans. 1845-60 with Hyde & Goodrich; 1861, Thomas, Griswold & Company; 1865-70, A. B. Griswold & Company. Imported Tranter revolvers among other arms, but also manufactured firearms. Griswold died in 1877 at age 48, but the firm continued until 1924 when it sold to Hausmann, Inc. [Gorman; Census; *Dirs*.]. Samuel Griswold was born December 29th 1790 in Windsor, Connecticut, in 1835 when he was 45 he purchased 5000 acres of land in Jones County, 10 miles south of Macon in Georgia. On this land he built several buildings including a soap, candle and cotton gin factory along with employees dwellings, a church, a post office and a general store. He suitably named this new township Griswoldville.

Griswold and Gunnison decided to replicate the Colt Navy 1851 model as it was easier to manufacture than the popular Remington 1858. At first glance the Griswold and Gunnison below could be mistaken for Colts original as seen beneath it. The big differences between the Colt and their own design was the forging and machining of the frame and trigger guard out of solid brass instead of graded and case hardened steel as Colt had done. The reason for this was not an aesthetic one but instead out of necessity, because there was a shortage of graded steel in the Southern States. The cylinders on many Griswold and Gunnison revolvers were cast out of iron and it promoted rust. The metal was not even chemically blued a treatment that acts as a rust inhibitor, but just left in its bare metal state. Almost all Griswold and Gunnison revolvers have a slight pinkish coloration in the brass, this is because they mixed in a large copper content to make the available metals go further and make more guns. Confederate weapons manufacture was limited to many of these factors during the Civil War and they actually did rather well to produce weapons in any great quantity._The barrel was cylindrical as opposed to Colts distinguished hexagonal design. It was fabricated this way as it was easier and less time consuming to produce. The barrel housing lug was made in two versions, a rounded type and one that had a more octagonal top. They were .36 caliber cap and ball black powder guns equipped with accurate 7½ inch barrels, with the smooth well finished grips made from walnut. Even with often limited resources, Griswold and Gunnison still did their best to produce quality revolvers and consequently they were all marked with a serial number along with assembly numbers, inspectors stamps and benchmarks for quality control. The cylinder and indeed the barrel and housing was made of iron instead of graded steel. It was a process called twisted iron, in that iron bars were heated up and twisted to strengthen them, which leaves small twist lines visible on almost all Griswold and Gunnison cylinders. The barrel was rifled with six clockwise twisting grooves, with more tightness in the amount of twist in the latter half of the barrel. The hammer had a roller kingpin, and the cylinder, surprisingly, was over engineered with six integral safety pins unlike the Colt that only had the one.

Jewelry & Fancy Goods. A. B. Griswold & Co., old firm Hyde & Goodrich, established in New Orleans 50 years, manufacturers and importers of Watches,

Jewelry, Silver Ware, Cutlery, Fancy Goods, Guns and Pistols – corner of Canal and Royal streets [*Galveston News*, 9 June 1869].

Gross, John. locksmith. 1851, Rousseau St., New Orleans [*Dir*.].

Guardia, John (1853--1928). gunsmith. Thibodaux, Lafourche Parish. John was born in Hancock County, Mississippi, on 15 September 1851, a son of Pierre N. and Euphrosine Guardia. Census of 1880: John Guardia, 27, works in gun shop, born in Mississippi; Lizzie, 29. Census of 1900: John Guardia, 48, gun smith, widower; Edward, 14; May, 15; and Nita, 11. John died on 22 February 1928 and was buried in St. John's Cemetery, Thibodaux [Ancestry; Find-a-Grave].

John Guardia, Watchmaker, Jeweler and Gunsmith. Dealer in fine Watches, Jewelry, Guns, Spectacles, Clocks and Accordions, all kinds of Sewing Machines. A full line of attachments for all kinds of sewing machines. Watches, Clocks, Jewelry, Sewing Machines, Firearms, Etc., carefully repaired and guaranteed [Thibodeuax *Sentinel & Journal*, 31 January 1885].

Guidry, Moise. (1873—1934). gun- and blacksmith. Raceland, Lafourche Parish. Noted as assisting in apprehension of several robbers [*New Orleans Times*, 12 March 1919]. On 4 January 1894 Moise Guidry married Lydia Morris in Lafourche Parish. Moise died on 29 December 1934 [Ancestry].

Guarino, Frank. gunsmith. 1885, 50 Marais, New Orleans [Dir.].

Guilfoux & Lee. gunmakers. 1873, 132 Chartres, New Orleans [*Dir*.]. Leroy E. Lee and Joseph B. Guilfoux.

Guilfoux, Joseph B. (1844--1884). gunsmith. New Orleans. Joseph was a private in the 8th Louisiana Infantry during the Civil War. Census of 1870: Joseph B Guillfoux, 26, clerk in store; Carmilite, 24. After 1874 he left the profession. 1871, gunsmith at A. Tegniere's shop, house rear 276 Villere. 1870 directory listing: 132 Chartres St., gunmaker and dealer in firearms. [Gorman; D*irs*.]. Pl;ace of burial is unknown.

Guillot, Johany (1836-). gunsmith. Orleans Parish. Census of 1860; Johany Guillot, 24, gunsmith, born in France. Presumably he worked for someone else since is not listed in directories. On 22 April 1861 Johany enlisted in the 7th Louisiana Infantry. Not located after the war.

Guion, Thomas F. (1815-1865). gun dealers. 1838-65, St. Charles, New Orleans. While Guion was a proprietor of a "fancy goods" store, Gorman pointed out that his estate inventory showed many firearms and that sales of guns clearly constituted a major portion of his business. It does not appear that Guion made any firearms or was a gunsmith. W. J. Duval, an employee, and J. W. Smith bought the store [Gorman; *Dirs*.]

Gunnison, Arvin W. (1824-1882) originally manufactured guns in New Orleans, but when the city fell to the Union army in 1862, he quickly relocated and settled in Griswoldville, Georgia. He met up with Griswold and they both transformed the cotton gin factory to make revolvers at the behest of the Confederate Ordnance Department, who put in an order for as many revolvers as possible.

Gunter, A. gunsmith. 1867, 263 Chartres, New Orleans [*Dir*.].

Gurralin, G. gunsmith. 1865, 121 Bourbon, New Orleans. He was drafted by the Union Army.

Guyot, Jean Baptiste. cutler. 1842, 19 Madison St., New Orleans [*Dir*.].

Guzau, Louis. gunsmith. 1873, south side St Claude bet Frenchmen and Union, New Orleans [*Dir*.].

Gys, Florent. locksmith. 1861, 66 St. Louis, New Orleans [*Dir*.].

Haas, Jacob. gunsmith. 1874, 124 S. Rampart St., New Orleans [*Dir*.].

Hack, Adam. locksmith. 1861, 83 Marais, New Orleans [*Dir*.].

Hackenberg, Frank. gun- and locksmith. 1861, 801 New Levee, New Orleans [*Dir*.].

Haley, Jeremiah J. gunsmith. 1865, 106 Liberty, New Orleans. He was drafted by the Union Army.

Hall & Cook. gunsmiths, sporting goods. 1880-82, 24 St. Charles, New Orleans [Dirs.; Gorman]. Louis Cook & Louis Hall.

Hall, Oragile (1861-). armorer. 1880, Bayou Sara, West Feliciana Parish. Census of 1880; Oragile Hall, 19, gunsmith, was a son of Thomas and Louisa Hall. Not located after 1880.

Hall, Thomas Hicks (1834-1910). gunsmith. Hall was born near Bayou Sara, about 1834. He was the son of Burr S. and Elizabeth (Garnheart). In

1857 Thomas married Louise Rosella Mourain, in the Diocese of Baton Rouge. He was a gunsmith or armorer. He survived his wife by 22 years, and died in 1910. He is buried in the St. Joseph's Catholic Cemetery, Baton Rouge. Census of 1880, West Feliciana Parish: Thomas Hall, age 47, armorer; Louisa, 45; Oragile, 19; Olile, 17; Bowman, 10; Rosalie, 8; and Bertha, 3 [Family; Ancestry].

Ham, Reuben James. (1832-1887). before 1887, Union Parish. Reuben James Ham was the son of William Ham (1801-1867) and Clarinda Seale (1811-1897), who moved to north Louisiana in February 1837 from Lowndes County Alabama. Reuben had originally joined the Stars of Equality, a unit of men from eastern Union Parish that later became Company E, 19th Regiment Louisiana Infantry. However, Reuben was discharged "for want of physical ability" from the unit before it officially entered the Confederate service in December 1861. Estate of Reuben Ham, deceased, late a resident of the Parish of Union included: 1 set of blacksmith tools appraised at $35.00; 1 set gunsmith tools appraised at $20.00; another lot of gunsmith's tools, $37; 1 lot carpenter's tools, 2 planes, 1 saw, 1 iron square $2.50; 1 Enfield rifle, without lock appraised at $1.00; 1 fine rifle and case and shot pouch appraised at $30.00 [*Union Parish Estate Book*].

Hamby, Thomas J. (1815--1896). gunsmith, bell hanger, blacksmith. Cherino, Nacogdoches County, Texas. Thomas Hamby was a son of Roda and John Harvey Hamby, Sr., born about 1815 in Tennessee while they were on the way to Texas. He lived in 1836 in Louisiana. He married, first, Rose Ann Calhoun from Mississippi. He brought his wife and family to Nacogdoches County, Texas, about 1837. He and Rose Ann Hamby had one daughter, Frances born 1842 in Nacogdoches, Texas. Census of 1860 of Cherino: Thomas Hamby, 45, bell maker, born in Tennessee, value $400. Thomas married, second, Catherine F. Holt of Denning, San Augustine Texas, on December 28, 1869. Thomas' occupation was gunsmith and blacksmith. He served the Confederate as a private in the Texas Volunteer Infantry. Census of 1880 of Cherino, Nacogdoches County: Thomas J Hamby, 65, gunsmith; Catherine, 33; Enos, 7; and Walter, 2. Thomas died in 1898 and was buried at the Clarks Ferry Cemetery in Angelina County [Ancestry; Family].

Hamelton, R. P. (1827-). gunsmith. East Carroll Parish. Census of 1850: R. P, Hamelton, age 23, born in Kentucky, gunsmith, value $300, single.

Hammel, Charles. gunsmith. 1842, 241 Tchoupitoulas, New Orleans [*Dir.*].

Hammond, Job (1820-). gunsmith. Blossom Hill ward, Caddo Parish. Census of 1850: Job Hammond, 30, born in Kentucky, value $100; Margaret, 23, born in North Carolina; Wesley, 7, born in Louisiana.

Hammond, Mark. locksmith. 1861, New Orleans [*Dir*.].

Handrachy, C. gunsmith. Lake Charles, Calcasieu Parish. Unlocated.

We call special attention to the advertisement . . . of C. Handrachy, blacksmith in general, and gunsmith in particular. Mt Handrachy has worked at this business for many years , consequently is a good mechanic, and says he can and will give satisfaction. We advise those who have work in his line to give him a trial, as he is a deserving, hard-working man and merits a share of the public patronage. His shop is located at the foot of the ferry wharf [*Lake Charles Echo*, 26 September 1885].

Hanley, James. armorer. 1865, home at 10 Poydras, New Orleans. He was drafted into the Union Army. [*New Orleans Times,* 17 March 1865]

Hanson, Charles H. armorer. Private, Company B, 14th La. Infantry. Enlisted June 3, 1861, New Orleans. Employed on extra duty as armorer. Hanson was born in Kentucky. Residence New Orleans [*Booth's Index*].

Haran, N. locksmith. New Orleans. 1851, 37 Elysian Fields; 1861, 401 Chartres. [*Dir*.]. Also seen as Harran.

Harkenburg, Frantz. gun- and locksmith. 1859-61, 765 New Levee, New Orleans. Frantz married Victoria Joerger [*Dirs*.]. Nothing else in Ancestry.

Harrington, Joseph (1838-). **armorer.** Private, Company K, 10th LA Infantry. Joseph enlisted on. July 22, 1861. Active from February 1862 until January1864. He deserted from the hospital on January 11, joining General J. H. Morgan's Command from May to August 1864. Missing since October 19, 1864. Noted on federal roster of prisoners of war, captured at Strausburg, Virginia, on October 19, 1864 and sent to Point Lookout, Maryland, from Harpers Ferry, West Virginia, on October 25, 1864. Paroled and transferred for exchange. Received. at Coxes Landing, James River, Virginia, on 14-15 February 1865, and exchanged. He was born in Mississippi, occupation gunsmith, Residence Lake Charles, Louisiana, age 23, single. Name also seen as K. J. Herrington, [*Booth's Index*].

Harrison, Thomas. gunsmith. 1866, 136 Girod, New Orleans [*Dir*.].

Hartleb, Frederick K. gunsmith. 1873, Levee St., New Orleans [*Dir*.].

Harvay, John. 1811, master armorer of the Arsenal, 60 Ursulines, New Orleans [*Dir.*].

Hauck, Valentine. locksmith. 1861, 401 Magazine, New Orleans [*Dir.*].

Hauser, ---. gunsmith. New Orleans. A charge of arson was brought against a gunsmith named Hauser for attempting twice to burn down his gunshop at 25 St. Philip St. Bail was set at $1000 [*Daily Crescent,* 14 March 1854].

Hausman, Gustav. gunsmith. 1861, 234 S. Charles, New Orleans [*Dir.*].

Haynes, Nero. gunsmith. 1922, 1418 Julia, Baton Rouge [*Dir.*].

Heath, James Harvey (1814-1904). gunsmith & farmer. James Harvey Heath: James was born March 26, 1814 in Crystal Springs, Washington Parish. Crystal Springs is located just south of Mississippi on the toe of Louisiana. It may have all been part of the same territory at one time or another. It is not far from Jackson, Mississippi but located on the Gulf. James married Teresa Jane Rigdale in June of 1835 in Raymond, Hinds County, Mississippi. She was born in England and was an immigrant. James was converted to Mormonism and the Heath clan family sold out and went up the river to Nauvoo, Illinois. In 1840 we find James living with his family in Augusta Iowa working in a stone quarry to provide stone for the temple in Nauvoo. He did courier work for Joseph Smith bringing messages back and forth from Missionaries and political workers. Through the winter of 1843 he did mission work in Louisiana and Mississippi. After his arrival in Nauvoo, Illinois, in 1840 tragedy struck his family. His wife Teresa and four children died, probably of cholera. In Nauvoo he married a woman from his birth place. Huldah Maria Holden was born in Crystal Springs, Washington Parish, LA, on March 26 of 1814. She went with him to Utah in 1851. James was listed variously as a wagon maker, gunsmith and farmer. James died on October 21, 1904 [Mormon Genealogy; Ancestry].

Hebert, Alexis S. (1836--1902). gunmaker. New Orleans. Alexis was born on 8 February 1836 in Assumption Parish. 1870, 404 Conti. 1874-75, 12 Commercial Place. He was a native of Assumption Parish. During the Civil War Alexis served as a member of the 26th Louisiana Infantry. He was captured at Vicksburg, paroled, and served in the Ordnance Department for the remainder of the war. He returned to New Orleans where he was a gunsmith until 1878. 1878, partner in Simmons & Hebert, machinists. He then went to work for the U.S. Mint in New Orleans and eventually was promoted to foreman in 1882. He married Hester Beasely by whom he fathered four daughters. Alexis died on 20 July 1902 in New Iberia, Iberia Parish, but was buried in Masonic Cemetery No. 1 in New Orleans [*Dirs*.; Gorman].

Mr A S Hebert, the gunsmith of Commercial Alley, has just completed . . . one of his new telegraphic machines. . . . Mr Hebert is at work on a pair of them, and they are as creditable to his skills and pains as the invention is to the skill of the inventor [New Orleans *Republican*, 26 October 1873].

Hedzer, John (1820-). gunsmith. Galveston. Census of 1860: John Hedzer, 40, gun smith, born in Switzerland; wife Augusta, 30; 2 children born in Louisiana. Not located after 1860.

Heibark, Friedrich (1832-). gunsmith. 1853. arrived on 12 October 1853 from Bremen, Germany. Heibark, age 21, gunsmith, bound for New Orleans.

Hendry, Micajah B. (1802-c.1855). gunsmith. Copiah County. The first Micajah Hendry (1765-1838) and Lydia Moarlin married by 1789, probably in North Carolina. In the first census ever taken in the United States in 1790, they were living in Chatham County, North Carolina. Between 1790 and 1803, the Hendry family moved to Lincoln County, Georgia, a county adjoining South Carolina. Perhaps they moved when Lincoln County was first created in 1796. The first child was born in North Carolina, and the last three were born in Georgia. Since there are gaps of several years between the known children, there may have been others. In 1805, Georgia had its first land lottery to settle the counties of Baldwin, Wayne, and Wilkinson. Micajah Hendry had two draws. He drew two blanks; thus he remained in Lincoln County. When the Creek Nation ceded land to the United States in 1805, another Land Lottery was planned. In 1807, there was a land lottery to settle Baldwin and Wilkinson Counties. The land was between two rivers and was good fertile land for crops. The price was $12.15 per 202-1/2 acre lot. This time Micajah was more fortunate, drawing Lot #173, District lived on it for a short time. In 1812 he was gone from Georgia to Louisiana. When his daughter married in 1812, she stated that she was of Amite County, Territory of Mississippi. The senior Hendry lived in Louisiana at the time of the Battle of New Orleans in 1815. In 1820, Micajah was still in Feliciana Parish, but by 1826 he had moved to Copiah County, Mississippi. Micajah, Jr., the gunsmith, received two land patents: on 10 December 1840 and May 25, 1841. In 1850 he owned four slaves, ages 13, 11, 5 and under 1 year. Land records show he bought 39.9 acres on December 10 1840, Copiah County, Mississippi. Micajah was born on 11 January 1803. Census of 1830 of Copiah County: Micajah Henry head of family of three persons; one male 30 to 39; and one male 70 to 79. Census of 1850: Micajah Hendry, age

48, value $300, gunsmith, born in Georgia; Sarah, 48, his wife; Mary, daughter, 21; Nancy, 19; Savisa [f], 14; Satella [f], 7, all born in Mississippi. Ancestry has several postings giving his date of death as 1850.

Henry, Pierre D. (1797-1862). gunsmith. 1822-32, 209 Tchoupitoulas above Julie, New Orleans [*Dir*.]

Hetchie, Julius. gunsmith. 1865, 194 Tchoupitoulas, New Orleans; drafted.

Heuser, J. (1820-). gunsmith. 1850-54, New Orleans; born in Switzerland. In 1850 he was associated with Armand Soubie [Gorman, *Dirs*.; Census].

Hidden, Enoch. gunsmith. 1822-32, 170 Levee below Champs Elysees, New Orleans [*Dir*.]. 1820, 293 Cherry St., New York City. 1849-51, brass foundry and cannon lock maker, C & 12th Sts, New York City. On 16 December 1831 Enoch Hidden patented a percussion lock and assigned it to John P. Moore, 302 Broadway, New York City [Gorman; Dirs.; Gardner, *Small Arms Makers*, 91 & 135].

Hill, Allen. locksmith. 1842, 206 Baronne, New Orleans [*Dir*.].

Hille, Charles (1811-1860). gunsmith. 1837-59, 79 Magazine St., New Orleans. 1842, same address as Allen & Hill. His association with Joseph Allen began about 1841 and lasted until Hille's death. Hille died in Orleans Parish in July 1860 of diarrhea. Census of 1860: Charles Hille, born in Germany, age 48, gunsmith [*Dir*.; Ancestry].

Hille, Charles G. (1844-1924). New Orleans. Charles G was the son and apprentice of Charles Hille. 1867, in partnership with Thomas Bailey, Jr.. He soon left gunmaking and became an auctioneer [Gorman; *Dirs*.].

Hoff, Victoin (1826-). locksmith. 1851, New Orleans. Admitted to charity hospital with diarrhea. Hoff was born in Baden, Germany.

Holloway, James. gunsmith. 1866, 225 Terpsichore. New Orleans [*Dir*.].

Holmes, John. cutler. 1851, Nuns below Levee & Religious, New Orleans [*Dir*.].

Honzinan, Benjamin. gunsmith. 1875, Gretna, New Orleans [*Dir*.].

Hopkins, William. locksmith, brand cutter, and bell hanger. Sign of the Cross Keys. New Orleans. Census of 1840: William Hopkins head of a household of five slaves and four white persons, male age 20 to 29 engaged in commerce. 1841, late of Camp Sr., now on 10 Julia St.; 1842-43, 110 Camp; 1851, 93 Carondelet "iron chests repaired." He warned against loaning money to Alex. Duncan, never a partner, once in his employ [*Times Picayune*, 9 March 1841, 7 June 1842, 1 August 1843; *Dir.*].

Hough, Franklin T. (1848--1812). gunsmith. Keatchie, DeSoto Parish. Census of 1880: F. T. Hough, born in Mississippi, 30, gunsmith; wife Susan, 27; Bessy, 5; Benny, 3; Katy, 1, all born in Louisiana. Hough died in Rusk, Cherokee County, Texas, in 1912 and was buried in Cedar Hill Cemetery [Find-a-Grave; Ancestry].

Houlné, Edward (1860-). gun- and locksmith. 1880-1900, New Orleans [*Dirs.*; Census; Gorman]. Gorman noted that he was listed as a gunsmith only in 1886.

Huckel, Joseph. gunsmith. 1903, 618 St. Louis, New Orleans [*Dir.*].

Huet, Auguste. gunsmith. 1827-30, St. Paul near Gravier, New Orleans [*Dir.*]

Hughes, J. H (1825-). gunsmith. Pointe Coupe Parish. Census of 1860, J. H. Hughes, age 35, born in Kentucky, gunsmith; Mary, 28, born in Mississippi; Jane, 8 and Mary, 2, both born in Louisiana. There was James Harvey Hughes (1824-1899) in Boone County, Kentucky, noted as a farmer. That man shows in the censuses of 1850, 1870, and 1880, but not 1860.

Hunt, Alban (1830-). locksmith. 1850, New Orleans. Hunt was a patient in the charity hospital. Hunt was born in Germany, age 20.

Huston, Guy (1822-1875). gunsmith. 1850-53, 172 Circus, New Orleans [*Dir.*]. Also seen as Huieston. After working in San Francisco a few years Guy moved to Victoria, British Columbia, Canada, where he died in 1875 [Gorman; Shelton]

Hyatt, James S. (1840-1867). gunsmith. Hyatt was born in Baton Rouge and worked in both Baton Rouge and New Orleans. 1867, 577 Dryades, New Orleans. Hyatt lived in Brookstown, an historic neighborhood of Baton Rouge. Hyatt was considered to be a mechanical genius and expert gunsmith. He was murdered by some Negroes while on route from Baton Rouge to his home [*State Times Advocate*, 29 January 1915; Gorman; *Dirs.*].

Yesterday morning another sad accident occurred from the careless holding of a revolver, which will probably have a fatal result. Mr James Hyatt, son of Sylvester Hyatt, the gunsmith near the capitol, had been shooting at a mark with John Morrison. He thought he had entirely discharged the contents of the weapon and commenced examining, turning the cylinder, when the weapon went off, the ball entering the side of Morrison, passing entirely through his body, and lodging in the wall of a building in which they were standing [New Orleans *Daily Crescent*, 11 March 1861, citing Baton Rouge *Comet*].

Hyde & Goodrich. military supply store. 1829-61, New Orleans. Hyde & Goodrich imported Tranter revolvers and sold all sorts of imported and even American made firearms and military goods. On 1 July 1861 it became Thomas, Griswold, & Company [Wikipedia].

Icard, Joseph. gunsmith. Donaldsonville, Ascension Parish. Joseph Icard was in partnership with Joseph Ferrier. Notice in the *Louisianais* of 6 October 1877 that the partnership was dissolved. The multi-functional firm performed services in the following fields: blacksmithing, wheelwright, locksmith, coach maker and gunsmith. Ferrier continued the businesses. On 27 April 1876 Joseph Icard married Caroline Butler in Ascension Parish. Census of 1880: Joseph Icard, 36, blacksmith and wheelwright, born in France; Caroline, 23; and Henry, 2. Not found after 1880.

Ilault, Jacob. gunsmith. 1866, 220 St. Mary, New Orleans [*Dir.*]. Name is unclear.

Irwin, Jacob. gun- and blacksmith. 1813-35, smith to the Caddo tribe of Amerindians, on Caddo Lake [State of Louisiana]. He was a gunsmith at the Caddo Indian Agency at one time and moved to what is now Bossier Parish and established a home and plantation at Irwin's Bluff, on the river just outside of Benton. He was married to Mary, the daughter of Larkin Edwards who was the interpreter for the Caddo Indians. Larkin Edwards is said to be buried at Coates Bluff, just across Burt Boulevard from the courthouse in Benton. Coleville is about 5 or 6 miles east of Benton. Noted in the 1834 report of Bureau of Indian Affairs, salary for one year $508, J. Brooks, Indian Agent on the Red River, Louisiana.

Major Jacob Irwin, one of the first settlers of this section of Louisiana, died at his residence, in this parish, on last Saturday at 5:30 PM in his 95th year. Maj. Irwin located here many years before Bossier parish was organized, and was, at the time of his death, the oldest citizen of Bossier Parish. Indeed, a venerable landmark has fallen – Bossier's pioneer has been called home and his earthly labors are ended forever. He has been prominent as a business man and done faithful work in the service of his country. His deeds of charity have been numberless and as noiseless as the falling snow and he goes to his long home now amid expressions from the lips of every class of the community of the love and esteem he has inspired. As a friend and neighbor he was a model in any community. But with it all he was quiet and unostentatious. Major Irwin was a truly good man, in the broadest meaning of that word, and his good deeds and life of usefulness will long be remembered by his relatives and friends "And to live in hearts we leave behind is not to die." Last Monday morning, at Colveille cemetery, amid many expressions of regret from sorrowing relatives and friends, the mortal remains of Major Jacob Irwin were laid, solemnly to rest in the city of the dead, in faith and hope of the glorious resurrection morning. [*Bossier Banner Progress*, March 26,1885]

Isaac. gunsmith. African-American tradesman. September 9, 1838, Isaac, gunsmith and slave, was sold to Andrew Hynes [LSU, Gay Papers].

Isouard, J. B. lock- and gunsmith. 1841-56, New Orleans. 1841-42, 94 Bourbon; 1846, as Isoir, 51 Bienville [*Dir*.]. Unlocated in Ancestry.

Ittman, Jacob (1840-1906). gun- and locksmith. New Orleans. Ittman was born in Germany. 1867, doing business as Lee & Ittman with John J. Lee, 243 Camp [*Dirs*; Gorman].

Jackson, E. T. (1805-). gunsmith. 1841-42, Carondelet near Common, New Orleans. 1834, Bangor, Maine; 1838-39, St. Louis; 1840-42, New Orleans; Census of 1840 of Orleans County: E T Jackson, living alone, age 30 to 39. Census of 1850, Limestone County, Texas. Jackson was born in Massachusetts [*Dir*.; Hanson; Paul; Demerit]. Not located after 1850.

Jackson, Joseph. gunsmith. 1902, 1801 Bayou Rd., New Orleans [*Dir*.].

James & Coates. locksmiths & bell hangers. 1861, 75 Lafayette, New Orleans. Thomas James & George Coates. [*Dir*.].

Janotzek, S. locksmith. 1861, 112 St. Andrew, New Orleans [*Dir*.].

Jaub, Joseph. lock- and gunsmith. 1877-79, New Orleans [Gorman; *Dirs*.]. Also seen as Jaud.

Jeforgul, Pierre. gunsmith. 1851, 21 St. Ann, New Orleans [*Dir*.].

Jerome, Jean. locksmith. 1861, Elysian Fields near Royal, New Orleans [*Dir*.].

Johnson, John. gunsmith. 1890, Gretna, New Orleans [*Dir.*].

Johnson, James Lemuel (1830--). gunsmith. James Lemuel Johnson was born on 28 May 1830 in Chester, Vermont, a son of Lemuel Johnson. Census of 1850 of Worcester, Massachusetts: James L. Johnson, 20, cabinet maker, born in Vermont, single. Massachusetts state census of 1855: James L. Johnson, living in Ashburnham, Worcester County. Massachusetts state census of 1865: James L. Johnson, 35, born in Chester, Vermont; Harriet, 27; and Mason, 3.

Curtis Johnson, *Gunmakers of Illinois*, listed J L Johnson 1870-72 in Young America [Kirkwood], Warren County; and 1878-88 in Keithsburg, Mercer County. Census of 1870: James L Johnson, 40, born in Vermont, gunsmith; Harriet, 33, born in Massachusetts; Susan, 10; Mason, 9; Nellie, 5; and James, 1, all born in Massachusetts. Census of 1880 of Keithsburg: James L Johnson, 50, born in Vermont, widower; James, 11, born in Massachusetts. 1884, Weeping Water, Nebraska.

1888, Schamber, Acadia Parish. E. N. Marsh, from near Schamber, accompanied by J. L. Johnson, his brother-in-law, called at the Signal office Wednesday. Mr. Marsh has been a resident of the parish for only a few months and is very highly pleased with the country and climate. Mr. Johnson is an expert gunsmith formerly of Keithsburg, Illinois. [*Acadia Signal*, 8 December 1888].

Curt Johnson also noted that James Johnson was in Fort Madison, Lee County, Iowa, beginning about 1892. Iowa state census of 1895: James L. Johnson, born in Vermont. Census of 1900 of Lee County, Iowa: James L Johnson, 70, janitor, widowed, born in Vermont, living alone. Last, Curt noted that Johnson was handicapped in some way.

Johnson, William, Sr. machinist and gunsmith. 1874-94, New Orleans. 1875-77, gunsmith, Gretna; [*Dirs.*; Gorman].

Johnson, William, Jr. gunsmith. 1881-84, New Orleans; working with his father.

Jones, Gilbert (1842--). armorer. New Orleans. African American tradesman. Gilbert Jones, a black armorer, was appointed to serve in that capacity with the Continental Guards, a wholly white militia. One Cottom, a wealthy lieutenant, was missing his gold watch and some money and accused Jones and another Negro. When the real culprit was located Cottom refused to apologize, but Jones was reinstated as company armorer [*St. Louis Republic*, 25 March 1890]. The following is probably the armorer: Census of 1870: Gilbert Jones, 28, mulatto, carpenter, born in Alabama; Martha, 24; and David, 2. Census of 1900: Gilbert Jones, black, age 57, blacksmith; Susan,

28; and Lotta, 5. Also George Morris, 22, brother-in-law. Not located after 1900; not in Find-a-Grave.

Jones, William Thomas (1888-1978). gunsmith. Washington Parish. Buried in Nobles Cemetery near Pine, Louisiana. William "Gunsmith" Jones was born on 24 March 1888, a son of Harvey Jones of Salem, Mississippi. He died on 13 April 1978 and his tombstone carries the gunsmith nickname [mortality schedule].

Jonte, Eugene. locksmith, edged tool maker. 1851, Annunciation below Basin & Robin, New Orleans [*Dir.*]. Best known as a saw maker.

Joustan, Henry. gunsmith. 1849-53, Levee between 6th and 7th, New Orleans [Gorman; *Dirs.*]. Also seen as Jourdan.

Jufforgue, Pierre Rossignol (1805-1872). gunsmith. 1838-53, 24 St. Ann, New Orleans. African American tradesman. Born in Cuba [*Dirs.*]. Pierre appears in only one U.S. Census, that of 1840: P R Jufforgue, free colored male, age 25 to 35, engaged in a trade. He died on 12 October 1872 [Death Records; Ancestry].

Juge, Pierre Adolphe (1833-1900). gunsmith. 1867-78, Chartres, New Orleans. Census of 1880, 5th ward, St. Landry Parish: Adolph Juge, gunsmith, 45, born in France; wife Ann, 30; Leo, 6; Mary, 4; Fred A., 2, all born in Louisiana. Paul Juge sold a pistol to a murderer whom he had not previously known. He died in Assumption Parish [*Cincinnati Gazette*, 23 February 1877; Census; *Dirs.*; Gorman; *Times Picayune*, 20 February 1877].

Notice. The owners of guns and pistols left with me to repair are notified that if not claimed before 60 days they will be sold for their account. A. Juge, Gunsmith [*Opelousas Journal,* 20 March 1874].

Adolph Juge (formerly of Washington) Bellevue street, adjoining Frank the Baker's, Opelousas, LA, has always on hand a fresh stock of groceries which he will sell cheap for cash. He is now ready for work at his old gunsmith trade and invites his friends and the public to try him again. Particular attention paid to repairing all kinds of firearms. Will give prompt and substantial work at moderate prices. He has on hand a good stock of breech and muzzle loading guns and pistols and ammunition for all. Manufacturer and sole agent for St. Landry and Lafayette of Wildermuth Bed Springs [*Opelousas Courier*, 2 January 1886].

Jules, L. gunsmith. 1912-18, 1723 Governor Nicholls Hwy, New Orleans [*Dirs.*].

Jusselin, Antoine (1803--1880). gunsmith. 1834-49, New Orleans. 1849, doing business as Pessou & Jusselin. On 2 July 1833 Antoine Jusselin married Marceline Mayeux. Census of 1860: Antoine Jusselin, 61, gunsmith, born in France, $1000 real estate, $500 personal value; Marceline, 45; Marie, 17; Gaspard, 15; Leon, 12; and Julie, 9. Census of 1870 of Avoyelles Parish: Antoine Jusselin, 67, gunsmith, living alone. Census of 1880 or Marksville, Avoyelles Parish: Antoine Jusselin, 76, gunsmith, widower; living with his daughter Amelie. Antoine died in 1880 in Avoyelles Parish, burial unknown [*Dirs.*; Gorman; Ancestry].

Justin, Louis. gunsmith. 1877, rear 19 Toulouse, New Orleans [*Dir.*]. See Louis Juzan.

Juzan, Genereux. (1856--). gunsmith. New Orleans. 1878, Genereux lived with Joseph Juzan at 19 Toulouse, New Orleans [*Dir.*]. There was also a Numan Juzan, blacksmith, in the household. Census of 1860: L. Juzan, 41, gunsmith; Odille, 30; Arsine, 8; Judith, 6; Genereux, 4; and Ida, 3, all born in New Orleans. Genereux disappeared after 1878.

Juzan, Joseph G. (1856-1909). gun- and locksmith. 1880-1908, New Orleans; born in Louisiana; son of Louis and Adile Juzan. 1872-73, St. Claude St. corner of Reuchmen St. 1874, 543 Dauphine St. 1878, worked for P. Bouron, lived at 19 Toulouse. 1879-1901, home at 19 Toulouse St. 1908, 1317 Monroe St., locksmith. Census of 1880, Louis Juzan, gunsmith, 66; Odille, wife, 51; Joseph Juzan, gunsmith, 24; Samuel, blacksmith, 18, all born in Louisiana [*Dirs.*; Gorman]. 1904, 1019 Foucher St. [*Dir.*].

Juzan, Louis (1815-1899). gunsmith. 1838-99, New Orleans. Census of 1860: L. Juzan, 41, gunsmith, $1600 real estate, $100 personal value; Odille, 30; Arsine, 8; Judith, 6; Genereux, 4; and Ida, 3, all born in New Orleans. 1861, armorer at the Armory, 337 Orleans; 1869, 85 Frenchmen St. Census of 1870: Louis Juzan, 52, mulatto, born in Alabama, tinsmith; Odille, 39; Judith, 14; Joseph, 12; Newman, 8; and Emelia, 1, all mulattoes, all born in Louisiana. Census of 1880, New Orleans; Louis Juzan, 66, gunsmith, born in Louisiana; wife Odille, 51; Joseph Juzan, 24; and Samuel Juzan, 18, all listed as white. Louis died on 29 September 1899 [*Dirs.*; Gorman]. Not located in any census before 1860; in 1870 listed as mulatto but white in 1880; birthplace in given as Alabama in 1870, Louisiana in 1860 and 1880. No mention of race in 1860 census. African American tradesman?

Kaiser, John (1804-1877). gun- and blacksmith. New Orleans. Census of 1860: John Kaiser, 56, tinsmith; Eliza, 56; Jacob, 33; John, 28; Mary, 21;

Julia, 19; Eva, 15; Margaret, 12, all born in Bavaria. 1871, 24 8th St.; 1878, rear, north side Toledano between Chippewa and St. Thomas. John died on 12 October 1877 [*Dirs.*; Ancestry; Gorman].

Kaiser, John, Jr. (1832--). gunsmith. 1900-02, 917 Decatur St., New Orleans. John was a son of John and Eliza Kaiser, born in Bavaria [*Dirs.*].

Kauffman, John (1810-). gunsmith. Baton Rouge. Census of 1850, John Kauffman, age 40, gunsmith, value $500, born in Germany; Parmelia, 28, his wife; Mary, 9; Keziah [female], 6; Araline [female], 4; Benjamin, 2, all born in Louisiana. Not located before or after 1850.

Kault, Joseph. gunsmith. 1876, 207 St. Mary, New Orleans [*Dir.*].

Keifer, Joseph. gunsmith. 1874, 99 Marais St., New Orleans [*Dir.*]. See Joseph Kiefer.

Kellerman, Charles C. (1805-). gun- and locksmith. New Orleans. Census of 1850: C. Kellerman, 46, blacksmith; M, 42, wife; Julie, 15; Charles, 10, all born in France; Albertine, 6; Emily, 3, both born in Louisiana. 1870-77, 130 Frenchman St., New Orleans. Census of 1870: Charles C Kellerman, 65, locksmith, single, born in France [*Dirs.;* Gorman]. Not located after 1870; not located in 1860 Census.

Kelly, Daniel L. (1825-1885). armorer. New Orleans. 1881, Barrone St., [*Dir.*]. Census of 1880, Daniel L. Kelley, age 55, widower, armorer, born in Ireland; Daniel J.,22; William H., 16; Thomas Kelley, 13; Maria Benny, 35 [Census]. Kit Gorman notes that he was never noted as a gunsmith in civilian life. State armorer [*Times Picayune*, 30 January 1879].

Kelly, Daniel L. Jr. armorer. 1875-84, New Orleans; with Washington Artillery; rank of Major [*Dir.*; *Times Picayune*, 21 November 1875].

Kelly, William. locksmith. 1881, 459 Magazine, New Orleans [*Dir.*].

Kernaghan. arms importer. New Orleans. Kernaghan was a major importer of English shotguns up to the beginning of the Civil War and ended only when the Union blockade went into effect. There are several New Orleans Kernaghan-marked shotguns known.

Kevol, J. B. gunsmith. 1866, 280 Royal St., New Orleans [*Dir.*].

Kidd, Forbes. locksmith. 1876, rear 117 S. Johnson, New Orleans; worked for J. H. Reynolds [*Dir*.].

Kiefer, Joseph (1835--1900). lock- and gunsmith. 1861-81, New Orleans. 1861, 50 St. Peter; 1879, 144 S. Rampart; 1881, 112 S. Basin. He died on 16 November 1900 in New Orleans [*Dir*.; Ancestry]/

Kingston, Charles (1840-). gunsmith. 4th ward, Lafourche Parish. Census of 1880: Charles Kingston, born in Maryland, 40, gunsmith; wife Mary, 37, born in Kentucky; Logan, 14; Edward, 11; George, 4; Lillie, 1, all born in Louisiana. Not located before or after 1880.

Kittredge & Folsom. gun store. 1857-61, 55 St. Charles, New Orleans. George Folsom & Benjamin Kittredge. Successor to Ben Kittredge & Company [Gorman; *Dirs*.]. Reportedly the largest gun store of its time in New Orleans.

Kittredge, Benjamin (1825-). gun store owner. 1852-57, 55 St. Charles, New Orleans; doing business as Ben. Kittredge & Company. He also owned a store in Cincinnati, Ohio, established in 1845, doing business as Eaton & Kittredge, with Daniel E. Eaton. That store produced 250 rifles in 1851. In 1859 Ben form B. Kittredge & Company in Cincinnati. In his shop at 134 Main St. Kittredge sold arms to the federal government. He also invented a spring-back system to retain flash-back from percussion caps used on the Manhattan navy model revolver, patent 41,848 of 8 March 1864. The Cincinnati firm was open on Main St. until at least 1891. The New Orleans branch reopened after the war and was active at 55 St. Charles until at least 1876 [Gardner, *Small Arms Makers*, 108].

Kline, Louis B. gunsmith. 1907, 405 Gen. Myers Ave, New Orleans [*Dir*.].

Kling, Frank F. (1881—1942). gunsmith. 1901, Meridian. Shop at 507 25th Ave; home at 2301 6th Ave. [*Dir*.]. Frank was born in August 1881, a son of A. Frank, a blacksmith, and his wife Margaret Kling and resided with them. Frank died on 5 October 1942 in Rapides Parish, Louisiana, and was buried in Semmes Cemetery, Lauderdale County, Mississippi [Find-a-Grave; Ancestry].

Knaeble, Anton. locksmith. 1861, 319 Carondelet, New Orleans [*Dir*.].

Knopp, John H. locksmith. 1861, 160 Basin, New Orleans [*Dir*.].

Koch, Francis A. (1825-1873). cutler and gunsmith. New Orleans. 1887-1908, cabinet maker. Koch died on 23 February 1909 [Ancestry; Gorman].

Koch was listed by Gorman but all entries I can find indicate cabinet-maker.

Koehler, George (1815-1877). gunsmith. 1870-77, Rayville, near Monroe, Ouachita Parish. "Dealer in Guns, Pistols, Caps, Tubes, Cartridges, Powder Flasks, Patent Elastic Gun Wads. Repairing of all kinds neatly done, at 25% below former prices and work guaranteed" [*Ouachita Telegraph*, 8 October 1870; 7 September 1872]. He ran an ad offering his services as late as 20 April 1877. On 31 August 1877 the executors of George Koehler offered at public auction his house, lots in Monroe, and "all the gunsmith tools and other tools of the deceased; also a lot of pistols and guns; and a lot of gun-smith materials and iron; also a lot of unredeemed guns and pistols held for repairs done thereon. . ." On 3 September he ran an advertisement seeking an apprentice who would be "afforded every advantage to learn the trade and be treated kindly."

Notice! George Koehler, Gunsmith, gives notice that he has permanently located in Monroe and is prepared to make or repair Guns, Pistols, etc. An experience of 15 years in the most celebrated manufactories in Germany enables him to do work superior to any found in the South-west. His work is already known, as a residence of six years in Farmerville has given his work much celebrity. All his work is guaranteed and with proper care will last a generation. He keeps on hand Guns, Pistols, and Hunting Apparatus generally. Office two doors south of the post office [*Monroe Register*, 10 March 1859].

Apprentice Wanted. At Koehler's Gunsmith shop. An industrious boy will be afforded every advantage to learn the trade and will be kindly treated. Apply soon. Monroe [*Ouachita Telegraph*, 17 September 1870].

George Koehler, Gun Smith, Monroe, LA, dealer in Guns, Pistols, Caps, Tubes, Cartridges, Powder Flasks, Patent Elastic Gun Wads, Repairing of all kinds neatly done as 25% below former prices, and work guaranteed [*Ouachita Telegraph*, 22 October 1870].

Mr. George Koehler died at his residence in this city on the 16th after an illness of several weeks caused by an affection of the throat. Mr. Koehler was a native of Baden, Germany, and was born in 1815. He came to the United States in 1851, having taken an active part in the revolution of 1849 in Germany. He was an an excellent mechanic, well-known as a gunsmith, in which trade he was thoroughly skilled. At one time he was a member of the city council. He leaves two little boys, for whom ample provision is made in property left by the deceased and by a life insurance policy in the Knickerbocker company [*Ouachita Telegraph*, 18 May 1877]

Koult, Joseph. gunsmith. St. Mary St., New Orleans. City council voted to allow Joseph Koult to open a gunsmith shop [*New Orleans Daily Crescent*, 7 January 1862]. Presumably the restrictions existed because of occupation by Union Army.

Kraunerich, George. locksmith. 1851, Benton below Clio & Calliope, New Orleans [*Dir*].

Kuhnert, Edouard (1802-). gunsmith. 1851, New Orleans. Edouard Kuhnert, 49, was admitted to the charity hospital for rheumatism. He had been born in Berlin, Germany.

Kuntzmann, Jules H. lock- and gunsmith. 1865-81, New Orleans. 1877, 848 Magazine St. Originally he was a barber [*Dirs*.; Gorman].

Labat, M. gunsmith. 1841, 186 Barracks, New Orleans; same address as Latil gunsmiths [Gorman; *Dir*.].

Labour, Grasset (1799-). gunsmith. African-American tradesman. Census of 1860, Opelousas, St. Landry Parish: Grasset Labour, gunsmith, age 61, widower, born in France; Homere A., 27, deputy clerk at court; Emile, 21. See LaTour.

Labau, Justin (1826--1870). gunsmith. Iberia Parish. Justin was born on 18 December 1826. Hubertville, about a mile above Jeannerette, on the Bayou Teche. Labau, also a native of France, who had removed to Louisiana in 1857. Labau after locating in Louisiana, was for some time engaged as salesman in W. F. Hudson's general mercantile store. At the beginning of the war he joined an independent company of cavalry organized by Captain D. Kerr, and afterward commanded by Captain A. A. Pecot, which was afterward consolidated with General Harrison's command as Third Louisiana Cavalry. He was taken prisoner of war and paroled at New Iberia on 11 June 1865. Justin Labau was a gunsmith by occupation, and served in that capacity during a portion of the war. He was, however, in active service during the Red river and Mississippi campaigns. He served until the close of the war. Before coming to America he had served seven years as a soldier in the French army. Justin died on 20 November 1870 [Perrin, *Southwest LA: Biographical and Historical, 100*].

Lafitte, Jean 9c.1776-c.1823). gun- and blacksmith and pirate. Pirate Alley, near Jackson Square, New Orleans. Reportedly he melted down much of his treasure in silver and gold at his shop. Jean and his brother Pierre started on Bourbon Street as blacksmiths. Following their assistance to Andrew Jackson in his destruction of the British Army near New Orleans in the War of

1812 President James Madison granted both Lafitte brothers and the other pirates full pardons with restoration of citizenship. Lafitte later lived at Galveston, Texas. Reportedly, he died in a pirate engagement off Yucutan in 1823 [*Times Picayune*, 27 November 1927]

Lagé, Julien (1815-). gun smith. Lafourche Parish. Census of 1840 of St. Landry Paris: Julien Lagé head of household of 5 persons, one male 20 to 29. Census of 1850: Julien Lagė single, gunsmith; age 35, value $1000; born in France. Not located after 1850.

Lamal, Prosper. agent. 1885-88, 15 Carondelet, New Orleans. Prosper represented several Belgian manufacturers of shotguns [*Dirs*.; Gorman].

Lambert & Paulhemus. gun- and locksmiths. 1850, 107 Charles St., New Orleans [*Dir*.]. Henry Lambert & Cornelius Polhemus.

Lambert, Henry. gunsmith. 1848-50, St. Charles St., New Orleans [*Dirs*.]. 1849, J. H. & Henry Lambert, 105 St. Charles. 1850, Lamberty & Polhemus, 107 St. Charles.

Lambert, L. lock- and gunsmith. 1851, Ursulines below Conde & Old Levee, New Orleans [*Dir*.]. A justice of the peace attempted to serve a writ on Lambert, but Lambert threatened him so the man applied for and received help from the city police. Lambert fired on them so they requested help from the Zouaves and were thus able to subdue and arrest Lambert [*Times Picayune*, 21 July 1859]

Lambert, P. (1831--). gun- & silversmith. 1857, Congress Ave., Austin. 1859-60, C & 22nd Sts, Galveston. Census of 1860, Galveston, P. Lambert, jeweler and silversmith, 29; Odile, 23, both born in France; Phyllis, 4, born in Texas [Hirsch; *Dirs*.]. The Census of 1880 in Louisiana showed P. Lambert, born in 1831 in France, physician, but spouse and children are wrong. Otherwise not located in Ancestry or Find-a-Grave.

Lambert, Pierre (1756-1836). gunsmith and cutler. 1778-1834, 39 St. Peter & Bourbon Sts.; 1832, 59 Toulouse, New Orleans [*Dirs;* Gorman.].

Lambert, Pierre Joseph, Jr. gunsmith. One important way in which the Spanish sought to retain the allegiance of the Quapaws was by providing them with a gunsmith to keep their weapons in good order. Some years after 1771, Captain Balthazar de Villiers informed Governor Gálvez that the Quapaaws' gunsmith had died, and he asked the governor to appoint Pierre Joseph Lambert Jr. a young man of good conduct who was born at the Post but who was then living in New Orleans, to the vacancy. Pierre was the son of (Pierre Jopseph Lambert, Sr., who was noted as a soldier in the French garrison on 31 December 1758. The governor responded that the Quapaws who had recently visited him had asked him to name Antoine Lepine to the position and he had acquiesced in the request, but he directed Villiers to choose whichever of the two seemed more likely to please the Indians. Villiers appointed Lambert to the position because he had left his home in New Orleans in reliance on Villiers's assurance that he could have the job and had built a house and a forge at the Post. Although Villiers appointed Lambert to the post, it appears that Lepine eventually succeeded him. [Ancestry].

Lambert, Xavier (1820-1868). gun- and blacksmith. New Orleans. Noted as a gunsmith only in 1846; remainder listed as blacksmith only. Census of 1850: X Lambert, 30, mechanic [?], value $23,000; Charles, 26; Charlotte, 18, all born in Louisiana. The will of Pierre Francois Xavier Lambert was probated in 1868 [Ancestry; Gorman; *Dirs.*].

Lambot, Fred. gunsmith. 1883, New Orleans; worked for Julien Saget [*Dir.*].

Lamote, Etienne. gunsmith and gilder. 1822-32, 14 St. Ann, New Orleans [*Dir.*]. Not in Ancestry.

LaMothe, Louis. cutler. 1861, 209 Chartres, New Orleans [*Dir.*].

LaMothe, P. goldsmith. 1811, corner of Toulouse & Royale, New Orleans [Dir.]

Landrum, Benjamin (1756-1825). blacksmith, farmer. Benjamin was born in 1756 in Chatham County, North Carolina. He moved to Louisiana after 1816 and died in 1825 in Quachita Parish, Louisiana. He was a veteran of the Revolutionary War and the Creek War [Family; Ancestry].

Landry, Pierre. gunsmith and cutler. 1822-32, 59 Toulouse, New Orleans [*Dir.*]. Census of 1810: Pierre Landry head of household of 5 free whites, one male and one female, ages 26 to 44. Census of 1820: Piere Landry head of household of four free whites, and one m,ale slave; male and female over age 44. Census of 1830: Pierre Landry head of household of five persons, one male slave, one white male and one white female, ages 70 to 79.

Larenaudie, Hippolite (1838--). gunsmith. Iberia Parish and San Antonio, Texas. Census of 1870 of Iberia Parish, Louisiana: H Larenaudie, 32, gunsmith, $1000 real estate, $100 personal value, born in France; Coralie, 26.

1883-94, 228 S. Flores, San Antonio. 1887, Gun & Lock Smith, Sewing Machine Repairer, fruits, cigars. 1892, 402 W Neuva [Ancestry; Hirsch; *Dirs*.]. Not located in 1880 Census or after 1894. Not in Find-a-Grave.

Lange, Moritz. gun- and locksmith. 1866-68, 148 Basin, New Orleans; same address as Mathias Laska [Gorman; *Dirs*.].

Langne, J. J. gunsmith. 1873, rear west side St. Anthony between Marals and Urquhart, New Orleans [*Dir*.]. See Jean J. Lavigne

Largnon, Nicholas. gunsmith. c. 1740-64, Natchitoches Parish. A building was erected by a gunsmith named Nicholas Largnon and a blacksmith named Jean Baptiste Martin. [*Natchitoches Times*, April 3, 1958]

Laska, Frank (1873-1943). lock- and gunsmith. New Orleans. Frank was a son of Mathias Laska, and brother of Joseph. 1902, Laska Bros., gunsmiths, 616 N. Basin St. [*Dirs*.; Gorman; Ancestry].

Laska, Joseph O. (1863-1911). lock- and gunsmith. 148 Basin St., New Orleans; born in Austria. Joseph was a son of Mathias and a brother of Frank [*Dirs*.; Gorman; Ancestry].

Laska, Mathias A (1837-1900). gun-, lock-, and blacksmith. 1872-99, 148 Basin St., New Orleans; born in Moravia; wife Theresa. 1866-68, Moritz Lange worked for Laska. In 1899 the firm became M. A. Laska & Sons. Primarily blacksmiths. 1886-87, 148 N. Basin, gunsmith. 1915, 737 S. Rampart St. Census of 1880, Mathias Laska, 43, lock- and gunsmith; Theresa, wife, 50; Annie, 19; Joseph, 17; Mary, 15, all born in Moravia; Mathias, 9; Frank, 7, both born in Louisiana [Gorman; *Dirs*.].

LaSalle & Glesner. gun-, lock- and blacksmiths. 1841-43, New Orleans. Leonard LaSalle & J. Glesner [Gorman; *Dirs*.].

LaSalle, M. lock- and blacksmith. 1851, 16 Jefferson, New Orleans [*Dir*.].

Lassére, J. P. (1788--). cutler, manufacturer of surgical instruments. 1834-55, New Orleans. 1842, 34 Conde; 1851, 29 Conde, [*Dir*.]. Census of 1840: J P Lassére, head of family of 6 free white persons, one male 30 to 39, engaged in manufacture. Census of 1850: J B Lassére, 62, cutlery manufacturer; Josephine, 50; Leon, 13; Sophia, 10, all born in France. There is a problem: if children ages 10 and 13 were born in France, how could J P have been practicing his trade as early as 1833 in New Orleans? There was another J P Lassére (1832-1898) born in France, living in New Orleans.

Latil & Brother. gunsmiths. 1832-34, Barracks, New Orleans [*Dir.*]. Joseph & Louis.

Latil, Achille Azael (1833--1883). gunsmith. 1877, Hallettsville, Lavaca County, Texas. Achille was born on 16 January 1833 in Baton Rouge, Louisiana, and baptized at St. Joseph Cathedral. Achille was primarily a school teacher. He married, first Elizabeth Korwin Jaholkowski on 19 August 1861 in Baton Rouge. They had a son, Julius Achille Joseph. He married, second, Lucinda Ann Dixon on 13 February 1866 in Baton Rouge, and they had 2 children. Census of 1880 of Baton Rouge, East Baton Rouge Parish, Louisiana: Achille Latil, born in Louisiana, gun smith, 47; Lucinda A., his wife, 34; Julius, 18; Annie E., 13. He died on 5 October 1883 in Baton Rouge and was buried at St. Joseph's Catholic Cemetery, Baton Rouge [Find-a-Grave]. The directory entry and newspaper ad of 1877 apparently marked his one brief foray into Texas.

GUNSMITH. Hallettsville, Texas (near Turner's Hotel). is competent to perform all work, in his line, to repair Pistols & Guns, re-stock guns, and put sewing machines in running order. He respectfully asks the patronage of the county and guarantees satisfaction A. Latil [*Hallettsville Herald and Planter*, 14 November 1877]

Postponed Sale . . . Parish of east Baton Rouge –in the matter of the succession of Achille Latil, deceased – will expose to public sale, on the premises whereon deceased last resided in the City of Baton Rouge, at the corner of North and Church streets, Monday the 7th day of January, A.D. 1984, . . . One lot of Gunsmith's Tools and material and old Guns and pistols; also 2 barrels . . . 8 undressed gunstocks, . . . 1 gun sign, . . . one grindstone, benches and Gun *Racks [Daily Advocate,* 27 December 1883]

Latil, Hector Lawrence (1827--1915). gunsmith. Baton Rouge. Hector was born on 18 March 1827 in Baton Rouge. Census of 1870: Lawrence H. Latil, 43, gunsmith, value $100, white; Mary, 40; Helena, 17; Willie, 14; Estelle, 12; Emma, 6; and Florence, 1. Census of 1900: Hector Latil, 73, gunsmith, living with William H. Latil, 45. Hector died on 26 February 1915, and was buried in Magnolia Cemetery, Baton Rouge [Ancestry; Find-a-Grave]. See Laurent Latil.

Latil, Joseph Thimecour (1796-1857). gunsmith. New Orleans. Joseph was born on 7 May 1796 and baptized at St. Louis Cathedral on 7 July 1796. Joseph served in the Battle of New Orleans. On 21 July 1816 he married Marie Marcelite Clermont at St. Louis Cathedral, and fathered 9 children.

Early in his career he was a carpenter and cabinet-maker. 1827, gunsmith, 323 Burgundy. 1832-34, worked with his brother Louis, Latil & Brother. Noted in 1850 Census as being blind. He died on 13 February 1857 [Census; *Dirs*.; Gorman].

Latil. Julius Achille Joseph. gunsmith. Julius was a son of Achille and Elizabeth (Korwin Jaholkowsi) Latil Church & Main Sts., Baton Rouge [*Daily Advocate*, 1 March 1902]

Latil, Laurent Hector (1827-1915). gunsmith. Laurent was born on 18 March 1827 in Baton Rouge, a son of Louis Azael and Maria (Gonzalez-Ruiz) Latil. On 4 July 1848 he married Mary Elizabeth Blanchard.1850, Baton Rouge. 1850, Hector, age 23, gunsmith, value $300, born in LA; Mary, 20, born in NY; Mary, 1, born in LA [Census]. 1860, Hector, 33, value $200; Mary, 29, born in NJ [sic]; Mary, 11; Ann, 9; Carmolite, 8; William H., 4; Sarah, 2; Mitchel Clara, 26, born in IL [Census]. Known as Hector, he was a son of Louis and Carmelite (Ruiz) Latil, born on 18 March 1827 in Baton Rouge. On 4 July 1848 he married Mary Elizabeth Blanchard (d.1908). During the Second War for Independence he served in the LA infantry, Company B, 4th Regiment. 1880, Hector, 53, gun smith, born in LA; Mary E., 49; Florance, 11; Caladonia, 8; Robert L. Smithson, 33; Louisa E. Smithson, 17. He died on 26 February 1915 in Baton Rouge and was buried at Magnolia Cemetery, Baton Rouge.
[Census; http://www.latil.org/eng/eng_latil_louisiane.htm]

Hector Latil made an affidavit before Justice Nephler of the first ward, against Pat. Dougherty, charging him with larceny. The affidavit asserts that the accused stole a pistol from the gunsmith shop of the complainant on Lafayette street last Tuesday [*Daily Advocate*, 8 November 1883]

Mr. Louis Hector Latil, one of the oldest members of the community, died at 1:30 o'clock Friday morning, following an illness of only a few hours. Mr. Latil was quite active for his 88 years and was apparently in the best of health and spirits before this stroke which ended his long and useful life. Mr. Latil was born in Baton Rouge and was the descendent of a French armorer and gunsmith who came to Baton Rouge in the Spanish-French regime to take charge of the garrison armory, which is now our beautiful university. Mr. Latil, like several generations before him, continued in the trade of his forefathers until age and ill health forced him out of active service. He was a veteran of 2 wars: Mexican and Civil wars, where he served with honor to himself and his country. He was a good citizen and took an active part in the affairs of the town in years passed. Five generations of the Latil family are residents of this city. Mr. Latil is survived by 7 living children, 44 grandchildren, 31 great-grandchildren, and 2 great-great-grandchildren. . . . [*State Times Advocate*, 27 February 1915].

Latil, Louis Azael (1798-1877). gunsmith. Louis was born on 8 November 1798 in New Orleans and baptized at St. Louis Cathedral in New Orleans on 8 May 1800. On 20 March 1824 at St. Louis Cathedral he married Maria Gonzalez-Ruiz. 1850, Baton Rouge. 1850, Louis, gunsmith, age 52; Carmalite, 40, his wife; Algier, 20 [female]; Achille, 18; Arthur, 16; Carmelite [female] 13; Azina [female], 11; Elmina, 8; Louis, 6; Edgar, 4; all born in LA [Census]. Louis was a son of Lazare and Heanne (Esteve) Latil, born 8 November 1798. On 20 March 1824 he married Maria Carmelite Ruiz in New Orleans. He died July 30, 1877, Baton Rouge. Congress considered granting L. A. Latil a pension because he incurred a disability while serving as master armorer at Baton Rouge [14 August 1856]. His daughter married gunsmith William H. Doyle who died young. Robbers attempted to break into his gunshop on Main St. between St. Francis and st. Anthony Sts. [Family ; *Daily Advocate,* 13 June 1902].

Ingenious Invention. We were shown yesterday a gun, the invention of a citizen of Baton Rouge, which is a most ingenious contrivance. It has 4 chambers and 1 barrel, and is so arranged as to shoot as rapidly as the triggers can be pulled ; and yet in size and weight, is not heavier or more cumbersome than an ordinary gun. The inventor is Mr. L. A. Latil, of Baton Rouge, a Creole, who has for many years held the post of armorer at the Baton Rouge Arsenal [*Augusta Chronicle*, 15 October 1849]

Ingenious Invention. We were shown yesterday a gun, the invention of a citizen of Baton Rouge, which is a most ingenious contrivance. It has 4 chambers and one barrel and is so arranged as to shoot as rapidly as the trigger can be pulled ; and yet, in size and weight, is not heavier or more cumbersome than an ordinary gun – The inventor is Mr. L. A. Latil of Baton Rouge, a Creole, who has for many years held the post of Armorer at the Baton Rouge Arsenal {New Orleans Delta, 10 November 1849].

Latil, Thimecour Lazare (1764-1845). gunsmith. Lazare was born on 30 December 1764 in New Orleans and baptized on 17 June 1768 at St. Louis Cathedral. 1822, home 137 Burgundy; 1832, 323 Burgundy St., New Orleans [*Dir.*]. He was a son of Alexander and Maria Jeanne (Goujon) Latil. He married Jeanne Sophie Esteve (1768-1830). She was a *mulata libre*, a free woman of mixed racial heritage. They had given birth to children before their marriage and they were made legitimate by the marriage. He died on 15 December 1845 and was buried at St. Joseph Catholic Church Yard, Baton Rouge on 17 December.

Latil, William H. (1856-). gunsmith. Baton Rouge. William was a son of Lawrence and Mary Latil. Census of 1880, William H Latil, gun smith, born in Louisiana, 24; Mary, his wife, 24; William H., 11 months. Census of 1900: William Latil, 45, watchman, widower, white; living with Lawrence Latil, 73, gunsmith, white, his father.

LaTour, Homér A. (1833-1873). politician, gunsmith. Homer was born in Opelousas, St. Landry Parish, on January 24, 1833, one of eight children. His grandfather, Captain Jean (Jérome) Grasset LaTour and his father Pierre Grasset LaTour were born in France. The family migrated to Louisiana. As a child growing up, he worked in his father's gunsmith shop. Homér married Emilie Pasquier, but had a relationship with an Cajun woman, Heléne Richard (1830-). She was of the Acadian Richard family who was exiled during the Acadian Expulsion. Census of 1860: Gracest LeTour, 61, gunsmith; Homer LaTour, clerk at court, $1500 personal, $800 real estate; Emily, 21, born in Ohio. Census of 1870: Homer LaTour, 37, dry goods merchant, real estate $2000, personal value $500; Emily, 27; Emily, 9; Alice, 3. Census of 1880: Homer LaTour, 47, noted with a disability; Emily, 37; Emily, 18; Alice, 13. Homer died in 1873 [Ancestry]. African American.

LaTour, Ozéme (1869-). gunsmith. Opelousas, St. Landry Parish. LaTour was born on October 14, 1869, the son of Homér A. (Omér) LaTour, and Heléne Richard. In his youth he trained as a gun- and blacksmith. Ozéme LaTour was the product of a French Creole Mulatto and a Cajun. Census of 1900, LaTour, black, Police Jury Ward 7, Saint Landry Parish, age: 30; Osema Lataur 30; Marie Lataur 25; and 6 small children.

Latour, Pierre Grasset (1798-1860). gunsmith. On 9 November 1846 his owner emancipated Grasset Latour and several other St. Landry Parish inhabitants. Several men certified that "the slave has at all times led a good conduct, and we further declare that the considerations upon which the above petition [for emancipation] is grounded are well known to us, and that therefore, as far as it lies in our power, we support the same and pray for this emancipation of the slaves therein described." Census of 1850 St. Landry Parish: Gracest Latour, age 57; Felicie, age 39; Homere, age 18, and Alfred, age 12. All born in France [*sic*]; occupation, gunsmith; value of real estate: $700 LaTour born in the Bergerac, Dordogne, France. 1830, left Bordeaux, bound for New Orleans on ship *James and Isabella*, age 21, native of France [ship roster]. Pierre, gunsmith by profession, married Felicia Franchebois July 4, 1826 in Opel. Felicia was the daughter of Jean Franchebois and Felicite Vige. She was born in Iberville Parish on the River. 1850, Opelousas, St. Landry Parish, Gracest, age 57, gunsmith; Felice, 39; Homer, 18; Alfred, 12, Census says all born in France. Property value $750. Grasset died on 4 December 1860 at age 62, and was buried at St. Landry Catholic Church, Opelousas, Louisiana. Latour, Grasset, age 21, occupation gunsmith, native of France on the ship *James & Isabella,* port of departure, Bordeaux, arrival in New Orleans on 13 December 1830 [Fontenot, *Southwest Louisiana Courthouse Inventory,* 1:. 427-428; Census]. African American tradesman.

Laureaudac, Henri (1837-). gunsmith. 1880, 6th ward, Iberia Parish. Henri, 43; born in France, gunsmith; Provost, his wife, 35; Albert Provost, 13 [Census].

Laurent, Michael (1788--1863). gunsmith. New Orleans. Census of 1850: Michael Laurent, 62, gunsmith. Michael died on 22 July 1863 [Ancestry].

Laurenty, Pierre (1744-). gunsmith. New Orleans. Laurenty was a German, gunsmith, 41, with Marie Videt, his wife, 42; and Pierre, their son, shoe-maker, 17. The Layrenty family arrived on the *L'Amitie,* a 400 ton ship led by Captain Joseph Beltremieux, which left France on August 20, 1785. After 80 days at sea, they arrived in New Orleans on November 8, 1785. There were 270 people in 68 families on board On the way, there were 6 deaths after some sickness spread [Ancestry].

Lavigne, Jean Jacques (1819-1891). gunsmith. African-American tradesman. New Orleans. 1858, noted as a free man of color. Only occasionally shown in directories, he was noted in the censuses of 1850, 1860, and 1870, born in LA. 1876-91, 86 St. Anthony St.; [*Dirs*.; Census; Gorman].

Leatherman, Thomas S. (1829-1923). gunsmith. Leatherman, one of the early settlers of what is now Morrow County, Oregon, died at the advanced age of 92 years 10 months and 22 days. Had he lived until Christmas day he would have rounded out his 94th year. Leatherman was born at Alexandria, Louisiana, in 1829. When grown he migrated to Hot Springs, Arkansas, where he lived until 1875 when he brought his family to Oregon settling on a ranch on Rhea Creek where they lived for a number of years later going to Chico, California, where he remained until 1910 when he returned to this county. When the civil war broke out Mr. Leatherman was living in AR and although of southern birth and ancestry, he was always loyal to the old flag and when the vote was taken in that state on the question of secession he was one of the two men in his county to vote against the measure, casting his vote on the side of the government of the United States. Later, however, he was drafted into the southern army and, being a gunsmith by trade he was put at work making guns to help equip the Confederate Army. He was married to Mary Logan, at Arkadelphia, Arkansas, in 1859 and to them ten children were born. Mr. Leatherman was a man of a kindly, benevolent disposition and possessed to a marked degree the high ideals and qualities of honor which go to make up the true Christian gentleman. He was predeceased by his wife in 1883 [Heppner, *Oregon Times*, November 27, 1923].

Ledoyer, V. M. (1810-). gunsmith. 1860-66, 309 Old Levee, New Orleans [*Dir*.; Census].

LeDuc, A. gunsmith. 1838, New Orleans [*Dir*.].

LeDuc, Philippe. locksmith. 1740, New Orleans. Philippe was a witness in the marriage of Marie Jeanne Drapeau (1719-1782) with the surgeon general of Louisiana [Ancestry].

LeDuc, Louis T. gunsmith. 1841, New Orleans [*Dir*.]. May be same as Theodore.

Leduc, Louis Theodore (1799-). gunsmith and cutler. 1837-1861, New Orleans. 1842, 38 Conti; 1851, 98 Conde; 1861, 214 Chartres. Associated with Jean Marie Breffeihl (-1838) engraver. 1861, T. LeDuc & Son as Eugene Leduc joined the firm. On the eve of the Civil War he advertised hundreds of Colt pistols and other firearms and thousands of waterproof percussion caps. In 1860 he owned real estate valued at $6000 and had a personal value of $4500 [*Dir*.; Gorman; Census]. Two men were wounded, one fatally, by the accidental discharge of a firearm in Leduc's shop [*Daily True Delta*, 10 April 1862]

Guns and Pistols. with every article of superior quality connected with the Gun Trade, imported from England and France of the best manufacturers, by LeDuc & Co. Gun Makers. 93 Chartres Street, between Bienville and Conti. Mounting and repairing done on the lowest terms [*Times Picayune*, 17 March 1846]

Leduf, Jacques. goldsmith. 1811, 23 Royale, New Orleans [*Dir*.].

Lee & Ittman. gunsmiths. 1872, 243 Camp, New Orleans [*Dir*.]. John Lee & Jacob Ittman [Gorman].

Lee, John J. gunsmith, metal worker, gunsmith. 1867, 248 Camp St.; 1884, 380 Lafayette, New Orleans; same address as Louis Gertieis, Jr. [Gorman; *Dirs*.]. Burglars entered J. J. Lee's gunshop on the night of March 5 and ransacked the establishment [*Times Picayune*, 13 March 1867]

Lee, Leroy E. (1835-). gunsmith. 1867-80, New Orleans; born in Mississippi, lived alone. 1871, employed by gunsmith Carson Mudge, 75 Magazine St. 1872, Guilfoux [Grilfoure] & Lee, 132 Chartres. 1878-85, S, Rampart St.

1871-72, 55 St. Charles St., New Orleans. 1867, 149 Baronne. 1871, gunsmith at Carson Mudge's shop, residence rear 356 Dryades. "He is always ready to make, repair, and clean guns, Pistols, and Shot Guns" at Charleville's Sportsmen's Depot." 1874-79, rear 356 Dryades. Census of 1880, L. E. Lee, gunsmith, 45, born in Mississippi, single, living alone [*Dirs.*; *Times Picayune*, 17 March 1872; Gorman]. J. Grilfoure and L. E. Lee. Grilfoure and Lee sued the city of New Orleans for loss of guns and accouterments incurred when on 6 March a mob broke into their gunshop. [New Orleans *Republican*, 25 March 1873].

Lee, Michael. locksmith & bell hanger. 1851-61, New Orleans, 1851, 106 Circus; 1861, 90 Rampart. 1867, 168 Rampart [*Dir.*; Ancestry].

Lee, Zachariah Z. (1828-1902). blacksmith and gunsmith. Lee was born on 28 December 1828. His first wife was from Pike County, Mississippi, and was named Safronia Courtney. She died sometime before the Civil War. He was active in the Glorious Cause. Initially he was stationed with the 39th Mississippi Infantry at Corinth, Mississippi, where he made cannonballs. Later he worked at the armory at Port Hudson, Louisiana. He was on leave when town was enveloped and thus avoided capture. He then operated with partisan rangers in Felcianas until war's end. After the war he lived in Slaughter, Louisiana, where he acted a official of Baptist Church. His headstone reads, "Asleep In Jesus, Blessed sleep; From which none ever wake to weep." [Ancestry]

Leeds & Company. New Orleans. This firm which apparently made a single 8-inch Columbiad, which burst, and from then on produced bronze field calibers until fall of the city in April, 1862. Charles J. and Thomas L. Leeds, proprietors. Several 3.3-inch caliber bronze cannon were manufactured. One example is located in the Museum of the Confederacy in Richmond, Virginia [O.R. Series I, Volume 6, Serial No. 6, page 621-6].

Question. Were any heavy guns made at Leeds & Co.'s establishment or were any rifled or banded?
Answer. We made a few heavy guns for the Navy and one for the Army. We rifled quite a number of old 32 and 42 pounders for the Army, and we banded one 7-inch gun. I do not recollect whether any more were banded..."

Lefebvre, Jean Baptiste Modeste (1762-1837). merchant & gunsmith. New Orleans [Dirs.; Ancestry].

Lefevre, Jules. gunsmith. 1893-94, 90 Chartres, New Orleans. 1923-24, 1723 Governor Nicholls Hwy [*Dir.*].

Lefevre, Louis. gunsmith. 1854, 159 St. Peter, New Orleans [*Dir*.].

Lefevre, T. B. gunsmith. 1834, 195 French, New Orleans [*Dir*.]

Leglaize, ---. gunsmith 1827, Old Levee, New Orleans [*Dir*.].

LeGrand, Jean Baptiste. cutler & gunsmith. 1814, New Orleans [Gorman].

Lehne, Frederick. gunsmith. 1891, rear Washington, north east corner 9th, 7th district, New Orleans [*Dir*.].

Leicht, Henry. gunsmith. 1874, New Orleans. Leicht, gunsmith employed by Jacob Myers, and boarded at 90 N. Peters St. [*Dir*.].

LeMat, Jean Alexander Francois (1821-1895). inventor. New Orleans. Patent 15,925 of 21 October 1856 for a revolver; 16,124 of 25 November 1856 for a revolver; 24, 312 of 7 June 1859 for a revolver; 24,313 of 7 June 1859 for a cannon lock; 97,780 of 14 December 1869. Dr LeMat is best remembered as the inventor of the famous LeMat revolver, much prized in the Confederacy, but strangely issued mostly to its navy. The revolver was developed in New Orleans in 1856 by Dr. Jean LeMat and backed by Pierre G. T. Beauregard, who was to become a general with the Confederacy. Roughly 2,900 were produced. The distinguishing characteristic of LeMat's revolver is that its 9 shot cylinder revolves around a separate central barrel of larger caliber than the chambers in the cylinder proper. The central barrel is smoothbore and can function as a short-barreled shotgun with the shooter selecting whether to fire from the cylinder or the smoothbore barrel by flipping a lever on the end of the hammer. Flipping the lever down caused the moveable striker to fall upon the primer set directly under the hammer, discharging the lower barrel, while leaving it in the standard position would fire the chambers in the cylinder, much like any other revolver. LeMat died outside Paris where he lived after the war, dying at age 74 [Wikipedia].

Leonard, William (1825-). gunsmith. New Orleans. Census of 1850; William Leonard, 25, gunsmith, born in England.

LePage, Gregoire (1812-). gunsmith. 1842-58., New Orleans. 1851, St. Peter below Chartres. Census of 1850: Greg. LaPage, 38, gunsmith, born in Belgium, living alone.

Lepine, Antoine. gunsmith. 1771, The Quapaw Indians who had asked that the governor to name Antoine Lepine to the position of armorer to the tribe

[Ancestry].

Lepape, Desbois. gunsmith. 1842, 87 Bourbon, New Orleans [*Dir.*].

Lerenaudie, H. gunsmith. New Iberia, Iberia Parish. On 27 June 1870 a fire consumed part of the business district of New Iberia. Lerenaudie lost his gunshop and its contents valued at $1000 [Opelousas Journal, 9 July 1870].

Levy, Nicholas. gunsmith. 1875, 210 Bienville, New Orleans [*Dir.*].

Lewis, Leo. gunsmith. 1902, 538 Common, Shreveport; home same [*Dir.*].

Libeau, V. G. W. gunmaker. Valentine Libeau was born in 1790, in Castle Hesse, Prussia. He later worked in St. Petersburg [Petrograd], Russia. In 1816 he emigrated to America, landing at Bristol, Rhode Island. In 1819 he was naturalized in Bedford. In 1819 and 1820 he was taxed as a single freeman in Bedford boro.

Gun Smithing. The Subscriber lately arrived from Germany, respectfully informs the publick, that he has opened a shop, next door to Mr. William Gibson in Juliana street, Bedford, where he intends making new Rifles, single and double barreled Fowling Pieces, Pistols, Guns, and Gun Locks of every description; as also to repair old Guns, Locks, &c., &c. From the perfect knowledge he has of the business he flatters himself to gain a part of the publick custom. VALENTINE LIBEAU [Bedford *True American*, 181 June 1818]

By 1825 he had moved to Cincinnati, Ohio. 127 Main St., Cincinnati [*Cincinnati Advertiser*, 17 March 1827] 1856-57 he had a shop at 215 Cutter St., Cincinnati, Ohio [*Dir*]. A man named Baptiste Libeau worked in St. Louis 1838. Libeau then moved to New Orleans. 1830, Valentine Libeau, gunsmith, 8 Camp; 1832, V. Libeau, gunsmith, 9 Camp; Same in 1834, 1835 and 1838, 7 Camp, Libeau was not listed in 1841; 1842, 7 Camp. He was not in 1843, 1846 or 1849 directories. 1840, Valentine G. W. Libeau, Orleans Parish [Census; *Dirs.*]. V.G.W. Libeau is listed in New Orleans No. 9 Camp Street, in the city directories from 1832 through 1845.

The undersigned offers for sale rifles, guns, belt and other pistols, and a complete set of gunsmith's tools, at a bargain. Persons wishing to purchase the whole or a part of the above will find it to their advantage to call on V. Libeau at Mr. Irwin's Tremont House, St. Charles St.[*Daily Crescent*, June 3, 1848]

Libeau was known as a maker of percussion derringers and half stock sporting rifles. His unique revolver is likely the only specimen made.

There is no serial number. It displays quality of manufacture. No other examples have been observed. Unlike the Colt Paterson which revolves clockwise, the Libeau turns counterclockwise. He worked also in Cincinnati together with Charles Libeau. Two guns made by V. G. W. Libeau are known from the Estate of Stanley Diefenthal auction catalog, lot 210: The title description of the gun is a "Unique and Important Hand Built Revolver with Gold Inlaid New Orleans Barrel Marking and Signed on Lock by V. G. W. Libeau, New Orleans; dated 1847." The gun is engraved in script in three lines on the lockplate: "V.G.W. Libeau /New Orleans/ 1847". Maker of percussion derringers and half-stock sporting rifles. Rare Derringer Pistol by V. Libeau of New Orleans circa 1840-45. The gun is a .50 caliber, 5-inch octagonal smoothbore barrel with two silver inlaid bands; patent breech; V. Libeau inscribed on back action lockplate; scroll and border engraved on barrel breech, patent breech and upper tang, trigger guard and trigger plate and butt cap with hinged lid and compartment for percussion caps; German silver mountings [Kit Gorman].

Engraved gunlock of Valentine Libeau pistol

Known pistol. V. Libeau percussion target pistol. caliber about 60 Smoothbore. High grade half stock target pistol with 8-3/4" octagonal barrel, marked *London* on the top flat. It has an engraved breech with a narrow gold and wide platinum band. The hammer, lockplate, trigger guard and tang are engraved to match. The hammer has dolphin head motif with a safety on the lockplate. It has single set trigger and a finger rest trigger guard with decorative pointed finial. It is mounted in a 1-pc stock with raised sideplates and checkered bag shaped grip. It has German silver nosecap and oval wedge escutcheons. It also has an engraved small German silver oval on the bottom of the butt. The exposed part of the bbl has an iron rail on the bottom with iron guide and iron nose pipe that contain the original brass tipped rammer with concealed worm. The condition was described as good to very good. Bbl retains a medium dark patina with some moderate pitting around the bottom rail and is cleaned on part of the top flat and on the lockplate. The trigger guard & hammer retain a dark patina.

Guns and Pistols. A Bargain. The undersigned offers for sale Rifles, Guns, brlt and other Pistols and a complete line of gunsmith tools at a bargain. People wishing to purchase the whole or part of the above will find it to their advantage to call on V. Libeau at Mr. Irwin's Tremont House, St. Charles street [*Daily Crescent*, 5 March 1848].

Lilly, Jno. T. (1843-). gunsmith. Lake Charles, Calcasieu Parish. Census of 1880: Jno T Lilly, single, born in Virginia, lived in a boarding house or hotel with 20 or so others. John was a son of Thomas Patrick Lilly of Grafton, Taylor County, West Virginia. In 1870 John was an inmate in the penitentiary in Fort Madison, Lee County, Iowa.

Lindsay, William B. (1806-1866). inventor. New Orleans. Lindsay was a physician who tinkered with various products. In May 1861 he reportedly invented a cannon capable of firing 30 shots a minute and was supposed to make a rifle with a similar capability. Nothing more is known of the cannon or rifle. No known U.S. or Confederate patent [Gorman].

Lischy, Edward (1821-1892). machinist, gunsmith. 1850-91, New Orleans; Edward was born in France and died in Baton Rouge [*Dirs*.; Gorman].

Livet, Louis (1868--1947). gunsmith. Vermillionville [Lafayette], Lafayette Parish. Livet was noted in passing in *Lafayette Advertiser*, 23 May 1891. Louis Livet arrived from France in 1885. Livet died on 27 May 1947 and was buried in St. John's Cemetery, Lafayette Parish [Find-a-Grave].

Locke, Samuel. hardware dealer and gunsmith. 1845, 7-8 Front Levee, New Orleans. Advertised gun parts, including stocks and dies [*Jeffersonian Republican*, 7 March 1845; *Times Picayune*, 31 October 1868].

Loftin, Benagh (1820-1895). gun- and blacksmith, plantation overseer. Benagh (pronounce Benja) was born in Lawrence County, Mississippi, and moved to Lauderdale County and then on to Jasper County. Prior to the Civil War he moved to Calcasieu Parish, Louisiana, and then to Beauregard Parish shortly after 1860. He then moved to Vernon Parish, Louisiana, on Sabine River near Evans, Louisiana, with son, William Loftin. During the Civil War he worked as a Blacksmith and Gunsmith in Sylvarena, which is a village in Smith County, Mississippi. He was also a farmer and at one time served as an overseer of 75 slaves on a Mississippi plantation [Ancestry].

Lorie, F. locksmith. 1861-66, 122 St. Peter, New Orleans [*Dir.*].

Louis. slave tradesman. 1828, New Orleans. Isaac L. McCoy sold a group of slaves among whom was "Louis, aged about 17 or 18 years, has been about 10 years in the country, speaks English and French fluently, has served an apprenticeship of two years to the tailoring business and about the same time with a gunsmith" [*New Orleans Argus*, 10 September 1828]. African American tradesman

Lucas, John. goldsmith. 1811, 46 Ursulines, New Orleans [*Dir.*].

Lucas, W. A. (1802-). gunsmith. division 5, Union Parish. Census of 1850, W A Lucas, 48, value $100, gunsmith, born in North Carolina; Ann, his wife, 48, born in Tennessee; Lewis, 16; Andrew, 12; Thomas, 10, all born in Mississippi. Not located after 1850.

Luce, George D. inventor. New Orleans. On 11 March 1873 he received patent number 136,660 for a magazine. On 3 November 1874 while in New Orleans he received patent number 156,431 for a magazine firearm, while in Tallahassee, Florida. Luce held other non-firearms patents. Kit Gorman reported that he was in New Orleans 1873-78 which raises the question of why one patent was issue to him in Florida.

Lyon, J. H. (1841-1879). gun store. c.1868-79, 55 St. Charles, New Orleans; born in CT. Lyon was a clerk for E. J. Watkinson, formerly Dart & Watkinson, when Watkinson died in 1869. Lyon took over the store and ran it until his won death at age 38 [Gorman]. It seems more likely that it was a general sporting goods store that sold, perhaps repaired, guns but made nothing.

McAvoy, Michael. armorer. 1865, 320 New Levee, New Orleans. The Union Army drafted McAvoy [*New Orleans Times,* 17 March 1865]

McBeth, James E. (-1870). inventor & attorney. 1866-69, New Orleans. A fair interpretation might be that McBeth was a carpetbagger from New York, an attorney by profession, and an inventor by hobby. On 2 October 1866 he received patent number 58,443 for a safety gunlock. On 14 January 1868 he received patent number 73,357 for a breech-loading firearm, assigned in part to Sheldon Sturgeon. Altogether he held 7 patents [Gardner, *Small Arms Makers*, 121; Gorman]. 1867, James E McBeth, U. S. Inspector of Distilled Spirits, 97 Levee. James married Gertrude Collins in New York. Census of 1870: James E McBeth, lawyer, 30, $13,000 real estate; Gertrude, 26, both born in New York; Gertrude, 4; and Agnes, 2, both born in Louisiana. On 1 October 1890 Gertrude filed for a widow's pension based on her late husband's service in the 131st New York Infantry and, later, the [Union] Second Louisiana Cavalry [Ancestry].

McClannahan, John H. (1838-1863). Filemon Parish. John served the Glorious Cause as a private in the Ninth Louisiana Infantry, enlisting on July 7, 1861 in Camp Moore, Louisiana. He was present on all rolls until August, 1863 until he was killed at Battle of Gettysburg on July 2, 1863. John was born in Georgia, occupation gunsmith; age when enlisted 23, single [*Booth's Index*].

McCoole, Dennis (1837--). armorer. Dennis was a private in the 6th Louisiana Infantry. He enrolled on June 4, 1861 at Camp Moore, Louisiana. He was present on all rolls to August 31, 1864. He became a prisoner of war, captured May 5, 1864. His name was on the list of prisoners of war, paroled at Staunton, Virginia on May 1, 1865. Dennis was born in Ireland, occupation gunsmith, age 24 years, when enlisted, single, Residence New Orleans. Ge may have been the Dennis McCool born in August 1838 in Irelands, in Census of 1900 in Schuylkill County, Pennsylvania.`

McCoy, Ambrose (1825-). gunsmith. New Orleans. Census of 1850; Ambrose McCoy, 25, gunsmith, born in Ireland. Not located after 1850.

McDaniel, Aaron (1816-). gunsmith. Dallas County. Census of 1850, Aaron McDaniel, born in North Carolina, 34, gunsmith; Mary, 25, wife, born in Louisiana; Emily, 6, born in Virginia; Stephen, 6; Maryetta, 5, both born in Louisiana; Susannah,1; and Henry, newborn, both born in Texas. Noted also on Dallas tax rolls, 1855-58. Not located after 1858; not in Find-a-Grave or Ancestry.

McDonald, Daniel (1827-). locksmith. 1851, New Orleans. Admitted to charity hospital with "int. fever" born in County Tyrone, Ireland.

McMahon, John (1799—1855). lock- & gunsmith. 1851-56, Tchoupitoulas below Gaiennie & Suzette, New Orleans. John died on 15 February 1855 and was buried in S t. Patrick Cemetery No. 2 [*Dir.*; Find-a-Grave].

Mace, P. locksmith. 1851, 115 Royal, New Orleans [*Dir.*].

Maier, Charles M. (1860-1926). gunsmith. 251 S. Rampart St., 1881-1926,

New Orleans; 1900-02, 734 S. Rampart St. Early in his career he had been a shoemaker [*Times Picayune*, 5 July 1893; Gorman; *Dirs*.].

Maillant, Jules. gunsmith. 1871, works at P. Bouron, rear 138 Chartres, New Orleans [*Dir*.].

Mairot, J. C. goldsmith. 1811, 9 St. Pierre, New Orleans [*Dir*.].

Malitz, Charles the Elder (1827-1853). gunsmith. 1860-53, Victoria, Victoria County. Census of 1860, Charles Malitz, 33, born in Prussia, gunsmith; children 9 & 11 born in Louisiana.1847-52, Melicerte, between Magazine & Constance Sts., New Orleans [*Dirs*.; Census; Gorman].

Tragedy. We regret to announce the occurrence of another murderous tragedy in this county. It seems that a gunsmith of our town, a German named Malitz, had his house broken open and robbed on Saturday night last, by 2 persons, supposed to be deserters from the army on the Rio Grande. Obtaining information of the route they had taken, Malitz pursued them, and is supposed to have been murdered by them. The officers having overhauled them, one of them surrendered himself, but the other declared his intention never to be taken. Finding resistance useless, he put a pistol to his head and blew his brains out. His accomplice is here in custody to await his trial at the next term of the District Court. [*Texas Ranger and Lone Star,* 16 June 1853]

Maletz, Charles the Younger (1848--1891). gunsmith. 1880-96, Victoria, Victoria County. Charles was born on 11 April 1848 in New Orleans Parish, Louisiana. He married Bertha Ida Selma Louise Malitz. Census of 1880, Charles Maletz, gun smith, born in Louisiana, 32; Bertha, wife, 22; Hortense, 2; Josephine, 1. He died on 8 February 1891 and was buried in Evergreen Cemetery, Victoria [Find-a-Grave; Ancestry].

Malone, Albert Sidney (1871-1902). lock- and gunsmith. New Orleans. Albert was a son of Michael Malone.

Malone, George, gunsmith. George was a private in the Tenth Louisiana Infantry. He enlisted on July 22, 1861 in Camp Moore, Louisiana. Present on all rolls to Feb., 1862 Absent, wounded Payne's Farm, Nov. 27, 1863. Rolls May, 1864, to August 31, 1864. He was wounded at Monocacy, Maryland. Federal rolls of prisoners of war, captured and paroled at Fairfax, May 19, 1865, by Lt. Moore, Provost Marshal. Malone was born in Missouri, occupation gunsmith, Residence: New Orleans, single.

Malone, Michael (1834-1916). safes, bell hanger, lock- and gunsmith. New

Orleans. Father of gunsmith Albert Sidney Malone; father-in-law of gunsmith Frederick Bush. 1887, 12 Commercial Pl [Gorman; Ancestry].

Marchal, Felix (1840-). gunsmith. 8th ward, St. James Parish. Census of 1880: Felix Marchal, gunsmith, 40, born in France; wife Anne, 41; Francois, 10; Albertina, 8, all born in France; Louis, 4; Hortense, 2, both born in Louisiana. Not located before or after 1880; not in Find-a-Grave.

Marine, Francois. locksmith. 1861, near Carondelet, New Orleans [*Dir.*].

Marques, Charles (1872--). gunsmith. 1892-1918, 114 Spain St., New Orleans [*Dirs.*]. Charles was a son of Vincent and Catherine Marques. Date of death and place of burial unlocated.

Martin, Julius (1839-). gunsmith. 14 July 1862, Enlisted in 3rd Massachusetts Cavalry in New Orleans, age 23; gunsmith. He was discharged on July 29, 1865 [Massachusetts Soldiers in Civil War].

Martinet, Gustave. (1845--). locksmith. 1877, 124 Bienville, New Orleans [*Dir.*]. Census of 1860: Gustave Martinet, 16, apprentice locksmith, born in France, living with Francois and Marie Josephine Laurier. Gustave married Theresine Pullen. Census of 1880: Gustave Martinet, 35, locksmith; Theresine, 36; Hy, 2; living with Josephine Pullen, 58. Gustave became a business partner of Jacques Bolet. In 1877, Bolet became ill and died at the age of 53. Gustave Martinet, refused to allow Marguerite Bolet, the widow, into the shop, or to give her any money to pay the medical and funeral bills. She asked the court to step in, and Gustave was served with a summons to force him to divide the shop assets with her. The court ordered that he must, and so a Sheriff's sale was held, and all the contents were sold for a total of $265.00, giving Marguerite $132.50 for her share of the estate. She was left to raise 4 children on her own [Gorman]. 1901, Gustave Martinet, machinist. Census of 1910: Gustave Martinet, 67, has own own locksmith shop; Theresine, 70; Helen Alexander, 24, granddaughter. Not located after 1910.

Maury, J. gunsmith. Ursaline street, New Orleans. City council voted to allow Maury to have a gunsmith shop provided he install a fireproof roof [*Daily Crescent*, 24 March 1853].

Mawk, E. armorer. 1876, New Orleans [*Times Picayune*, 4 March 1876]

Marx, Balthasar (1697-). smith. 1724, lived on the Mississippi River above New Orleans. Marx was from Wullenberg, Palatinate Germany; Catholic; 27 years old. smith. His wife, 22 years old. "His wife had a miscarriage last year on account of working at the pounding trough. He went to New Orleans to get some salt and had to give a barrel of shelled rice for three pounds. His affairs excellently arranged. Good worker." One and a half arpents cleared. Three years on the place. 1731 : Husband, wife, two children. One engage. One negro, three cows. In 1775 Jean Simon Marx, son of Balthasar and Marianne Aglae Marx, married Catharine Troxler, daughter of Nikolas T. and Catharine Matern at St. James Parish.

Massoccia, J. (1828-). gunsmith. 1880, New Orleans. Census of 1880: J. Massoccia, 52, born in Louisiana, living with his 24 year old divorced daughter, a seamstress. Not located before or after 1880.

Mathias, Remy A. gunsmith. 1882-83, New Orleans; worked with Philip Bouron, 134 Chartres [Gorman].

Meisner, August. lock- and gunsmith. 1875-78, New Orleans. 1875 working with Frederick Busch, gunsmith. After 1878 Meisner was noted as a pipe fitter and plumber [*Dirs.;* Gorman].

Menge, A. copper- and gunsmith. 1846, 91 Poydras, New Orleans [*Dir.*].

Mentzel, Henry (1837-1872). brass finisher, gun- and locksmith. Old Levee, New Orleans. Census of 1870: Henry Mentzel, 33, gunsmith; born in Prussia, value $200, living alone. 1871, 909 Decatur St. Henry died on 29 July 1872 [*Dirs*.; Gorman; Ancestry]

Merritt, Jerome (1817-). gunsmith. DeSoto Parish. Census of 1850, Squire Pate, 40, carpenter, head of household, born in Tennessee; Pascal B. Reynolds, 38, carpenter, value $600, born in Georgia; Parmelia Pate, 30, born in Alabama; Susan Pate, 2; James Pate, 1, both born in Louisiana; John G. Graham, 45, born in North Carolina, carpenter; Richard Wood, wheelwright, 29, born in New York; Lawson Merritt, 31, blacksmith; Jerome F. Merritt, gunsmith, born in Georgia, 33; Martin Watson, 35, born in Virginia, cabinet maker. Not located after 1850.

Meyers, Jacob (1822--1879). gunsmith. 1850-74, New Orleans. 1851, 99 Front Levee; 1853, 69 Front Levee. Jacob died on 9 May 1879 in New Orleans [*Dirs*.]. Also seen as Meyer.

Mezeray, Joseph (1813-). locksmith. 1850, New Orleans. Joseph was a patient in a charity hospital. He was born in France, age 37.

Miller, J. H. gunsmith. 1850-56, Elysian Fields, New Orleans [*Dirs*.].

Miller, Jacob (1830--). gunsmith. Monroe, Ouachita Parish. "All kinds of repairing neatly and promptly executed. Shop on Grand street between shops of Thomas Naughton and Peter Ezelius [*Ouachita Telegraph*, 8 October 1870]. Census of 1870: Jacob Miller, 20, gunsmith, white, born in Nassau, living alone. Not located after 1850.

Miller, Martin. locksmith. 1842, 93 Conti, New Orleans [*Dir*.].

Miller, Miles (1825--1890). gunsmith. Franklin, St. Mary Parish. Census of 1850: Miles Miller, 24, gunsmith, born in Pennsylvania; living with Charles Johnson, 35, cooper. Census of 1880; Miles Miller, gunsmith, born in Pennsylvania, 55, single, living alone. Miles died on 18 July 1890 and was buried in Franklin Cemetery [Ancestry].

Miller, Peter. gunsmith. 1874-78, rear west side Delery between Delaronde and Bienvenue, New Orleans [*Dirs*.].

Miller, Pierre. gunsmith. 1832-38, Conde St., New Orleans [*Dir*.].

Millet, Jean Baptiste. gunsmith. c.1780-1800, New Orleans. There were at this time in Louisiana two men named Jean Millet. This Jean was a gunsmith, born in New Orleans, parents from Paris, married to Marian Frederick Also seen as Milet.

Milton, Nathaniel B. (1847-). gunsmith. Monroe, Ouachita Parish. On 1 May 1878 Nathaniel B Miller married Ella Newman in Monroe. Census of 1880, N B Milton, 33, gunsmith, born in Alabama; A.E., his wife, 20; Jerome, 10 months; Ann Hardy, 36; Charity Patrick, 53. Not located after 1880; not in Find-a-Grave.

Misland, Joseph (1821-). gunsmith. 1860, New Orleans. Census of 1860: Joseph Misland, 39, gunsmith, born in Germany; in household of Louis Gerteis. Not located after 1860.

Mitchell, Thomas Jefferson (1854--1939). gunsmith. Rayville, Richland Parish. Thomas was born in Bienville Parish. Census of 1880: Thomas J. Mitchell, 25, gunsmith, born in Mississippi, single. Thomas left the gun trade soon after 1880 and moved to Texas. He died in Tillman County, Oklahoma [Find-a-Grave].

Mon, Joseph (1820-). armorer. East Baton Rouge Parish. Census of 1850: Joseph Mon, 30, born in Pennsylvania, armorer [Census]. The name possibly was Won; census is unclear.

Monget, Antonio. gunsmith. Baton Rouge. Antonio was a free Negro servant and trained as a gunsmith. Antonio Monget settled in an area east of Fort San Carlos at Baton Rouge resettle from the Spanish families from Galvez Town in order to increase the population to help defend the fort site. African American tradesman [Ancestry]. Census of 1820: Antoine Monget, one male, one female, each ages 16-25. Census of 1830 of Baton Rouge: Antoine Monget head of household of ten persons: one free black male, age 10 to 23; 3 slaves; and 6 whites. Census of 1840: Antoine Monget, head of household of 31 persons: 8 free whites, 23 slaves.

Montague, ---. gunsmith. 1831, New Orleans. Kit Gorman found a most interesting ad run by Montague the gunsmith. He offered his wares, tools, and personal items for sale. He claimed to have been cheated in some way by the State. It is a curious item, a story without beginning or end.

Morchinveg, Jno M. (1853-). gunsmith. 1880, Opelousas, St. Landry Parish. Census of 1880: Jno M Morchinveg, 27, single, born in Louisiana; living with James Ray family. See Mornhinveg.

Moreau, E, V. gunsmith. 1841-42, Bourbon & St. Peter Sts., New Orleans [*Dir.*].

Morgan, Solomon. frontiersman, gunsmith, farmer. Morgan married Jemima Webb, daughter of a Baptist minister. Thee had a daughter born in South Carolina in 1762. They had another child, a boy named Isaac. Solomon was a gunsmith during the Revolutionary War. Payment was issued on 11 July 1785 were for his work "as a gunsmith and making horsemen's swords for General Marion's Brigade in 1781." He also served 242 days duty as a private in Colonel Baxton's Regiment, General Marion's Brigade. There is also a receipt "for a horse lost in service in 1781" consisting of the account itself. A large column of colonists from South Carolina, including the Morgans, moved into Ward 3 of East Feliciana Parish in 1806. Solomon's wife Jemima died on 8 October 1834 in East Feliciana Parish and was buried in the old Brian burial grounds near Jackson, Louisiana. Presumably Solomon was buried nearby [Ancestry].

Moriarity, George Washington. (1856--1935). gunsmith. St. Landry Parish. George was born on 5 March 1856 in Opelousas, St. Landry Parish, a son of William Ambrose and Aurora Moriatity. On 15 May 1877 George married Anna Lucinda Prather in Opelousas. A fire consumed his gunshop, stock, and tools along with most other buildings in the business district. In

1912 he advertised that he had been a professional gunsmith for 49 years [*Times Picayune*, 14 June 1904; 8 September 1912]. Census of 1910: George W Moriarity, 57, owns gun store, widower, living alone.1904, Bellevue St., George moved to Muscogee, Oklahoma, in 1918. He died on 6 January 1935 in Muscogee, Oklahoma, and was buried in Greenhill Cemetery

George W Moriarity, Gunsmith, Bellvue street, calls attention of sportsmen to his gun, pistol, and ammunition department, which he has just opened in connection with his regular repairing business. He has a complete assortment of breech and muzzle loading guns, pistols, all kinds of paper and metallic cartridges for guns, pistols, and rifles of every make and gauge, wads, powder, caps, primers, etc. Repairing in first class style and guaranteed. Shells loaded. Bottom prices assured [*Opelousas Courier*, 13 November 1886

George Moriarity, Gunsmith, successor to the late Sol. D'Avy. All work guaranteed. Terms moderate and strictly cash. Shop on Bellevue street between Main and Court [*Opelousas Courier*, 27 November 1880].

If you are in need of Guns, Rifles, Pistols, Ammunition of all kinds, pocket cutlery, scissors, razors, fishing tackle, etc,. you should call at George W Moriarity's gun store, where you will find the best selected and finest stock to choose from, and the guarantee of a practical gunsmith as to the quality of goods. Mr Moriarity's reputation as a first class gunsmith is well known through out the country [*St. Landry Democrat,* 19 October 1889]

George W Moriarity, Gunsmith, has moved into his new gun shop and gun store and it is a daisy [*St. Landry Clarion,* 11 July 1891].

George W Moriarity, our well-known gunsmith, has the most complete gun store and best equipped repair ship in southwest Louisiana. Having no rent or clerks to pay, and the largest repair business in the state to sustain him, besides the capital required to buy in quantities for spot cash, he defies all competition. Nothing succeeds like success. [*St. Landry Clarion,* 2 November 1895].

Mornhinveg, John M. (1852--). gunsmith. Opelousas, St. Landry Parish. [*Opelousas Courier*, 30 November 1878]. Census of 1880: John M Mornhinveg, gunsmith, 27; Amelia, 25; James, 3; John, 2; Margaret, infant. John Mornhinveg was the son-in-law of James Ray, 55, a physician. John Mornhinveg's two brothers-in-law, John and William Ray, were gunsmiths. The two families lived side by side. Census of 1900: John M. Mornhinveg, 48, gunsmith; Carrie, 24; and Ethel, 4. Spelling variations include: Mornhenieg, and Mornkimea. Not located after 1900.

If you have a gun broken or out of order in any way take it to John C. Mornhinveg, Main street, Opelousas; he will make it as good as new and not charge you much for it [*St. Landry Democrat,*20 December 1879].

J. C. Mornhinveg. The Live Gunsmith. Always willing to accommodate his customers at short notice; work done with neatness and dispatch and guaranteed. Main street, Opelousas [*St. Landry Democrat,* 17 January 1880].

J. C. Mornhinveg. Gunsmith. Bellevue street opposite Court House, Opelousas, work done on short notice and guaranteed [*Ibid.*, 5 February 1881].

Morphy, D. E. gunsmithing supplies. 1873, New Orleans. Apparently a hardware store, Morphy offered a variety of "trimmings" for gunsmiths along with many other items [*Times Picayune*, 13 November 1877]

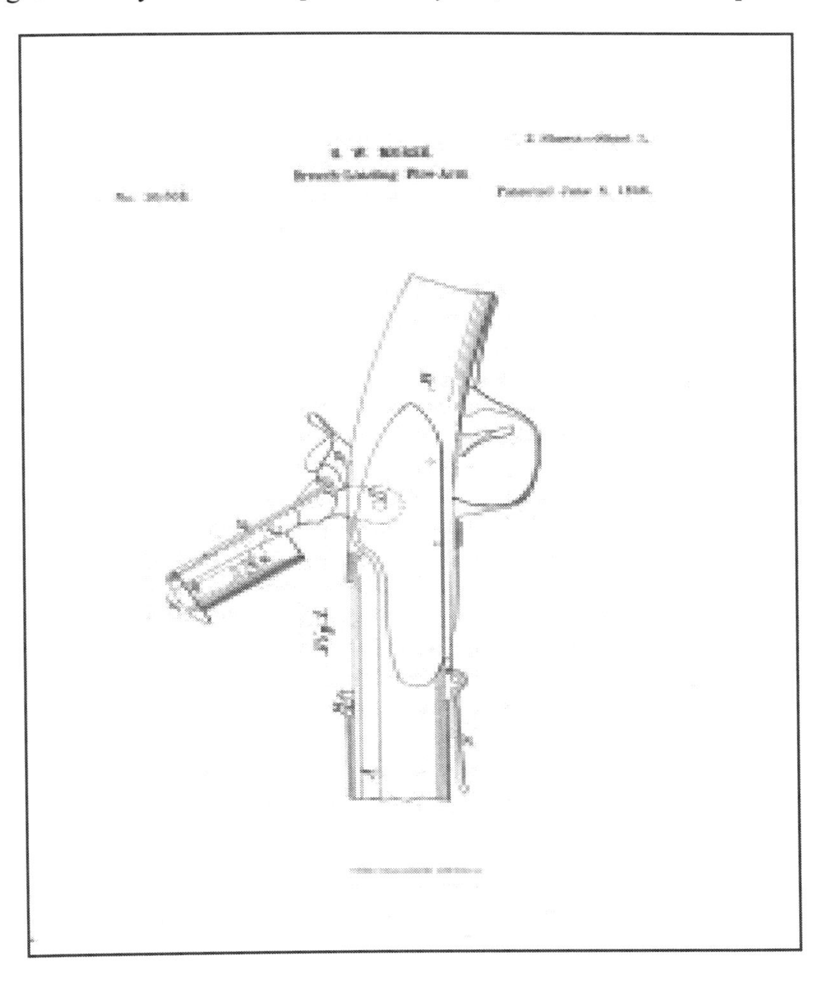

Morse, George Woodward (-1888). inventor. East Baton Rouge. Morse held patents 15,995 of 28 October 1856 for a breech-loading firearm; 15,996 of the same date for a cartridge for the gun; 20,214 of 11 May 1858 for a cartridge case; 20,503 of 8 June 1858 for a breech-loading firearm; and 20,727 of 29 June 1858. While the Springfield Armory made a limited number of Morse conversions to older muskets, it was the Confederacy that used the Morse muskets, rifles, and carbines. Hitchcock & Muzzy made a few sporting arms using Morse's patent [Gardner, *Small Arms Makers*]

Mudge, Carson (1839-1914). gunsmith. 1867-1914, New Orleans. Mudge was a carpetbagger, having served in the Yankee Army. 1867-80, gunsmith. He bought out Louis Gerteis. In May 1873 he lost nearly all his goods and firearms in the New Orleans riot. Thereafter he had a position at the U.S. Mint or was a law enforcement officer although his sporting goods store remained [Gorman]. Noted as having sold a Manton double barrel shotgun used in a murder [*Memphis Daily Appeal*, 4 July 1873].

Some men enjoying a respectable standing in the mercantile community . . . facilitated the obtaining of weapons with which to arm the rabble which attacked the police stations on the night of the 5th of March last, an act which facilitated the loss of several lives and destruction of several thousand dollars worth of property. . . . A frugal and industrious gunsmith . . . permitted his stock of goods to be placed in the hands of the mob, on the written promise of merchants of respectable standing to reimburse him for these losses. The arms were never returned to him and none of them were ever paid for. . . . The said Carson Mudge has furnished . . . from one to 300 arms and munitions to the value of $5000 [*New Orleans Republican*, 26 April 1873].

NOTICE All Persons having had Guns and pistols in my charge for repairs are requested to make themselves known to me immediately so that they may be indemnified. Carson Mudge, Gunsmith, No. 95 Magazine street [New Orleans *Republican*, 8 May 1873].

Műller, J. H. gunsmith. 1851, Victory street & Elysian Fields, New Orleans [*Directory*].

Nadler, Henry (1863-). machinist and gunsmith. Nadler, was born in Peru, IL, on February 26, 1863, a son of Joseph Nadler who was a native of Austria, and who came to the states about 1840. Henry was a gunsmith by trade. Henry Nadler received his education in the schools of Peru, during which time he learned the machinist's trade. In 1888 he came south and located in Plaquemine, where he became a partner of William Blackie [*Biographical and Historical Memoires of Louisiana*, 2: 294].

Nagebauer, Jean (1805-). 1850-53, Moreua, corner of Mandeville, New Orleans [Dirs.; Gorman]. Also seen as Neugbauer.

Nants, Albert (1816-). gunsmith. Census of 1840 of Ouachita Parish, Louisiana: Albert Nantz head of household of four free white persons. Census of 1860 of Jasper County, Texas: Albert Nance, 44, gunsmith, value $600; Malissa, 44; John, 22; Elizabeth, 18; James, 15; Mary, 13, all born in Louisiana; Thomas, 9; Irene, 6; Sil;as, 3; and William, infant, all born in Texas. Census of 1870 of Jasper County: Amos [*sic*] Nantz, 50, farmer; Malissa, 53; Thomas, 18; Irene, 15; and William, 10. Census of 1880, Newton County: Albert Nantz, 64; Malissa, 63; William, 20; Zina, 19; Ida Emma, infant. Not located after 1880; not in Find-a-Grave.

Newell, John David Stokes (1837--1899). inventor. Tensas Parish. J D S was born in Claiborne County, Mississippi, a son of David Newell. David Newell received U. S. Patent number 88,730 on 6 April 1869 and patent number 90,381 of 25 May 1869. Newell assigned the patent to himself, A G Brice, and Thomas Pickels, all of Tensas Parish [Gardner, *Small Arms Makers*, 140]. Census of 1870: J D S Newell, 31, value real estate $3475, farmer, son of David Newell, farmer. Census of 1880: J D S Newell, 43, farmer and lawyer; Nannie, 36; J D S, Jr, 13; Cecil, 10; Carroll, 6; and Edward, 4. He died on 5 March 1899 [Find-a-Grave; Ancestry].

Invention of a young Louisianian. The simplest breech-loader of all. The recent improvement of all improved firearms is the brain-work of Captain J D S Newell, of the late Confederate States Cavalry, a young planter of Tensas Parish, native and to the manner born. Casting about in his mind, for some royal road to wealth, he was induced to enter the unexplored fields of invent ion. He soon made the fortunate discovery that all breech-loading guns could be improved in simplicity of action and construction, weight, and durability and in less than three months of the time of the conception of his invention he had it perfected and a full size model made and tried. He applied for a patent immediately on finding the success of his gun, which has been very highly complimented by sportsmen, army officers, and machinists. He has now on exhibition in this city the second gun manufactured on his patent. It is the work of a gunsmith of this city, and is a neat and handsome arm. The perfect simplicity of the mechanism of this gun, its freedom from springs, levers, screws and brass work, surprises those who examine it critically [from *Louisiana Picayune*; published in *Bossier Banner*, 6 March 1869].

Neyrand, L. cutler. 1842, 20 Conde St., New Orleans [*Dir.*].

Nicholas, Bertrand. gunsmith. 1754-70, New Orleans; on militia list [Gorman]. Son of Jacques and brother of Jacques, Jr. and Jean Baptiste Nicolas.

Nicholas, Celestian. gunsmith. 1822-32, 153 Francis above Bon Enfants, New Orleans [*Dir.*].

Nicholas, Jacques (1721-1776). gunsmith. New Orleans. Jacques was born in La Rochelle, France, about 1721, a son of Francois and Marie (Flamanchet) Nicolas. On 8 May 1745 at Mobile he married Marie Anne Drapeau. A royal gunsmith, Jacques was the father of Jean Baptiste and Bertrand Nicolas. He died on 11 May 1776 at New Orleans [Gorman].

Nicholas, Jacques, Jr. (1756-). gunsmith. 1778, Burgundy, New Orleans. Son of Jacques; brother of Jean Baptiste and Bertrand Nicolas [Gorman].

Nicholas, Jean Baptiste (1746-). gunsmith.1770, St. Peter, New Orleans. Son of Jacques; brother of Bertrand and Jacques Jr. Nicolas [Gorman].

Nicholas, Laurent Valery (1774-1829). gunsmith. 1807-29, 19 Bourbon St., New Orleans [*Dir.*]. Son of Jean Baptiste Nicholas [Gorman].

Nieve, Francisco. cutler. 1832, 54 Conde, New Orleans [*Dir.*]

Noble, J. B. armorer. 1855, Continental Guards. New Orleans [*Times Picayune*, 31 October 1875]

Norton, Patrick. gunsmith. 1865, Erato near Franklin, New Orleans; drafted.

Nuttall & James. locksmiths. 1850-66, Lafayette near Camp, New Orleans [*Dir.*].

Oefinger, Bernhard (1828-). gunsmith. New Orleans and Castroville, Medina County, Texas. Census of 1860, Bernhard Oefinger, 32, master gunsmith, born in Württemberg. 1871, Bernhard Oefinger, gunsmith, boards at 226 Custom House, New Orleans [*Dir.*]. Not located after 1871.

Offrey, Philip (1815--1887). gunsmith. Houston County. Census of 1850: P Offrey, 38, gunsmith, born in France, single. Census of 1860 of New Orleans: Philip Offrey, 47, gunsmith, born in France, value $500; Ann, 54, born in Delaware; living with two unrelated public officers and their wives. 1861, gunsmith, 135 Royal, New Orleans [*Dir.*]. 1875-82, Crockett, Houston County. Census of 1880, P. Offrey, 65, born in France, gun smith, Ann, wife, 75. He died in 1887 and was buried in Glenwood Cemetery, Crockett [Find-a-Grave; Ancestry]. Posting on Ancestry: "Phillip Offery/Offrey was born about 1824 in France. He married Anne (Newcomb) Selby between 1850-1860 in probably New Orleans, Louisiana. He was a gunsmith and a farmer." The censuses agree that he was born c.1815, not 1824.

Oldis, G. locksmith. 1842, 129 Common, New Orleans [*Dir.*].

O'Quinn, William Araster (1833-1901). armorer. Natchitoches Parish. Served from 1861-1865, CSA. William was a son of Daniel (1800-1865) and Barsheba O'Quinn. William's brothers Jonathan and Zachariah had been captured at Vicksburg and died soon after their release from the Union concentration camp. William's tombstone lists him in Company C of Consolidated Crescent Regiment, he was a gunsmith by trade [Ancestry].

William was in the Civil War and traveled with a pick axe that he used to dig many graves during the war. . . .William was a gunsmith during the Civil War and he served some of his time in Shreveport, LA, William was a soldier but most of his service was as a gunsmith since this was a skill he previously possessed. He made guns for the Confederacy and sent his wife, Harriet, most of his earning which were apparently more than a regular foot soldier because of his skill, he sent Harriet instructions to "buy cattle and land" for the days when the war would be ended; but instead Harriet on advice from her father Thomas Thompson bought Confederate War Bonds. When the Civil War was over, William came home to worthless Confederate War bonds instead of land and cattle. Because of the advice given to Harriet there was severely bad feelings between William and Thomas and in November 1865 shortly after the end of the Civil War, William and Harriet moved to East Texas and lived there for 7 years before returning to southwest Louisiana. Ada O'Quinn once told Florence O'Quinn when talking about the hard feelings between William and his father in law Thomas Thompson caused by the purchase of the worthless confederate war bonds, Ada said " Our father knew we were going to lose that war". [Ancestry]

O'Riley, Charles (1810-). gunsmith. Catahoula Parish. Census of 1850, Charles O'Riley, age 40, gunsmith, born in New York; Harriet, 32, his wife, born in Louisiana; William, 11, Melchisadec, 9; both born in Arkansas; Peter, 9 months, born in Louisiana. Not located after 1850.

Paisson, J. (1812-). gunsmith. Natchitoches Parish. Census of 1850: J. Paisson, 38, gunsmith, value $1000; born in France; Marie, 30, born in Belgium; Jules, 2, born in LA; Louisa, 14, born in Louisiana. Not located.

Parish, George R. gunsmith. New Orleans. See George Farish.

Park, William (-1853). gun shop. 1853, Vidalia, Trinity Road, Concordia Parish. The bodies of Park and a gunsmith in his employ were found floating down the Tensas River, near Brushy Bayou, their throats cut and their heads bashed in. Park was not quite dead when pulled from the water but he was unable to speak. Murder weapon was a blacksmith's hammer which was found stained with blood. Suspicion fell on a shop clerk who was missing. [*Times Picayune*, 8 February 1853; 19 February 1853]

Pauly, J. gunsmith. 1843, St. Ann, New Orleans [*Dir.*].

Peck, Ossian Franklin (1836--). armorer. 1875, armorer to several centennial companies, New Orleans [*New Orleans Times,* 30 July 1875].Peck married Agnes Maitland. Census of 1870: Ossian F Peck, 34, clerk, born in Georgia; Agnes, 29; Augusta, 6; Sheldon, 3; and infant. Census of 1880: O F Peck, sewing machine repairman, 42, sick with measles; Agnes, 38; Augusta, 16; Milton, 13; and Robert, 3. Not located after 1880.

Peichatzel, John (1834-). gunsmith. New Orleans. Census of 1880, John Peichatzel, 46, born in Germany, gun smith; Sarah, 48, his wife; John. 32; Helena, 18; Anny, 10; Jane, 24. Not located before or after 1880.

Perrin, Casimir (1813-1881). lock- and gunsmith. 1842-81, New Orleans. 1842, 210 Dauphine; 1861, 124 Burgundy. Census of 1870: Casimir Perrin, 56, locksmith, $6000 real estate, $450 personal value; Annette, 56, both born in France; Maria, 32, born in New York; Rosalie, 22; Martin, 20; and Marie, 15, all born in Louisiana Casimir died on 6 April 1881 [*Dirs*.; Gorman; Ancestry].

Pesuchet. see Besuchet.

Pessou, Joseph Alphonse (1795-1875). gunmaker. African-American tradesman. 1832, Main St at Conde, as Pessou; home 109 Burgundy; 1842, shop at 18 Conti St; residence St. Claude St., New Orleans. 1867, Alphone Pessou, 369 St. Claude, gun maker. Pessou was born in Santa Domingo and died in New Orleans. 1849, Pessou & Jusselin with Antoine Jusselin [*Dirs*.]. Also seen as Pesson.

Removal. The Subscriber has removed his gunsmith shop from St. Louis street to Dumaine street between Conde and Levee streets, and avails himself of this occasion to return his sincere thanks for the liberal patronage he has received, and assures those who will favor him with their patronage, that their orders shall be executed with neatness and dispatch. [*New Orleans Argus*, 25 April 1828]

Pesson L., Sr (1790-).). gunsmith. 1842, St Claude near Esplanade, New Orleans. Census of 1850 of Mobile County, Alabama. L. Pisson, 60, gunsmith; L. Pisson, 21, gunsmith, both born in Louisiana; H. Cowen, 31, born in New York. All living with J. B. Fellows, merchant.

Pesson, L., Jr. (1829-).). gunsmith. 1850, Mobile County, AL. Census of 1850 of Mobile, Alabama: L. Pisson, 60, gunsmith; L. Pisson, 21, gunsmith, both born in Louisiana; H. Cowen, 31, born in New York. All living with J. B. Fellows, merchant.

Peters, F. H. gunsmith. 1857-66, 117 Greatmen near Mandeville, New Orleans [*Dir*.]. Also seen as H. F. Peters.

Petit, L. gunsmith. Lake Charles, Calcasieu Parish.

Mr. L. Petit, an experienced gunsmith, grinder and cutter, Received seven medals in France for skilled workmanship. His shop is on Ryan street near Philip Jacobs, where he will be pleased to have you call and see him [*Lake Charles Commercial,* 15 October 1892].

Pew, Julian W. (1825--1864). gunsmith. DeSoto Parish. Julian was born in Concuh County, Alabama. Census of 1850 of Desoto Parish: Jesse Pew, planter, 55, value $4000; Elizabeth, 55, both born in Georgia; Julian Pew, 25, gunsmith, value $400, born in Alabama; Aaron, 23. laborer; William, 21, laborer; Isaac, 19, laborer; John, 17, laborer, all born in Alabama; Stephen, 11; Elenora, 15; Hannah, 14, all born in Louisiana. Census of 1860: Julian W Pew, 35, farmer; Sarah, 25; Elizabeth, 5; Jonah, 3; and an infant. Julian served in the 12th Alabama Infantry. He died in Taylersville, Virginia, on 24 May 1864 [Ancestry; *Alabama Civil War Soldiers*].

Philinott, Charles. lock- and gunsmith. 1879, 49 Jefferson Street, New Orleans [*Dir*.].

Philipes, Francis (1801-). gunsmith. Baton Rouge. Census of 1850, Francis Philipes, 49, gunsmith, value $1500, born in Germany; Mary, 32, his wife; Mary, 9; Francis, 3; Elizabeth, 4 months; all born in Louisiana [Ancestry]. Not located after 1850.

Philippe, Auguste (1832-). locksmith. 1852, New Orleans; admitted to charity hospital with “int. fever.” Auguste was born in Vilaine, France.

Phillips, Francis (1797--1873). locksmith. East Baton Rouge. Francis was born on 26 May 1797. Census of 1860; Francis Phillips, 62, value $1500 real estate; $5000 personal; born in Baden. Francis died on 18 November 1873 and was buried in St. Joseph Catholic Cemetery, Baton Rouge [Find-a-Grave; Ancestry].

Phoenix Iron Works. Gretna (New Orleans). Sylvester Bennett, proprietor. *New Orleans Picayune*, May 5, 1861, noted that the above had cast a heavy gun eight feet in length. The *New Orleans Picayune* of September 4, 1861, noted that several 18-pounder cannon had been turned out at the firm.

Pickett, W. J. (1821--1864). gunsmith. New Orleans. Census of 1860; W J Pickett, 39, gunsmith, born in North Carolina. Pickett died in February 1864 and was buried in Greenwood Cemetery, New Orleans [Ancestry].

Piechaczek, Johnann (1833-1903). gun- and locksmith. Johann [John] emigrated to New Orleans, from Breslau, Poland in 1866. 1875-1900, 2514 Decatur St. [*Dirs*.; Family].

Pierre, Matthew. gunsmith. 1861, 28 Elysian Fields, New Orleans [*Dir.*]

Pierreman, Jacques. cutler. 1842, 27 Conde St., New Orleans [*Dir.*].

Pigne, Louis. locksmith. 1851, 17 Madison, New Orleans [*Dir.*].

Pigrenet, Joseph. machinist, gunsmith. 1900, New Orleans [Gorman].

Pilet, James A. gunsmith. 1892, 149 St. Anthony, New Orleans [*Dir.*].

Pinet, Jean. gunsmith. 1727, New Orleans [church records, Gorman].

Pinet, Yves. gunsmith. 1727-32, New Orleans [French Census cited by Gorman].

Pingeon, Antoine. locksmith. 1861, 202 Bayou Rd, New Orleans [*Dir.*]

Piny, Joseph. goldsmith. 1811, 9 St. Pierre, New Orleans [*Dir.*].

Pinta, Jean Baptiste. goldsmith. 1811, 35 Bourbon, New Orleans [Dir.].

Pitet, J. mult-facet dealers. Baton Rouge. See Petit.

J. Pitet & Company . . . They besides keep a shop where they will execute all kinds of blacksmith, gunsmith and locksmith work. . . . They have a complete assortment of ready made Tombs. . . . J Pitet & co. have now to announce to the public that they have received an assortment of elegant and capricious Marble Coffins. . . . [*Baton Rouge Gazette,* 4 September 1847]

Pittman, J. I. (1842--1904). state armorer. 1880, New Orleans. Census of 1880; J I Pittman, 35, state armorer, single; born in New York. Pittman died on 17 February 1904 in New Orleans [Ancestry].

Pobts, David (1820-). gunsmith. Shreveport, Caddo Parish. Census of 1880, David, 60, gun smith, born in Ohio; Jane Pobts, his wife, 54; Robert Watts, 11 [Census]. Not located before or after 1880; not in Ancestry. See Probst.

Pooley, C. locksmith. New Orleans. In a fire near the levee Poley's shop and tools, along with those of another locksmith named Lombert were damaged but not destroyed [*Times Picayune*, 21 February 1849]

Poreaux, N. cutler [*coutelier*]. 1811, 6 Ste. Anne, New Orleans [*Dir*.; M.E.S.D.A.].

Porre, Edmunde Lucien. gunsmith. 1721-32, New Orleans. Porre with his wife; born in Paris [French Census].

Porter, Ezekiel. gunsmith. 1832, Philipa near Poydras, New Orleans [*Dir*.].

Potine, Louis. locksmith. 1865, New Orleans; drafted in 2nd district.

Pouly, Claude (1814-1874). gun- and locksmith. 1841-74, New Orleans. Poly operated an ice house and also blacksmith [Gorman; Ancestry; *Dirs*.].

Powell, G. W. locksmith. 1861, 178 Tchoupitou, New Orleans [*Dir*.].

Powell, Thomas (1812-). gunsmith. 1850, convict in penitentiary, Baton Rouge sentenced for burglary; born in England [Census].

Probst, David (1821-). gunsmith. Shreveport, Daddo Parish. Census of 1850, David Probst, gunsmith, value $750, single, born in Ohio. Census of 1880, David, 60, gun smith, born in Ohio; Jane, his wife, 54; Robert Watts, 11. The Lancaster [PA] *Daily Intelligencer* of 1 April 1881 carried a story of a D. Robst, gunsmith, corner of Milan and Market Sts., victim of a fire that caused total $15,000 in damage with $6000 in insurance. Not located in Ancestry or most censuses. Date and place of death not found.

Pumillia, Giuseppe (1825-). gunsmith. 1872-80, Dauphine, corner of St. Peter, New Orleans; born in Italy. 1874, rear 103 Conti. 1873-74, worked for J. F. Dittrich. On 18 March 1874 Giuseppe married Marie L Briolli in New Orleans. Census of 1880, Giuseppe Pumilla, gunsmith, 55, born in Italy, single. On 19 March 1890 Giuseppe Pumilla married Lorenza Careca in New Orleans. Not located after 1890.

Raeser, Johan Georg (1692-). blacksmith. 1724-41, lived on the Mississippi River above New Orleans. Raeser was from Biebrich, in the Electorate of Mayence, Germany. Catholic; 32 years old. Blacksmith. His wife, an orphan girl of 18 years. Three years on the place. "Well arranged. Good worker." 1726: Husband, wife, three children, brother-in-law. One pig. 1731, Husband, wife, one child [http://genealogytrails.com/lou/1724census.html]

Ramelli, Camille (1841-1888). gunsmith. 1874-88, New Orleans. 1874, rear 75 St. Peter. Also a bartender. 1880, 2nd ward, Jefferson Parish. Census of 1880, Camille, born in Switzerland, gun smith, 38; Leonie, his wife, 36; David, 12; Agath, 8; Theodore, 4; Camilla, 2 [*Dirs.*; Gorman].

Rault, Henry E. (1860-1936). gun- and locksmith. 1880, New Orleans; son of Joseph and Julie Rault; born in Louisiana. 1886, 616 Magazine St. A

Joseph Rault a French immigrant opened a gunsmith shop at the age of 18 here in New Orleans the year was 1845. Very early in it's history the shop was located in the French Quarter, then moved to Magazine Street, where it has remained for over 160 years. His son Henri E. Rault, was not only a gunsmith, he also learned the trade of locksmithing as well and after the death of his father in 1881, he took over the shop. Twenty-one year old Henri added the H and the name of the business H. Rault Locksmith evolved into the business it is today. In 1936 at the age of 75 Henri Rault was struck by a Model T Ford crossing Magazine Street en route to New Orleans latest amusement, the motion picture matinee, a local theater located at the corner of Magazine and Washington Streets. His daughter Isabella Rault became the owner/operator of the lock shop until her son Russell E. Staub was of age to take over. Russell ran the shop then located at 3027 Magazine until his death in 1993. The shop was moved in 1926 from 3013 Magazine Street to it's present location which was purchased for $9,000.00. In 1992 the shop building and inventory were sold to a local businessman Jim Miller. Mr. Miller had the huge task of cleaning up piles of "stuff" after years of neglect. The backyard held pens for pit bulls and the second floor had been converted to a coop for fighting cocks. The property was in complete despair. Huge flat bed trucks took 18 loads of junk away and still so much more was left behind as well as a large inventory of antique locks and accessories.. [http://hrault.com/history.html]

Rault, Joseph (1827-1881). gun- and locksmith, bell hanger. 1854-80, 3027 Magazine St., New Orleans. Seen as J. B. Rault, gunsmith. 1861, 220 St. Mary St. Census of 1880, Joseph Rault, gunsmith, 53; Julie, 53, wife, both born in France; Henry, 19, gunsmith; Joseph, 15, cigar maker; Eugene, 12, all born in Louisiana [Gorman; *Dir.*]. Unlike many locksmiths who only repaired guns Rault advertised that he was an "arms manufacturer." Rault was repairing a revolver when the cylinder dropped out onto the floor and a bullet discharged wounding him in the breast but slightly [*Times Picayune*, 24 March 1872]

Rault, Julia (1827-1901). lock- and gunsmith. New Orleans. Whether Julia actually did any of the smithing is impossible to say. She did continue the business after Joseph's death in 1881 until c. 1890 [Gorman; *Dirs.*].

Ray, James O. (1857--1912). gunsmith. Opelousas, St. Landry Parish. Census of 1880: James O Ray, 23, gunsmith, born in Louisiana; son of James Ray, age 55, physician. Census of 1910: James Ray, 53, physician; living with his aunt and niece, apparently never married. James died on 21 May 1912 in Opelousas [Ancestry].

Ray, William M. H. (1862--1930). gunsmith. Opelousas, St. Landry Parish. Census of 1880: William H Ray, apprentice gunsmith, 18, born in Louisiana; son of James Ray, age 55, physician. William died in May 1930 in Saint Landry [Ancestry].

Raymond, Charles. gunsmith. 1873, boards 153 Decatur, 2nd district, New Orleans [*Dir.*].

Reim, Thomas. lock- and gunsmith. 1841-42, 93 Conti, New Orleans [*Dirs.*].

Revol, Jean Baptiste (1799-1886). gunmaker. 1846-49, 19 Conde; 1861, 280 Royal St., New Orleans. 1880, New Orleans. in home of J. B. Revol, 81, gunsmith; Joseph L. Revol, 49; Henrietta, 52, Joseph's wife; Josephine, 12; Amelia Revol, 28; Eugene Gerard, 18; Louis Fannier, 20, apprentice [Census; *Dirs.*].

March 20. Jean Baptiste Reval, aged 87 years, and for more than half a century one of the best known gun dealers and gunsmiths in this city, committed suicide this morning by shooting himself through the brain. The old man was a wonderfully hearty and sturdy veteran and had never been sick until lately, when he was troubled slightly by asthma. This seemed to worry and annoy him greatly and he doused himself with all sorts of medicines; but they did him no good. He told his doctors that he was not willing to stand his sickness, and in vain they endeavored to persuade him that it was a small matter. On first opportunity he committed suicide [*Fort Worth Daily Gazette*, 31 March 1886]

Revol, Joseph Leonard (1830-1917). gunmaker. New Orleans. Census of 1880, J. B. Revol, 81; Joseph L., 49; Henrietta, 52; Josephine, 12; Amelia, 28; Eugene Gerard, 18; Louis Fannier, 20. Fannier and Gerard were apprentices. 1887, 90 Chartres. Census of 1900: J L Revol, 69, gunsmith, born in Mexico, widower, born in November 1830; living with Jean and Josephine Jonet, son-in-law and daughter. Census of 1910: Joseph L. Revol, born in Mexico, 79, widower, living on own income; Amelie, sister, 52; living with son-in-law Henry Jonet, 51. He doed in December 1917, age 86. His obituary said he was born in France but he told the census takers in four censuses that he was born in Mexico. In addition to making guns he was a talented competitive shooter [Ancestry; Gorman].

Rey, E. F. gunsmith. 1900-03, 412 Chartres St., New Orleans [*Dirs*.].

Reynolds & Hill. lock- and gunsmiths. 1867, 30 Gravier, New Orleans. James H. Reynolds & George B. Hill [*Dir*.].

Reynolds, James H. gunsmith. New Orleans.

Lock and Gunsmith. James H. Reynolds, 72 Baronne street, General hOuse and Steamboat Smith. Door and Window Grating. Iron Safes, Store and Vault Door Locks Iron Railings, Office and House Keys made [*New Orleans Bulletin*, 12 January 1876]

Rhodes, Charles L. locksmith. 1861, Camp, opposite Lafayette Sq., New Orleans [*Dir*.].

Rhodes, Richard (1830-1903). gun store. 1874-1903, 55 St. Charles, New Orleans. In 1874 Rhodes purchased F. Charleville's Sportsmen's Depot. Upon his death the store became J. A. Landry Sporting Goods. The firm retained excellent gunsmiths throughout its history, including Louis Gerteis and Louis and Auguste Cook [Gorman].

Ribriou, J. (1817-). lock- and gunsmith. 1860-66, 160 Basin street, New Orleans [*Dir*.].

Richard, A. armurier. 1811, 24 Dauphine, New Orleans [*Dir*.].

Richardson, George Washington (1828-1898). armorer. George was born in 1828 in Washington Parish, Louisiana; He died in 1898 in Spurger, Tyler County, Texas. He married (1) Matilda Bridges (2) Delitha Harvill (3) Mildred Williams Flowers (4) Gardner, first name unknown (5) Matilda Bridges on 30 October 1865 in Tyler County, Texas. George lived at Town Bluff was a blacksmith, and had a tannery. He was also a saddler, a shoemaker and a gunsmith. During the Civil War he was released by special order of General John G. Walker from duty in Company K, 13th (Burnett's) Cavalry Regiment to return to his home and business on special assignment for the Confederate war effort. To accomplish all he was expected to do he must have had a considerable establishment that employed a number of men. Every two months wagons brought shoes, saddles, harness and guns to be repaired. The train then picked up those left for repair on the previous trip. Besides the repairs, there was also a quota of new shoes, saddles, harness and so forth supposed to be ready. George W. had bad luck with his wives. The first, Lettie Bridges of Liberty County, had 3 children before her death. The second wife was Lettie's sister, Matilda, who died at the birth of her first child, Richard. The third, Delitha Harvill, had 3 children before her death; the fourth, Mildred Williams [Family].

Richtor, Albert (1828-). gunsmith. 1850, Baton Rouge. Census of 1850; Albert Richtor, gunsmith, age 22, born in Germany, living alone.

Richoux, Eugene (1815-). gunsmith. Bayou Lafourche, Lafourche Parish. Census of 1850, Eugene Richoux, 35, born in France; Rosella, 23; François, 3; Eugenie, 2; all born in Louisiana. Not located before or after 1850.

Rils, Thomas (1856-). gunsmith. 3rd ward, Iberville Parish. Thomas was a son of John M and Terzile Rils. Census of 1880; Thomas Rils, 24, gunsmith, born in Louisiana; J. M. Rils, 65; J. M. Rils, 55; several others. Not located after 1880; not in Find-a-Grave or Ancestry.

Robeltaz, L. locksmith. 1851, 142 Dauphine, New Orleans [*Dir*.].

Roberts, H. gunsmith. Covington, St. Tammany Parish.

H. Roberts, Gunsmith and Machinist. Restocking and repairing of every description. Wok guaranteed and prices moderate. Orders left with William Baden, Mrs Charles Keller, F B Martindale, or at the shop, 6 miles from Covington, east of the Lee Road, will be promptly executed [*St. Tammany Farmer*, 23 October 1886].

Robert, J. B. gunsmith, wheelwright, blacksmith. 1893, Carencro, Lafayette Parish [*Lafayette Gazette*, 13 May 1893].

Roch, Lewis. cutler. 1865, 685 Market, New Orleans. The Union Army of Occupation drafted Roch.

Rochon, Hilaire (1823-). gunsmith. 1st ward, St. Martin Parish. Census of 1850: Hilaire Rochon, 20, son of, living with, his parents Narcisse and Charlotte Rochon, all born in Louisiana. No occupation or race given for any family member. Census of 1860 of Attakapas, St. Martin Parish: Hillaire Rochon, 33, gunsmith, unmarried, living alone. Census of 1880; Hilaire Rochon, 57, born in Louisiana, mulatto, single; living with his brother, Leon Rochon, 47, and his wife Odile, 3. African American tradesman.

Rodler, Johan (1689-). locksmith. 1724, above New Orleans on Mississippi River; from Rastadt, Baden. Catholic; 35 years old, locksmith. Works at his trade. His wife. Two years on the place. Eight verges cleared. Deaf. By 1726 he had four arpents cleared. [http://genealogytrails.com/lou/1724census.html]

Roof, Charles. gunsmith. New Orleans. 1868, 70 Girod St.; 1870, 172 Dryades St. [*Dirs*.].

Roos, J. L. locksmith. 1861, Prytania near Euterpe, New Orleans [*Dir*.].

Rose, Leonard. locksmith. 1861, 110 Prytania, New Orleans [*Dir*.].

Ross, Philip. goldsmith. 1811, 24 Main, New Orleans [*Dir*.].

Ross, William Jackson (1830-1878). gunsmith, machinist and blacksmith. Vermillionville, St. Landry Parish. During the Second War for Independence Ross made guns for the Confederacy. After the war he settled at Brandon, Mississippi, and later at Star, Mississippi. He married Sarah Jane Harvey. After their marriage, William J. Ross and wife started to return to Mississippi. While stopping in St. Landry Parish, their son, William Ray, was born. They then moved on hack to Meridian, Mississippi. W. J. Ross was a gunsmith, machinist and blacksmith. After the war he settled at Brandon, Mississippi, and later at Star, Mississippi, and died in 1878 at the age of forty-eight. He was a member of the Masons and the Baptist Church. [Chambers, *History of LA*, 2: 9].

Rouyer, C. (1813--1865). goldsmith. 1849-61, New Orleans. Rouyer plated guns, did galvanizing, made buttons and buckles and in all ways into military hardware. Kit Gorman noted that he died c.1865, but his widow kept the business going until c.1886.

Rovel, J. B. gun smith. 1851, 316 Royal, New Orleans [*Dir*.].Manuel Espinoza stole a gun from Rovel at 280 Royal St., but was captured [*Times Picayune*, 3 October 1860]. See J B Revol.

Rowell, Johnny Carl (1886-1958). gun- and blacksmith, farmer. Johnny was born 26 March 1886 in Sparta, Bienville Parish, and died on 2 May 1958 in Jamestown, Bienville Parish. He married Sarah Jane Basinger (1893-1963) on 24 January 1909 in Bienville Parish, daughter of William and Cornelia (Miller) Basinger. Johnny was a farmer who owned 48 acres, blacksmith, and gunsmith and Sarah a housewife. They are buried in Pleasant Grove Baptist Church Cemetery, Ringgold [*Bienville Parish History*, I].

Roy, Mathurn. gun- and blacksmith. 1721-27, New Orleans, apparently single [French Census].

Rueff, Charles (1828-). gunsmith. 1862-71, New Orleans. 1867, 106 St. Philip St. [*Dir*.].

Sachet, Arthur. gunsmith. 1873, rear 100 Orleans St., New Orleans [*Dir*.].

Sacriste, Louis Clement (1812-1860). gunmaker African-American tradesman. 1849-60, New Orleans. Free man of color. [*Dir*.]. See also Siegrist.

Sage, J. gunsmith. Thibodaux, Lafourche Paris. A fire broke out on the night of 23 June 1856 and consumed most of the public square businesses, including the gunshop of J. Sage [New Orleans *Crescent,* 25 June 1856]. Not located in censuses or Ancestry.

Saget, Arthur Edmund (1849-1896). gunsmith. New Orleans, Census of 1880: Arthur Saget, son of F. Saget; born in Louisiana. 1884, J. Saget & Son. Arthur took over his father's gunshop when the latter died in 1885. 1887, 198 Chartres [*Dirs*.; Ancestry; Gorman].

Saget, F. (1812--1885). gunsmith. New Orleans. Census of 1880: F. Saget, gunsmith, 68; Arthur Saget, 31, gunsmith; Maria Saget, 24, all born in France; Emma, 21, born in Louisiana Ancestry; Gorman].

Saget, Julian (1812-1885). gunsmith. 1860-90, 198 Chartres St., New Orleans. Saget was a gunsmith in New Orleans from about 1860 to 1890. He imported most of the guns he offered from Europe. "patent gun nipples, his own trade mark" There is a J Saget 16 gauge double barrel with 44 inch long barrels, imported from Liege, Belgium, with an engraving of ducks on the water surrounded by *J Saget, New Orleans, LA*. Census of 1880, New Orleans: J. Saget, 68, born in France; Arthur, 21; Maria, 24; Emma, 21. 1884, J. Saget & Son. [*Times Picayune*, 9 November 1879; Census; Gorman; *Dirs.*]. In 1923 Mrs. Robert Sager Hager, daughter of Julain Saget, died. In the news item in the 25 March 1923 issue of *Times Picayune*, the writer claimed that her father's gunshop in the Pontalba Building was the first gun-shop in New Orleans. He had earlier worked, and Mrs. Hager was born, in Laforche Parish. Her mother, Julian's wife, was Ursula Heolise Maria de-Masse, daughter of Marquis deMasse, who had been driven from France during its bloody revolution.

Attempted Burglary. The gun store of Saget on Chartres street, a square below the police station, was on Saturday night assaulted at the door by burglars, and 2 or 3 auger holes bored, preparatory to cutting away some of the wood work. At this juncture, a pointer dog, belonging to Dr. Espinola, whose store is upon the opposite side, commenced a furious barking in the street. His master, supposing that the noise originated simply from the efforts of the dog to obtain entrance from the street, got up to admit him, and while at the front door, saw two of the robbers at work upon the opposite side. The latter now took to their heels, closely followed by the dog, who returned shortly afterward, wounded in one of his legs. Neither of the parties was arrested. The attempt to commit the burglary doubtless originated in the fact that a large amount of arms had been received at the store during the preceding day [*New Orleans Times*, 25 January 1870]

Saget, Jules (1875-1942). gunsmith. New Orleans. Jules was a son of Julian Saget [Gorman; Ancestry]. gunsmith. Hospital St., New Orleans. Successor to Julian Saget. Patent of 4 September 1906 number 830,370. Patent number 817,937 of 17 April 1906 for a firearm.

Gunsmith's Invention. J. L. Saget, a New Orleans gunsmith, in Hospital Street, is being congratulated by his friends of his accomplishments and genius. He has invented combination sporting guns and has made duplicates of the old flintlock musket used in 1776, the percussion cap of 1861, and the Krag rifle. He has secured patents for the United States government [*Times Picayune,* 27 February 1907]

Saloman, Davy (1813-). gunsmith. 1850, St. Landry Parish. Census of 1850: Davy Saloman, gun smith, value $500, born in Louisiana, age 37.

Salamone, Raffaele (1837-1860). gunsmith. Raffaee Salamone, age 23, gunsmith, native of Palermo and resident of Ustica, Jefferson Parish. Death Certificate. Place of Death: Marrero, Jefferson Parish. Son of Antonio, age

48, gunsmith, resident of Palermo [http://www.ustica.org/cgi-bin/get_reference.pl?27478].

Salerno, Dimitrio. gunsmith. 1900, 818 S. Rampart St., New Orleans [*Dirs*.; Gorman].

Sanches, Jacob. gunsmith. 1778, St. Louis St., New Orleans [French Census; Gorman].

Saucier, Adolph Victor, Sr. (1820-). gunsmith. Marksville, Avoyelles Parish. Census of 1860, Adolph Saucier, 40, gunsmith; Armentine, wife, 30; Louis, 11; Lodiska, 7; Freemont. 5; Adolphe, 2; all born in Louisiana.

Saucier, Adolph Victor, Jr. (1857--1921). gunsmith. Marksville, Avoyelles Parish. Adolph Jr was born on 31 October 1857. Census of 1880, Adolph Saucier, 22, gunsmith, born in Louisiana; Helena, 18; Moore Saucier, 6 months; Hermantine Sancier, 45; Mary Danyette, 14. Adolph was married twice. His first wife was Helena Brouillette who died in 1893. His second wife was Helena's sister, Marie Blanche Brouillette. He died on 15 April 1921 and was buried in St. Joseph Cemetery. Also seen as Sancier.

Saucier, J. gunsmith. 1838, 34 Main St., New Orleans [*Dir*.].

Saulet, Armand. gunsmith. 1842, 24 Toulouse St., New Orleans [*Dir*.]

Schiell, Mathias (--1862). armorer. Mathias served in the First (Melligan's) Louisiana Infantry. He enlisted on April 5, 1861, at New Orleans. Present on Rolls to April, May and June, 1862. Enlistment time extended two years or the duration of the war in consequence of the Conscript Act passed April 16, 1862. Rolls to October 31, 1862. Mathias was killed in action at Battle of Sharpsburg, Maryland. According to a report dated September 8, 1869, Matthias was killed on September 17, 1862. He was born in Louisiana, occupation gunsmith and mechanic, Residence New Orleans, single.

Schneckenberger, John (1833-1893). gunsmith. 1861-93, New Orleans. Principally John ran a shooting galley although he was also a gunsmith [*Dirs*; Gorman].

Schneider, Martin (1835-). armorer. Martin served the Glorious Cause as a private, Company I, 10th Louisiana Infantry. He enlisted on. July 22, 1861, at Camp Moore, Louisiana. He was present on all rolls until February 1862. Record copied from Memorial Hall, New Orleans, by the War Department in June, 1908: he was born in Germany, occupation gunsmith, Residence

New Orleans, Louisiana, age when enlisted 27, single in August 1862 [*Booth's Index*]. Not located after the war.

Schuerer, Jacob (1829-). gun- and locksmith. 1851, New Orleans; admitted to charity hospital with a fever. Jacob was born in Germany.

Schuler, F. locksmith. 1861, 132 Ursulines, New Orleans [*Dir*.].

Schultz, Carl (1801-). locksmith. 1851, St. Louis St., New Orleans; admitted to charity hospital with "int fever." Born in Hamburg, Germany.

Schwardt, Martin. locksmith. 1854, near Levee, New Orleans [*Dir*.].

Schweitzer, S. locksmith. 1861, 234 Magazine, New Orleans [*Dir*.].

Searles, Daniel Captain (1782-1860). gunsmith. 1804-08, Cincinnati. Searles married Jean, daughter of John McFarland on 2 December 1807. 1836–1860, Baton Rouge. Census of 1850, Daniel Searles, age 68, value $5100, born in Maryland; Jane, his wife, 66; Sally York, 80, born in Ireland [Census]. Captain Daniel Searles was one of Baton Rouge's early gunsmiths and knife makers. Searles was a maker of the famed Bowie knife. His name is engraved on a knife made for Rezin Pleasant Bowie for presentation to a prominent local citizen. Searles died in East Baton Rouge Parish in March 1860, age 78, gunsmith [*Western Spy*, 17 October 1804; 16 December 1806; & 7 December 1807; Ancestry].

Removal. The Subscriber acknowledges with gratitude the many favors he has received from the citizens of Cincinnati and the public in general, at his late shop in Main street, and respectfully informs them that he has removed to a frame building on the corner of Water and Elm streets, adjoining Mr. Thomas McFarland's, where he continues the Gun, Pistol, Sword, and Dirk making business in all its various branches. Daniel Searles. N. B. Branding irons, stamps &c. lettered [*Western Spy*, 11 June 1808].

D. Searles, Gunsmith, informs the Public that, having employed an additional workman of the first order, he is now prepared to execute every kind of work in his line with neatness and dispatch [*Baton Rouge Gazette*, 22 June 1839].

Seecher, Daniel Francis (1805-). gunsmith. 1847, Calcasieu Parish; born in Maryland [Thomas Rigmaiden's diary]. 1850, Calcasieu Parish. Census of 1850; Francis Seecher, gunsmith, single; born in Maryland, age 45.

Seeger, Gustave. gunsmith. 1869, 247 Poydras, New Orleans [*Dir*.].

Segurs, Jehu H. (1797--). gun smith. ward 7, Morehouse Parish. Census of 1850, John Segurs, 53, value $700, born in South Carolina, gun smith; Cynthia, 23, born in Mississippi. Not located after 1850.

Serressol, Edouard. gunsmith. 1822-32, 276 Dauphine St.; home 147 Francis above Amor, New Orleans [*Dir.*]. See Ceressol.

Sheehan, M. J. gunsmith. 1883-88, New Orleans [*Times Picayune*, 3 January 1888]

Sheflin, John. gunsmith. 1851, New Orleans. Employed at Thomas Bailey's gunshop.. Caught a presumed customer trying to steal a pistol valued at $25 [*Times Picayune*, 17 June 1851]

Shrevtzer, Simon. locksmith. 1861, 24 S. Market, New Orleans [*Dir.*].

Sibley, John. physician and gunsmith. President Thomas Jefferson sent John Sibley among the Caddo Amerindians to assist in his two professions. Dr. John Sibley was sent by President Thomas Jefferson to Natchitoches in 1806 to be gunsmith for the Caddo Indians and to report on the area. He was married three times, outliving them all. 1803-14, Caddo and Bossier Parishes. John married Eulile Maliege. Indians of Orleans Territory, as well as Texas Indians, visited Sibley on many occasions during the years 1806 to 1812. The number of visitors gathered in Natchitoches at one time varied from a few to several hundred. They came to the post not only to settle problems, but also to sell their furs and to purchase goods at the factory, or government-operated trading post; to report on activities of the Spanish in Texas; to receive presents; and to have their guns and tools repaired. The gifts included powder, lead, guns, flints, combs, cloth of various kinds, mirrors, needles and thread, tobacco, buttons, handkerchiefs, beads, blankets, leggings, shirts, vermilion, agricultural tools, domestic utensils, bridles, saddles, plumes, earrings, and tobacco and snuff boxes. [*Louisiana History*, 5: 4 [1961], 401-19].

Siegrist, **Charles II**. gunsmith. 1879, 124 Poplar St., New Orleans [*Dir.*].

Sieverling, Heinrich C. (1828-). locksmith. 1851, New Orleans; admitted to charity hospital with "phthisis pulm". Born in Brunswick, Germany.

Simeon, J. goldsmith. 1911, Royale & Orleans, New Orleans [*Dir.*].

Siruguey, J. (1831--). gunsmith. machinist and gunsmith. 6th ward, Iberia

Parish. Census of 1880: J. Siruguey, 49, machinist, single born in France. Not located after 1880.

Gone to France. Mr J Siruguey, the excellent gunsmith and mechanic, last week started for a visit to his native France. Before doing so, he stated publicly that the few thousand dollars he has accumulated during the past four years he owed directly to the society the Friends of Temperance. We hope that Mr Siruguey has a pleasant trip and soon return to use permanently [*Louisiana Sugar Bowl* reprinted in *Lake Charles Echo*, 31 May 1879].

Skinner, Leodore (1831-). gunsmith. Landry St., Opelousas, St. Landry Parish. Census of 1850: Leodore Skinner, 19, blacksmith; son of James Skinner, 55, blacksmith; Judith, 53, his wife. Leodore is noted as mulatto, but not so for James and Judith. Census of 1880: Leodore Skinner; born in Louisiana; wife Julia H., 39 [*Opelousas Courier*, 5 January 1878]. African American tradesman. He was almost certainly the gunsmith listed as Joe Skinner, 38, value $400; wife Julia32; son William, 6; in Opelousas in the Census of 1870. Census of 1900: Joseph Skinner, 64, gunsmith, widower.

Smith, J. gunsmith. 1869, 205 Mandeville, New Orleans [*Dir*.].

Smith, J. B. (-1889?). machinist and gunsmith. 1880-85, Colfax, Grant Parish. On 6 April 1889 the *Colfax Chronicle* carried a notice that Smith had contracted "bronchitis and a complication of other diseases and is expected to die." Not located in census or Ancestry.

J B Smith, machinist, boiler maker, and gunsmith. Engine setting and repairing, boiler patching executed with promptness. Work in my several lines solicited [*Louisiana Democrat,* 13 April 1881].

J.B. Smith, whose card will be found in another column, offers his services as repairer of machinery and gunsmith to the people of this section. Mr. Smith is a practical engineer and understands his business in all its details. He has done a great deal of work where skill and a thorough knowledge of every branch of mechanics was required and has always given satisfaction. In the course of 25 years experience his skill has been attested by hundreds of persons, and he can give any number of references among the businessmen and farmers of Rapides, Grant, and adjoining parishes.

J. B. Smith, machinist and gunsmith, Grant's Point opposite Colfax. Is prepared to repair Machinery or take any job in that line that can be done outside a foundry. Also guns and pistols repaired or made to order. All orders addressed to me at Colfax will receive careful and prompt attention. [both from *Colfax Chronicle*, 13 June 1885]

Smith, James R. (1862-). boiler maker, carpenter, machinist, and gunsmith. 1880, Pineville, Rapides Parish. 1880, James, 18, single, born in LA, gun smith, son of John B., 57, and Margarite Smith, 45 [Census]. 1881, Alexandria, Rapides Parish. "engine seating and repairing, boiler patching, work in my several lines solicited" [*Louisiana Democrat*, 26 January 1881].

Proclamation by the Governor. $300 Reward. Whereas at the fall term of the honorable the 12th Judicial District Court, sitting in and for the Parish of Rapides, James Smith was indicted for arson, was subsequently admitted to bail, and afterwards forfeited his bond and left the parish; and whereas all efforts in procuring his arrewst have proved fruitless. Now, therefore, I, Samuel Douglaas McHenry, Governor of the State of Louisiana, have thought proper to issue this, my proclamation, calling upon the people of this State to aid and assist in procuring the arrest of the said James Smith, so that he may be brought to justice and dealt with as the alw directs, and by virtue of the authority vested in me by law I do hereby offer a reward of $300 for the arrest and conviction of said James Smith. This proclamation to be in full force and effect during sixty days. James Smith is a native of Pineville, parish of Rapides, has a bright complexion, light or sandy hair, blue eyes, about 5' 6 or 7" high, small and slender, predisposed to consumption, occupation that of a gunsmith and carpenter combined. . . . [*Daily Advocate*, 14 January 1885]

Smithwick, Noah (1808-1899). blacksmith, miller, and memoirist. Noah was a son of Edward Smithwick, born on January 1, 1808, in Martin County, North Carolina. The family moved to Robertson Countyturned to Matagorda in the fall of 1835, after four years in the Redlands of East Texas and Louisiana. He arrived at Gonzales the day after the battle and remained to repair guns. Joining the volunteers marching towards Bexar, Smithwick took part in the battle of Concepción. In January 1836 he joined Capt. John Jackson Tumlinson, Jr.'s newly formed ranger company to defend the Bastrop area from roving bands of Indians. He arrived at San Jacinto after the battle. In May Gen. Thomas J. Rusk ordered gunsmiths to follow the Texas army from the battleground to Victoria. Smithwick did not pursue the Mexican army south of the Rio Grande. Smithwick returned to Bastrop to work as a smith and serve in the volunteer ranger corps from the fall of 1836 through 1838. Understanding Spanish, he occasionally served as interpreter-agent with Plains Indians seeking treaties and trading posts. In 1839 Smithwick married Thurza N. Blakey, the daughter of widow Nancy Blakey and the widow of Richard Duty, settling in southeastern Travis County. By 1850 they moved to Brushy Creek in Williamson County. Smithwick applied for a job in Burnet County as armorer at Fort Croghan (present Burnet). That year he paid $5,000 for the nearby saw and grist mill built by the Mormons in 1850. He and his nephew and partner, John R. Hubbard, sold their interest in 1857-58. Smithwick began a new mill on 320 acres he bought ten miles east of Marble Falls in the Hickory Creek settlement. A Unionist in sympa-thy in 1861, Smithwick received threats and decided to abandon Texas. Smithwick and a number of friends left Burnet County on April 14, 1861, in wagons for southern California. By 1870 he and his wife and four children, ages 19-29, were living in Kern County, formerly part of Tulare County [Texas on Line; *Dallas Morning News*, 8 December 1896, 3 October 1935]., Tennessee, in 1814.. Having moved to Hopkinsville, Christian County, Kentucky, in 1827, Noah left his job as a blacksmith and traveled by flatboat to New Orleans and schooner to Matagorda Bay. He worked as an itinerant smith before settling in San Felipe. On July 9, 1830, he applied for a league of land in Stephen F. Austin's colony, saying he had immigrated from Tennessee in 1827, was twenty-two years old, and a gunsmith. A friend, Hiram Friley from Gonzales, sought refuge in San Felipe after killing a man. San Felipe authorities ordered him chained with leg irons, but Smithwick provided a file and a gun so he might escape. Tracked down, Friley was shot, and Smith-wick's gun implicated him. The authorities tried him, declared him "a bad citizen," and on December 7, 1830, banished him from Austin's colony and Texas, providing an escort to the Sabine. Smithwick re

Finding a pastoral life unsuited to my taste, and the sparsely settled condition of the country in my vicinity rendering a blacksmith shop unremunerative, when the commander at Fort Croggin advertised for an armorer, I went up and worked a short time, long enough, however, to get an insight into the workings of the government machinery. There was a little upstart of a non-commissioned offi-cer, who, having been made a sergeant, appropriated another fellow's wife and put on more airs than did the department commander. He set up a carriage and his wife had to have a servant and fine clothes. As his regular pay would not nearly pay his expenses he made up the deficit by cheating the government. He came into my shop one day with his scales, saying: "I wish you would fix these scales for me so they will weigh a trifle light. The men all draw more rations than they can eat and it is just wasted. Now, if I could manage to save a little from each one they would never miss it, and where I issue several hundred a day it would amount to a good deal to me." [Smithwick's, *Old Texas Days*].

Somne, Eubermin (1826-). gunsmith. Houston, Texas. Census of 1870, Eubermin Somne, 44, gun smith; wife Louisa, 39, both born in France, Leona, 15, born in Louisiana. Not located after 1870 or in Louisiana.

Soncey, Bee (1845-). gunsmith. East Carroll Parish. Census of 1880, Soncey Bee, gunsmith, 35, boarder, single.

Sookal, Korziman (1885-1947). lock- & gunsmith, tailor. 1910-47, Winnfield, Winn Parish. Funeral services for Sookal, 62, a resident of Winn Parish since 1910, were held at the Southern Funeral Home chapel on Tuesday afternoon, December 22, with the Rev. Alwin Stokes officiating. Burial was in Winnfield Cemetery. Sookal died at his home on Jones Street, Winnfield, on Friday, December 19, after an illness of several months. He was born in Lithuania, Europe on March 4, 1885, and came to the United States in 1905. He moved to Winn Parish about 1910 and several years later established his several businesses in Winnfield.

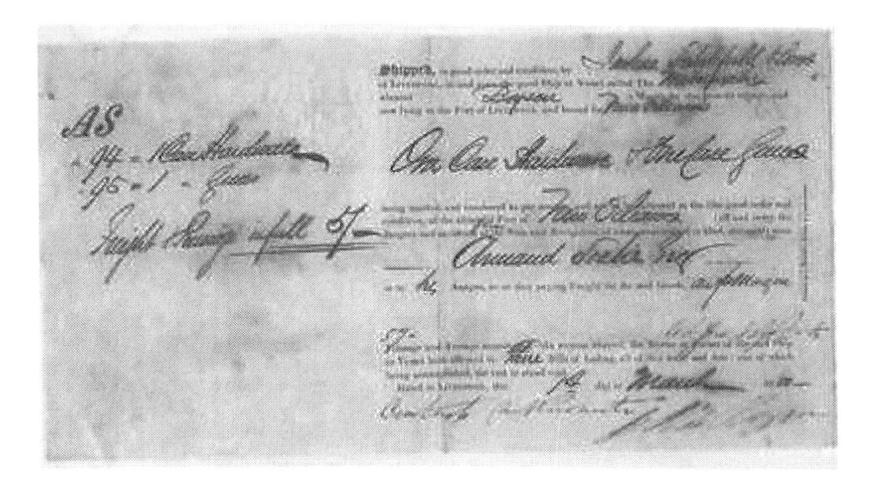
AS
Shipped,
New Orleans
Armand Soubie Esq
March

Soubie, Armand (1815-1889). gunsmith and major dealer. 1842-55, 24 Toulouse; home 11 History St., New Orleans. Soubie was a New Orleans gunsmith and gun dealer with wide-ranging business interests, including supplying weapons to the Texas population and people traveling to California [*Dir.*]. A known letter, dated 2 April 1852, from the Colt factory discusses various shipments of revolvers being sent to Armand Soubie and problems in receiving them. Colt promises that one box of 24 naval model pistols will be shipped very soon. The small pistols Soubie ordered had not yet been manufactured, and it will be some months before they are ready for shipment. They also promised that they will investigate the first shipment, which had been sent in February but apparently was not received. University of North Carolina has Soubie's papers, including some with his successor Phillippe Bouron.

Chiefly records, 1852-1900, of Soubie, a New Orleans, La., gunsmith and gun trader, including a monthly stock inventory, September 1859-April 1861; accounts with Pierre Cazelar of Paris, 1852-1856; a ledger of sales and repairs for individuals, 1855-1857; and scattered other records. Also included are twenty-five letters, 1854-1857, from Charles Hummel, gun dealer of San Antonio, Tex., to Soubie concerning their business dealings, Indian raids, and other news.

Soubiran, Etienne (1818-). gunsmith. New Orleans. Census of 1860: Etienne Soubiran, 42, gunsmith, value $1000; Antionette, 35; Martha, 12, all born in France; Eugenie, 7; and Albert, 4, both born in New Orleans. Not located before or after 1860.

Spohn, Heinrich (1825-). locksmith. 1851-61, New Orleans. 1851, St. Louis St.; 1861, 37 Rampart St. Spohn, age 27, born in Magdeburg, Prussia, admitted to charity hospital for rheumatism.

Stable, ---. goldsmith. 1811, 49 Ursulines, New Orleans [*Dir.*].

Stacy, Thomas. gunsmith. 1857-58, Carondelet, New Orleans [*Dirs.*].

Stader, William. lock- and gunsmith. 1873, works for J. Kuntzman. Rear Annunciation, between 6th and 7th Sts., New Orleans [*Dirs.*].

Stanley, Benjamin F. (1790--). gunsmith. near Harrisonburg, Catahoula Parish. Census of 1850, Benjamin Stanley, age 60, gunsmith, born in Louisiana; Sarah A., his wife, 28; Warren W., 10, both born in Mississippi; Joseph, 7; Louisa C., 5; male child, 1 month; all born in Louisiana. 1854,. Noted as "terror of the neighborhood" Stanly, aged about 61 years, killed John Pitt "an old man". The incident began with an argument about a barking dog. Stanley escaped and was described as being 5' 11" tall, gray hair, dark complexion. Seldom leaves home without his double barrel firearm, one barrel of which is rifled [*Daily Advocate*, 16 August 1854].

Starker, H. T. (1833-). lock- and gunsmith. 1861, New Orleans. Young Starker killed a man from Baltimore and was judged insane [*Alexandria Gazette*, 5 February 1861]. Also seen as Starks.

A Most Unaccountable and Deliberate Murder was committed in New Orleans in broad daylight on the 22nd ult. S locksmith named H. T. Starker, aged 28 years, deliberately shot dead a jeweler named Samuel Koplinger, aged 58 years, in the street in the sight of dozens of people. Not a word passed between the parties. They were not even to known to each other, except by sight, and even according to the statement of the murdered, there was not the slightest justification for the crime. Starker says he thought the deceased was going to kill him, so he drew a revolver and fired every barrel with deadly effect. [*Boston Herald*,

4 February 1861].

Starr, P. H. (1812-). gunsmith. 1842, New Orleans. P. H. Starr, gunsmith, age 30, born in New York, admitted to lunatic asylum.

Stephens, G. W. (1804-). gun smith. ward 3, Claiborne Parish. Census of 1870; G. W. Stephens, 66, born in Kentucky, gun smith; Phoebe, 35. Not located before or after 1870.

Stikes, George. locksmith. 1875, 320 ½ Felicity, New Orleans [*Dir.*].

Strong, Nathaniel (1816-1899). gun- and blacksmith. Nathaniel Strong was married to Mary Caroline Norton. He moved from Georgia to Claiborne Parish. in the 1850's. He was a blacksmith and a gunsmith who served in the LA 4th Cavalry Company F for the Confederate States of America. In his wife's 1903 application for a Confederate pension she listed him as having been buried at Pilgrims Rest in Shongaloo, Webster Parish. Several of his children are buried in the north east corner. He and his wife had 12 children. Nathaniel was a blacksmith and a gunsmith. Nathaniel's son Charlie Strong told his son Doyle that Nathaniel had two Muzzle loading rifles. One was a large caliber and it was named "Baldin" the other was a small caliber rifle and he named it "Little Joe Ree". [Ancestry].

Stubenrauch, V. armorer. 1873, New Orleans Turners [*Times Picayune*, 5 May 1873]. The Turners were a German athletic club.

Summers, Larentz (1809-). lock- and gunsmith. 1847, New Orleans. Summers was an inmate in the lunatic asylum, age 38, born in Bavaria, Germany, "softening of the brain" a patient for 7 years.

Swann, ---. gunsmith. 1797-98, New Orleans [M.E.S.D.A.].

Swatz, Henry. gunsmith. Henry was a private, in the 6th Louisiana Infantry He enlisted in 1862 at New Orleans for the duration of the war. He was born in Germany, occupation gunsmith; residence New Orleans. Detailed to work in Government Armory, Richmond, Virginia, in May 1862 [*Booth's Index*].

Sweeney, Philip (1815--). armorer. 1861, Orleans Artillery, New Orleans. A double barrel pistol fell from Sweeney's belt, discharging and killing a sergeant. The ball went through his wrist and into his heart [*Times Picayune,* 22 June 1861]. Census of 1860: P. Sweeney, 45, born in Galloway; Mary, 23; and Thomas, 4.

Tarr & Curran. On 23 May 1834, James McCamant of Wellsburg, West Virginia, shipped to Tarr & Curran in New Orleans, firearms valued at $90. The Brooke County Historical Society of West Virginia has additional bills of lading for firearms McCamant shipped on flat barges own the Ohio-Mississippi River complex.

Tarver, Samuel Wilson (1825-1919). mechanic, farmer, gun- and blacksmith. Samuel was born on 31 October 1825. 1830-53, Amite County. Served in Union Army in 1864, private, Company C, First Indiana Heavy Artillery. Census of 1860 of Holmesville, Pike County: Sam Tarver, 35, blacksmith; Mary, 28; Russell, 7, C C, 4; twins, age 1, all born in Mississippi. Census of 1870 of Pike County; Samuel Tarver, 46, farmer, born in Mississippi; Mary Ann, 40; Russell, 17, both born in Louisiana; six other children, ages 3 to 14, born in Mississippi. Census of 1880, Winn Parish, Louisiana; Samuel Tarver, 54, blacksmith; Mary, 53; four children, ages 9 to 15. Samuel Tarver died on 30 April 1919 in Boyce, Rapides Parish, Louisiana, and was buried in Alexandria National Cemetery. He married Mary Ann Lilly (1825-1917). She died in Caldwell Parish, Louisiana [Family]. Samuel Wilson Tarver applied for a military pension from his service with the Indiana Heavy Artillery. The date of the application, on which he lists all of his children with their birth dates, is dated by Samuel Wilson Tarver's signature June 7th 1899, and stamped by the pension office on June 12 1899. He married, second, Mrs. Nancy Delane (-1840) on May 1, 1880 in Rapides Parish, Louisiana. She was born 1840 [Ancestry; Family; Find-a-Grave].

Taylor & Churchill. major dealers. 29-39 Magazine St., New Orleans. The firm was a hardware store that sold many guns and carried an extensive inventory. Churchill bought out Taylor in 1861. Charles Churchill died in 1861 but his brothers Sylvester and Wiley took over the firm. Successors to Taylor & Hart. Gorman remarked that this firm was not the largest but certainly was the most aggressive in advertising.

Gun Store. Sign of the Golden Gun, 39 Magazine street, opposite the St. James Hotel. Our assortment of double barrel Shot Guns consists of 100 different varieties, made by the best English, French, and Belgian gun manufactories which we warrant to be good shots and free from flaws. Also an assortment of the Best Rifles and Pistols. Wholesale hardware dealers, Taylor & Churchill. Peter G. Taylor, New York. Charles H. Churchill, New Orleans [*Times Picayune*, 7 February 1861]

[and in the same issue an additional ad]. Five Shots in 5 Seconds. We are in receipt of a large lot of Revolvers which we are offering at the following low prices. Roger's Patent, self-cocking, $9 & $10; Beale's Patent, $9.40, $10, and

$12.75; Colt's Patent, 4 inch, $12.50, 5 inch, $15; 6 inch, $16.50; Colt's Patent, Ivory Mountings, 4", $20; 5" $22.50; 6" $24. Wholesale and retail. Discounts of 10% when purchased by the dozen. Taylor & Churchill.

Tessier, George D. (1830-1903). gunsmith. George was a private, in the 2nd Louisiana Cavalry. He enlisted on June 21, 1861 [or Aug. 21, 1862] at Natchitoches. He appears on muster roll dated September 14, 1862, without remarks. Again on rolls of January and February 1863, Absent from muster rolls of July and August 1863. He was detailed to Alexandria, to serve as gunsmith. Noted on roll of prisoners of war of detailed men, C. S. A., paroled Natchitoches, Louisiana, on June 6, 1865. Resident of Natchitoches, Louisiana [Ancestry; *Booth's Index*].

Tessier, John M. (1823-). gunsmith. Natchitoches Parish. John was a private in the 2nd Louisiana Heavy Artillery. He was taken prisoner and paroled on 6 June 1865. Census of 1870: John M Tessier, 46, gunsmith, $1500 real estate; Julia, 27; Angela, 8. Census of 1880: John M. Tessier, widower, 57, born in Louisiana; living with his 18 year old daughter Angela.

Teutsch, August. gunsmith. 1874-78, 22 St. Philip St., New Orleans [Gorman; *Dirs*.].

Theil, Philip (1808--1872). gunsmith. Baton Rouge. Philip was born on 25 March 1808. Census of 1850: Philip Thiell, 41, gunsmith; Mary, 28; Mary, 8; Amanda, 6; and Philip, 3. Census of 1860, Philip Theil, age 52, born in Germany, gunsmith; Mary, 37, his wife; Amanda, 16; Louis, 14; Joseph, 5; and Elizabeth Butler, 53, all born in Louisiana. Census of 1870: Philip J Thiel, 61, gunsmith, real estate $2000, born in Sachsen-Coburg und Gotha; Mary, 48. Philip died on 7 April 1872 and was buried in St. Joseph Catholic Cemetery, Baton Rouge [Find-a-Grave; Ancestry].

Thomason, F. locksmith. 1865, New Orleans; 2nd district draftee.

Thistle, Hezekiah L. inventor. 1834-38, New Orleans. On 1 August 1838 Hezekiah received patent number 843 for a firearm [Gardner, *Small Arms Makers*, 192]. Kit Gorman gave the patent number as 865. There is no evidence that it was ever manufactured. In 1853 Thistle demanded Congress indemnify him for the military use of his patented pack saddle; he lost. I failed to locate Hezekiah in any census or Ancestry or Find-a-Grave.

Tigniere, Auguste (1830-c.1890). gunsmith and shooting gallery. 1856-72, New Orleans. 1861, 48 St. Louis St., Kit Gorman gave his address for most years as 132 Chartres. Auguste enlisted in the French Brigade in the Glorious Cause. His business partner was Pierre F. Callier who may have been his brother-in-law or father-in-law Also seen as Tignieres. Census of 1880, Sedgwick County, Kansas: August Tignier, gunsmith, 50, born in France; Josephine, 39; Alice, 14; Ralph, 10, all born in Louisiana [Gorman; *Dir.*].

Sportsmen Attention. Tignieres, Gunsmith, St. Louis street, opposite St. Louis Exchange recommends himself to all those in need of a good gun. He has constantly on hand an assortment of guns, of the best make, at the most moderate prices. He repairs at the shortest notice all firearms entrusted to him. He has in his establishment a gallery of Pistol, Gun, and Rifle shooting. He makes all the Free Masonry ornaments and decorations [*Avoyelles Pelican*, 28 Dec. 1861]

Tralich, Heinrich (1822-). locksmith. New Orleans; Census of 1850: Heinrich Tralich in the Charity Hospital, age 28, born in Germany.

Treder, John F. (1805-1884). gunsmith. New Orleans. Census of 1870: John F Treder, 64, gunsmith; Anna, 62; Theodore 22, all born in Prussia; Louisa, 27, born in Baden; and Charles, 8, born in Louisiana. John died in December 1884 and was buried in Greenwood Cemetery, New Orleans.

Tremells, Robert. goldsmith. 1811, 26 Conti, New Orleans [*Dir.*].

Trombino, Francesco. gun- and locksmith. 1895-1923, New Orleans. 1898, 523 Hospital St. 1923, 514 St. Philip St. A Negro entered his shop and attempted to steal a revolver, but was chased away by Trombino's wife. The thief was soon caught hiding in some stalls [*Times Picayune*, 7 December 1923; Gorman; *Dirs.*].

Trucas, Charles. lock- and gunsmith. 1872-82, New Orleans. Noted in city directories as a gunsmith only in 1878 at 48 Bourbon St. [Gorman; *Dirs.*].

Turnbull, Walter Joseph (1860-1914). inventor. 1885-1900, New Orleans. On 8 August 1899 he received patent number 630,758 for a firearm, Half interest assigned to W. S. E. Sevey. Kit Gorman cites his obituary which said that Turnbull had invented a 21 shot pistol whose rights he sold to Colt [Gorman; Gardner, *Small Arms Makers*, 197].

Turner, Clint (1880-). gunsmith. 1930, Union Parish [Census].

Turner, Louis (1834-). gunsmith. New Orleans then to Lavaca County, Texas. Louis was born in Prussia, Germany, November 26, 1834, son of Christian and Mary (Buttermann) Turner. Louis served an apprenticeship at the locksmith and gunsmith trades. He then took passage for the United

States, landed at Baltimore, and went from there to Cincinnati, Ohio. He then worked in a machine shop for several months, after which he traveled for a time, looking for a location. After this he was on a steamboat on the Mississippi River a few months, and then located in New Orleans, where he worked in a gunsmith shop for nearly two years. On account of his health he came to Texas, and spent one year in Victoria, after which, in 1856, he located in Hallettsville, where he engaged with a gunsmith. After remaining with him eleven months, Mr. Turner bought the business out, and carried it on successfully until the spring of 1862. He then enlisted in the Confederate army, Whitfield Legion, and left Hallettsville with Company A, as chief bugler of the legion. He was captured and exchanged and then he joined Hardeman's Regiment. At the Battle of Poison Springs, he was shot in the leg, the bone broken, and the horse on which he was riding killed. From the time he was wounded, 9 o'clock in the morning, until 5 o'clock p.m, he remained on the battlefield, and while lying there wounded, two Indians came on the field and shot a wounded man. Turner only preserved his life by feigning death. A little later two men came on the field and robbed him of money and all valuables, and then a guard came, who remained until an ambulance made its appearance. In this three dead men were placed, with our subject on top of them, and in this manner he rode to Fort Smith, a distance of six miles. After the war he made his way to Hallettsville, Texas, from Little Rock, and arrived there July 27, 1865. When he fell from his horse on the battlefield near Fort Smith a friend saw, him fall and wrote home to his people that he had been killed. Now, when he made his appearance at home, a most exciting and pathetic scene ensued, for his friends thought he had been dead for a year. After recovering, Mr. Turner resumed business as a gunsmith in Hallettsville, and continued this until 1874. Being a superior workman, he had more work than he could do, and trade came from a long distance. About the year 1872 he began to erect an hotel. In 1861, previous to entering the army, Turner married. Josephine (Bragger) Dubois, a daughter of Jasper Bragger, a native of Germany He was the main organizer of the Hallettsville Shooting Club. He is one of the most prominent men of the county and is well liked [*History of Lavaca Co.*, 341-343].

Turpin & Company. goldsmiths. 1811, 8 St. Pierre, New Orleans [*Dir.*].

Varreuil, Jean. gunsmith. 1727, New Orleans [Gorman; French Census].

Verrier, Theodore (1828--). gunsmith. Thibodeaux, Lafourche Parish. On 14 September 1876 Theodore Verrier naturalized. He had arrived in America in 1851.Census of 1880: Theodore Vervier, gunsmith, 51; wife Johanna, 52, both born in France; daughter Octavia, 13, born in Louisiana. "The building on Main street lately occupied by J S Lann as a grocery is being repaired and has been rented to M Verrier, a gentleman from Lafouche who will open up a gunsmith shop and sewing machine depot [*Meridional*,, 7 November 1896]. The millinery store formerly occupied by Mrs Tom Sirmon is being remodeled by its owner Dr Kibbe to serve as a gunshop to be used by T. Verrier [Abbeville *Meridional*, 7 January 1899]. Census of 1900 of Bayou Vermillion: Theodore Verrier, 71, gunsmith, born in France, widower, born in August 1828; living with his niece, Octavia Devillard.

Verrier, Joseph. wagon-maker, blacksmith, wheelwright and coach-maker. Donaldsonville, Ascension Parish. Main between St. Louis & Green street [*Thibodaux Sentinel*, 14 April 1877; *La Louisianials*, 6 December 1879].Joseph Icard was in partnership with Joseph Ferrier. Notice in the *Louisianais* of 6 October 1877 that the partnership was dissolved. The multi-functional firm performed services in the following fields: blacksmithing, wheelwright, locksmith, coach maker and gunsmith. Ferrier continued the businesses. See also Joseph Ferrier.

Vial, Pedro (-1815). gunsmith. Pedro Vial, a native of Lyons, France, made the journey from Santa Fe to St. Louis, on behalf of the Spanish crown. Vial, who had worked in New Orleans and in San Antonio de Bexar (now San Antonio, Texas) was known as a trader and gunsmith with many talents, such as horseman, diplomat and linguist. Vial arrived in Santa Fe in May of 1787, after traversing a route from San Antonio to Santa Fe, an historic accomplishment because it marked the first European use of that route. Vial was then contracted by the Spanish governor, don Fernando de la Concha, to blaze a trail from Santa Fe to St. Louis. Vial and two companions, Vincente Espinoza and Vicente Villanueva, left Santa Fe on May 21, 1792. They were the first of European descent to traverse what later would be known as the Santa Fe Trail. The group arrived back in Santa Fe from St. Louis on Nov. 16, 1793. The Spanish frontier was defined at the time by the Mississippi River, from New Orleans to the Illinois area. The decision was made by the governor of New Spain, Fernando de la Concha, to open a trail from Santa Fe to St. Louis, which would serve Spain very well. The choice of Vial to lead this excursion was a good one because he was familiar with the majority of the Indian nations that populated the plains. The first detailed the journey from Santa Fe to St. Louis; the second from St. Louis back to Santa Fe. It is assumed that Vial stayed in Santa Fe to make his life. The last public record of him is found in the will that he signed on Oct. 2, 1814. His estate was settled on August 15, 1815 [*Santa Fe New Mexican*, 30 May 2009].

Vige, André. gunsmith. Baton Rouge. A Negro with several aliases was arrested and charged with stealing a revolver from Vige's shop several months earlier. Vige identified it as the one stolen about two months earlier. The robber had a nice double barrel shotgun he was trying to sell which is what aroused suspicion [*Daily Advocate*, 18 March 1886]. Unlocated.

Vinkin, William (1824--). gun- and locksmith. New Orleans. Census of 1870: William Vinkin, 46, locksmith, born in Holland; Virginia, 32, born in Prussia. Census of 1880: William Vinkin, gunsmith, 54; wife Sophia, 33, both born in Holland; son William, 3, born in Louisiana. Noted in city directories 1871 through 1876, usually as a locksmith. Not found after 1880.

Voebel, Charles (1822-1888). gun- and locksmith. 1852-88, New Orleans. Kit Gorman gave his date of birth as 1822; the Census of 1880 gave it was 1831. 1887, 30 Jackson Ave. Father of Frederick. Census of 1880, Charles Voebel, gunsmith, 50; Catharine, 46, wife, both born in Hesse Darmstadt; Louis, 16; Frederick, 14; Kate, 11; Louise, 8; William, 2, all born in Louisiana [Ancestry; Gorman; *Dirs*.].

Voebel, Frederick (1866-1925). gunsmith. 1885, 30 Jackson, New Orleans. Son of Charles [*Dirs*.; Census; Gorman].

Voebel, Jean B. gunsmith. 1872, 210 Chartres, New Orleans; same address as gunsmith Jean Baptiste Revol [*Dir*.; Gorman].

Vogt, Reinhard (1815-). locksmith. 1851, New Orleans; admitted to charity hospital with "remit fever" born in Prussia.

Wainwright, John. gunsmith. c.1809-1822, New Orleans. 1811, 45-7 South Levee; 1819, Conti St.; 1820-22, 20 Chartres below custom house. English [*Dir*.]. Census of 1820: John Wainwright head of household of two white persons, ages 26 to 44, one male, one female.

Wallace, James. armorer. Wallace was armorer to city guards, New Orleans. [*Times Picayune*, 22 October 1874; 26 February 1875]. There were many men by this name, none listed as smiths or allied trades.

Ward, John R. (1818-1880). gunsmith. Hempstead, Austin County. Census of 1860, John R Ward, 42. born in N.Y., value $1000; wife Mary Ann, 45, born in Tennessee. Census of 1870, John R Ward, 58, value $1000, son William H., gunsmith, born in Louisiana. John R. Ward, was born in County Cork, Ireland. He came to New York with his brother, (first name unknown), and sister, Fannie. He became a pilot on the Mississippi River. Eventually ended up in Lafayette, Louisiana, where he married a widow, Mary Ann Williams Kemper. They eventually moved to Hempstead, where they had one child, William Henry, born in 1854 [Ancestry].

Watkins, Edmund. gunsmith. 1869, residence 304 Jackson, New Orleans [*Dir.*]

Watkinson, E. J. (18270-1869). gun store. 55 St. Charles St., New Orleans. 1867 his partner Benjamin Dart died and Watkinson continued the store under his own name. Kit Gorman called this the most prestigious address for a gunshop or store in New Orleans. It is unclear if the store ever made guns or merely imported them. It sold some American made arms as well.

Watson, Charles A. (1807-). gunsmith. 1842, New Orleans; admitted in March 1842 to the lunatic asylum; born in Pennsylvania. Reason for incarceration: insanity and epilepsy; age 35.

Watson, Holland (1829-). armorer. Watson was a private in the 14th Louisiana Infantry. He enlisted at Camp Pulaski on June 30, 1861. He was born Scotland and was married. His occupation was occupation gunsmith. His residence was in Thibodaux, Lafourche Parish. His age when he enlisted was 32. For an unknown reason he was discharged in September 1861. [*Booth's Index*].

Watson, W. F. gunsmith and crook. Monroe, Ouachita Parish.

W F Watson, a gunsmith, and E J Davis, who worked for him, both living in Monroe, LA, have come to grief and are both now in the Monroe jail. They are two noted burglars who have been plying their nefarious trade of safe cracking in all the principal towns of north and middle Louisiana. They had a regular picnic of it. Watson fixed up the safes and Davis did the rest. This last one, when arrested, saved himself from being lynched by making a full confession of his deeds [*Meridional,* 18 June 1898].

Watts, W. T. (1837--). gunsmith. Shreveport. Census of 1870, ward 4 Shreveport: W T Watts, born in Georgia, 33, gunsmith; Martha, wife, 23, born in Illinois; W T, 4; Robert, 2, both born in Louisiana; Robert Cook, born in Illinois, 27, gunsmith. Not found before or after 1870.

Webel, Charles. gunsmith. 1853, Jackson St., New Orleans [Dir.].

Wehrmann, Henrietta Termier Dittrich (1834-1901). gun store. 1875-92, New Orleans. Widow of John F. Dittrich, she remarried to Herman Wehrmann. 1887, 75 Chartres. After 1892 she left the gun trade joining her second husband in the lithography business [*Dirs*.; Gorman].

Weiss, John A. (1842-). gunsmith. On 6 February 1862 at New Orleans John A. Weiss, born in Massachusetts, 20, gunsmith, enlisted in the 3rd Massachusetts Cavalry. Promoted to corporal on 1 May 1864. Mustered out on 19 May 1865 [*Massachusetts Soldiers . . . in the Civil War*].

Weiss, William. (1851-). gun maker. 1870-84, New Orleans. Census of 1880, William Weiss, 29, gun maker, born in Louisiana; Amilia, his wife, 24; Rosalee, 6; Mary, 5; William, 4; Georgiana, 2 . Among his several jobs he was an armorer for the Louisiana Field Artillery in 1884. In 1870 he worked for Louis Gerteis. In 1876 he had a shooting gallery at 82 St. Charles. 1878, lock- and gunsmith, 14 Commercial Place [Census; *Dirs.*; Gorman]. 1875, elected to Crescent Rifle Club. Ran shooting gallery at 80 St. Charles St. [*New Orleans Times*, 8 September 1875]. "armorer at Mechanics' Hall, won first prize among 200 competitors, shooting 14 or 15 offhand" [*Times Picayune* 7 July 1880; 1 August 1885]. Weiss invented a can opener [*Ibid.*, 16 October 1881]

West, William, Jr. (1778-1827). gunsmith. Natchez District, Spanish Louisiana [Family; Ancestry].

Weydert, Charles (1856—1936). wheelwright, blacksmith, locksmith, gunsmith. Bayou Sara, West Feliciana Parish. Charles was born on 10 March 1856. Boiler and gin stand repairing a specialty. [*True Democrat*, 5 December 1896]. Charles died on 11 May 1936 in Saint Francisville, West Feliciana Parish and was buried at Grace Episcopal Churchyard.

Wheeler, Albert W. (1847-1877). carpenter and gunsmith. 1874-77, St. Charles, New Orleans [Gorman; *Dirs.*].

Wieman, Albert (1829--1903). gun- and tinsmith. 1858-66, New Orleans [Gorman; *Dirs.*]. Census of 1860: Albert Wieman, 27, $4000 real estate, $1000 personal value, tin and hardware merchant; Lizzie, 25. Census of 1870: A Wieman, 36, tinsmith, $4000 real estate, $1000 personal value, born in Hamburg, Germany; E Wieman, 36, wife, born in Ireland. 1878, Albert Wieman, crockery and hardware, 68-70 N. Peters [Dir.]. Albert died on 15 April 1903 and was buried in Greenwood Cemetery [Find-a-Grave].

Wilson, George. armorer. 1861, Pelican Hook & Ladder No. 4, New Orleans [*Daily True Delta,* 20 January 1861].

Wiltz, Louis Clement (1849--1921). gunsmith. New Orleans. Usually most precise in all ways, this is by far the most obscure and inspecific listing in Kit Gorman's book. I have found absolutely nothing on Wiltz although Gorman said he was "a skilled gunsmith, having been trained by the leading gunmakers in New Orleans." On 26 July 1870 Louis C. Wiltz married L. Eugenie Ruffier in New Orleans. Noted in city directories from 1875 until 1918. Louis died on 30 January 1921 [Ancestry; Find-a-Grave].

Winders, Carl (1822-). locksmith. 1851, New Orleans. Carl was admitted to charity hospital. He was born in Hanover, Germany.

Winkler, Charles (1825-). gunsmith. 4th Ward, Morehouse Parish. Census of 1870 of New Orleans: Charles Winkler, 46, machinist, born in France; Louisa, 35, born in Baden, Germany; Louisa, 14; Clementine, 10; and Roseline, 1, all born in Louisiana. Census of 1880, Charles Winkler, born in France, gun smith, 55; Louisa, his wife, 45; Clementine, 20; Rosater, 11; Edward, 6. Charles Winkler, lock and gunsmith, Bastrop [*Morehouse Clarion*, 13 May 1881]. Not located after 1881.

Winkler & Ohle. blacksmiths and ferriers. Charles Winkler. William Ohle. Bastrop, Morehouse Parish.

Winkler & Ohle Blacksmith & Ferrier Shop. Bastrop, LA. The undersigned would respectfully inform the public that they have opened a shop at the Closson Old Stand and will do all work in their line such as repairing wagons, buggies, ploughs, etc. Repairing machinery made a specialty. We are also prepared to do all work in the lock and gunsmith line. Satisfaction guaranteed. Charles Winkler & William Ohle [*Morehouse Clarion*, 6 February 1880].

Charles Winkler, Lock and Gun Smith Bastrop, Louisiana. Will repair guns and pistols on short notice. Satisfaction guaranteed [*Morehouse Clarion*, 5 August 1881]

Winter, A. (1845-). gun maker. New Orleans. Census of 1880, A. Winter, 35, born in Germany, gun maker; C., 38, wife; Francis, 12; Peter, 10; Fred, 8; Albert, 7; Josephine, 2; Bertha Plaise, 46.

Wolfangel, William (1841-1875). machinist, black- and gunsmith. 1871-75, New Orleans. 1874-75, gunsmith at 260 S. Rampart St. [*Dirs.*; Gorman].

Wolff, Charles (1829-). locksmith. New Orleans; Census of 1860: Charles Wolff, 31, born in Baden, Germany; in the workhouse.

Wood, John. armorer. 1861, New Orleans, armorer to Washington Artillery [*Times Picayune*, 9 November 1861].

Yorston, Mathieu. armorer. Yorston enlisted in the 5th Louisiana Infantry on 9 May 1861. He was detached to the armory at Macon, Georgia, on 15 June 1862. He was captured on 20 April 1865 and paroled after the war.

Zabli, G. D. cutler. 1832, 92 St. Pierre, New Orleans [*Dir.*].

Zephernick, E. gunsmith. 1855-58, 18 S. Market St., New Orleans [*Dirs.*; Gorman].

The Society for Psychical Research in New Orleans set a trap for a ghost. "The next house was said to be haunted by the ghost of a one legged gunsmith who, according to tradition, had been murdered there by a Negro. He was heard by investigators stumping around the rooms, in the darkness of night. It was so strange and unratlike a sound that investigators did not believe that rats could have made it. Nevertheless, they set traps and that night caught 11 enormous rats. The ghost of the 'one legged gunsmith' was never heard again in that house, nor any other ghost." [*Columbus Sunday Herald*, 12 November 1899]

Zernott & Guardia. watchmakers and jewelers, gunsmiths. Thibodaux [*Thibodaux Sentinel,* 13 September 1882]. John Guardia was advertising alone in the *Sentinel* by 22 September 1883.

Confederate Manufactory

Cook & Brother. Ferdinand Cook arrived in New York from England, c.1840, at about the age of 16 and worked as a bondsman. He moved to New Orleans about 1845 and there learned the trade of metal crafting at the novelty works in Crescent City. He took employment as a city engineer in 1855, but was listed as an architect in city directories of that period. Francis L. Cook may have emigrated from England at the same time his brother arrived, c.1840, and worked as a commission merchant. About 1855 Francis moved to New Orleans, assisting his brother as a business manager in several enterprises.

When war came, the Brothers Cook displayed an ardent patriotism. They purchased the Fulton Warehouse on Fulton and S. Market Sts. in late 1861 and constructed a shop and installed machinery. They then operated the Cook & Brother Armory at 1 Canal St., New Orleans. Apparently the full cost was borne by the brothers. The initial investment in property, tools, and machinery was probably about $25,000. Had others financially supported their effort, it might have begun on a grander scale. As it was, they employed 27 men, many of whom Ferdinand trained himself. Initial production was probably about 10-12 guns per week. By January 1862, production had risen to about 20 rifles per day and the staff had increased to more than 400 men. In addition to the rifles, the armory manufactured musketoons, artillery muskets, and 3 band muskets. They also made artillery swords a saber bayonets for the rifles, musketoons, and artillery muskets. There was a rumor that they were going to manufacture General LeMat's patent revolvers but these were made in Paris and London and not by Cook. The initial production of rifles was delivered on state contract to Alabama. In 1862, the firm received a Louisiana state contract for 1400 pikes, although Union occupation may have precluded manufacture as well as delivery.

On 1 April 1862, the national government contracted with the Cook armory to manufacture 30,000 Enfield pattern two-band rifles complete with saber bayonets, sheath, and frog at $30 per stand. Delivery was to commence on 1 July 1862 and be completed by 31 December 1863. The government authorized the Ordnance Department to advance $150,000, with $55,000 being for the factory and $95,000 for tools and equipment. Allowing for the addition of the sword bayonets instead of spike type bayonets, the price was reasonably close to the contract price paid by the North.

Most C. S. contracts were optimistic concerning both the quantity to be delivered and the final delivery date, but in this case it might have been quite realistic save for three factors over which Cook had no control. First, there was a severe shortage of trained manpower which Ferdinand could only partially obviate by training the men himself. Many men whom he had trained were drafted into the army or state militia. Second, there was a severe shortage of both raw materials and transportation. Frequently, raw materials could be located, but the required military permit to obtain that transport were not forthcoming. Last, the Yankee navy arrived at about the exact moment the contract was finalized. Cook had insisted on the addition of an escape clause which allowed him to delay his deliveries if invasion threatened. The contract also guaranteed assistance in moving his men and equipment if he had to move from New Orleans.

With the assistance of the commanding general, Mansfield Lovall, their machinery was hurriedly taken away by boats up the Mississippi River toward Vicksburg. Had Lovall not given Cook priority, they would never have been able to commandeer all the boats necessary to move their extensive and heavy machinery. Ferdinand later reported that he had managed to remove all equipment from the armory, but that he lost all the tools and machinery from the machine shop. Cook also moved 130 tons of wrought iron and other raw materials and many parts of uncompleted guns. A schooner laden with additional raw iron and steel arrived just in time to join the flotilla moving toward Vicksburg. Reportedly, the schooner had bribed a Yankee guard $20 to allow it to pass through the canal he was guarding.

Upon arrival at Vicksburg, it was decided that this city, too, might prove untenable in the face of advancing Union forces, so the machinery and raw materials were unloaded and transported by land to Selma, Alabama. There is no evidence to explain why Cook did not establish there, and it is unknown whether Cook made the decision or whether it was superimposed from Ordnance in Richmond. In any event, after waiting a few weeks in Selma, he moved on to Athens, Georgia. Again, it is unknown how that town was selected. Athens was situated securely inland, had good railroad connections with Atlanta and other cities, and was populated by a considerable number of refugee Confederates from New Orleans. Finally, after many misadventures, they selected Athens, Georgia, as the city in which manufacture would again be undertaken.

Cook purchased Carr's old grist mill on Trail Creek, along with 25 outlying acres. Eventually, the Cook armory owned 240 acres of land. In addition to the factory itself, Cook had to construct housing for the men, some with their families, who had accompanied him from New Orleans. The total investment was about $300,000. The State of Georgia contracted with C. S. Ordnance and assisted the Cook Brothers to reorganize and extend their manufactory. Patriotic citizens contributed $145,000. Production resumed on 25 December 1862, Christmas Day. The renegotiated contract with the C. S. government specified 1 January 1863 as the first delivery date of the Enfield rifles Cook was making on contract.

By June 1863 the manufactory consisted of the following buildings: a three-story brick and stone flour and grist mill; a temporary planing and saw mill; a temporary finishing room; the main armory building of brick and stone construction, with two wings, valued at $90,000; a stone blacksmith shop; a race and break-head for water power to drive the machinery; a stone smokehouse and provisions storage building; and 85 acres of land. Machinery, both new and replacements for that abandoned in New Orleans, was purchased at a cost of $77,000. Suppliers included Hand & Son of Handsboro, Mississippi; Union Manufactory of Richmond; and the Athens Foundry and Machine Works. At that time, the total value of the physical plant, inventory, machinery, raw materials, and stock was $618,763.48. In January 1864 the Confederate government contributed an additional $100,000.

Cook clearly had the finest private armory in the South, whether in its original incarnation in New Orleans or afterward reconstruction in Athens. Nearly all gun barrels of the period were manufactured by bending iron skelps up and over a mandrel and then heat and hammer welding a seam that ran the full length of the barrel. Cook used 1.5 inch Swedish steel bars, heated and twisted, turned and bored, and finally rifled. This was known as the "Whitworth system," developed and long used in England. This virtually guaranteed none would burst either in the proving stage or in field use. On the other hand, many Cook rifles had weak main-springs, poor cones [percussion nipples], and hammers which, because of poor twist, did not hit upon the nipple directly. Army Ordnance made several recommendations for improvement. First, it suggested tempering the springs using charcoal instead of coal and tempering the other screws, specifically those in the tang. Last, it recommended using "go--no-go" gauges to assure perfect uniformity and fit of parts. This gauge system had long been used by federal inspectors, both in armories and in private contractors' facilities.

After the war, Francis Cook testified that the armory had manufactured between 3800 and 4000 arms at Athens. Cavalry carbine bearing serial number 7555 is shown in our first volume, suggesting somewhat higher production figures. Peak production of 600 per month could not be sustained because of shortages of labor, transportation, and raw materials. The firm also manufactured horseshoes, bayonets, agricultural implements, bayonets and sabers. One Cook naval cutlass has been reported. Cook also repaired various arms for Ordnance.

In April 1864, Colonel James H. Burton visited the armory and declared that it was ". . . the best fitted-up and regulated private armory that I have yet inspected in the [Confederate] States. . . . The establishment of the works reflects much credit upon the senior proprietor and he has exhibited a much better appreciation of the requirements of an armory than any other person who has attempted a like enterprise in the Confederacy." Burton recommended that Ordnance purchase the armory.

Late in the war, the government defaulted on payments, forcing Cook to suspend operations. Determined not to allow his armory fall without a fight, Ferdinand organized a local defense unit comprised of his employees. He sought a commission as colonel, with one as major for Francis, but was granted the rank of major, with his brother as captain. Their militia was placed under Colonel Rains of Augusta Arsenal. Although unhappy with the failure to receive the desired commissions, the Cook brothers forged ahead, preparing breastworks and even mounting a cannon obtained from Augusta. Cook's militia served with General J. G. Phillips at the Battle of Griswoldville, 12 miles east of Macon, on 22 November 1864. They then fought with C. S. forces at the Battle of Grahmville, S. C., in attempt to retain control of railroad lines from Charleston to Savannah. They joined the defense of Savannah and on 11 December Ferdinand was killed by a Union sharpshooter. Ordnance purchased the machinery and leased Cook's armory in January 1865 for $650,000 in depreciated Confederate currency, giving Francis bonds to cover the debt.

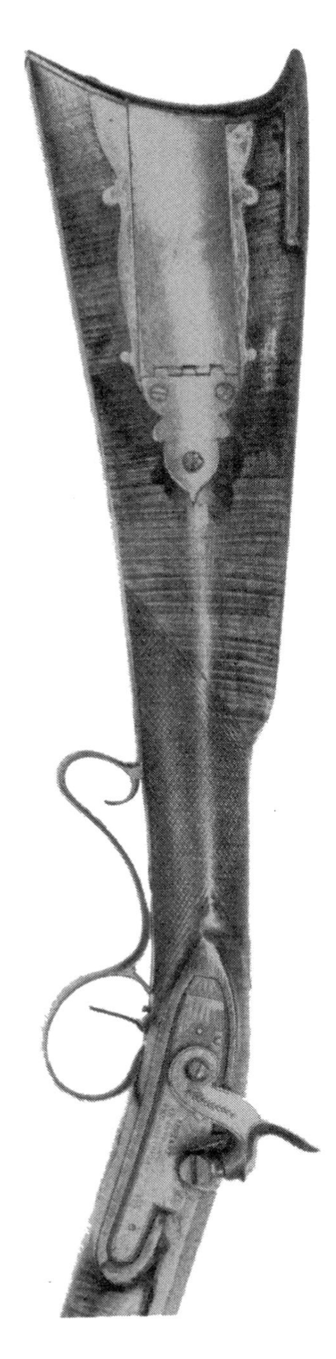

Valentine Libeau

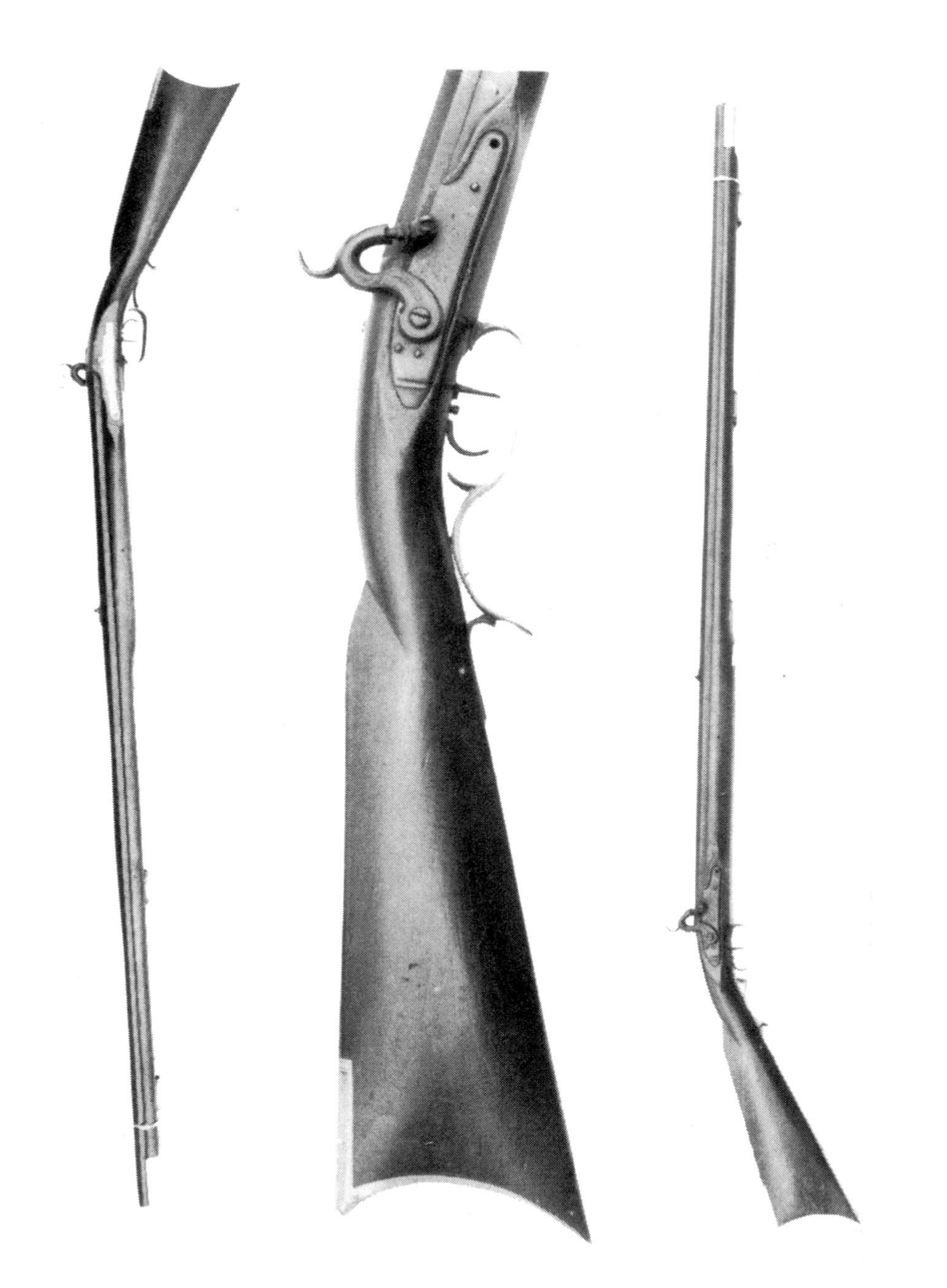

Valentine Libeau

Valentine Libeau

signed powder horn
probably made in Bedford County, Pennsylvania

Cook & Brother
serial number 634

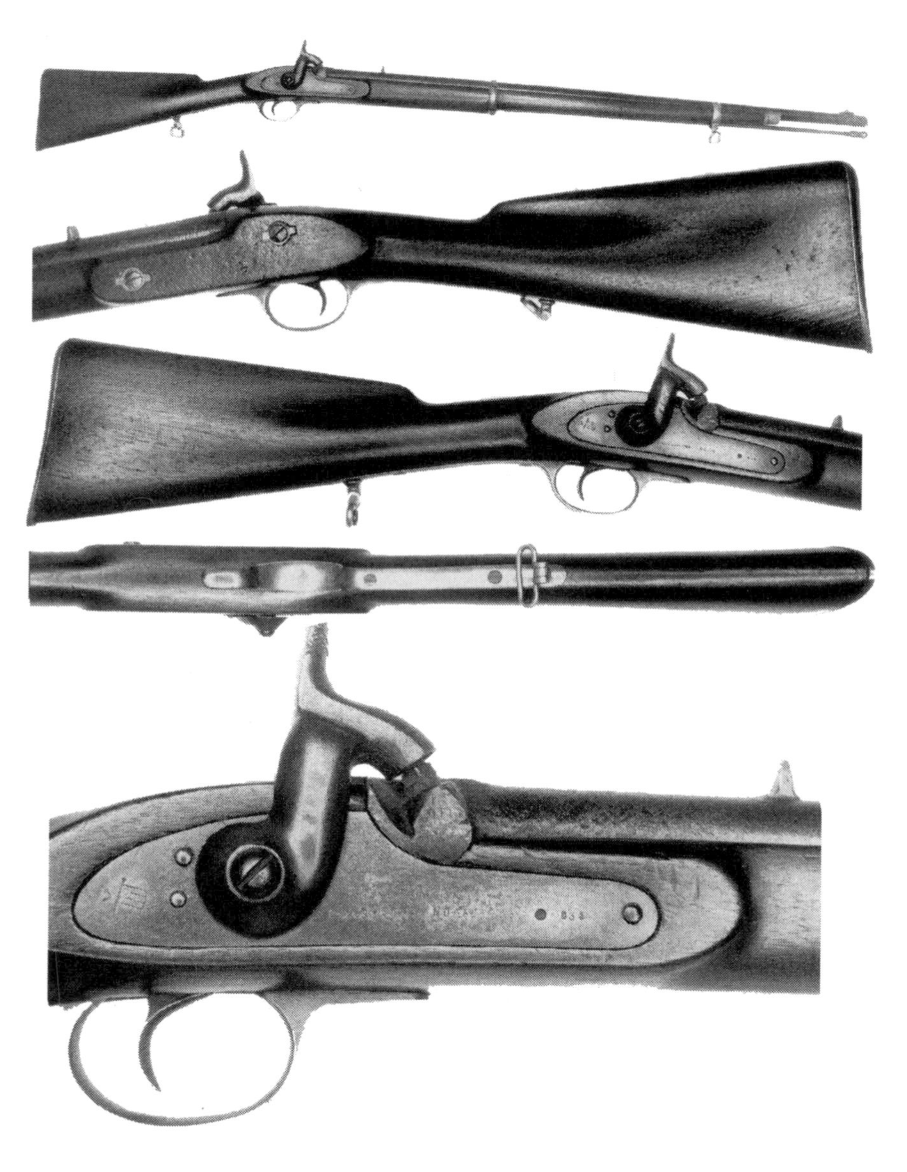

2 band rifle
made in New Orleans
Don Bryan Collection

Cook & Brother
made in New Orleans

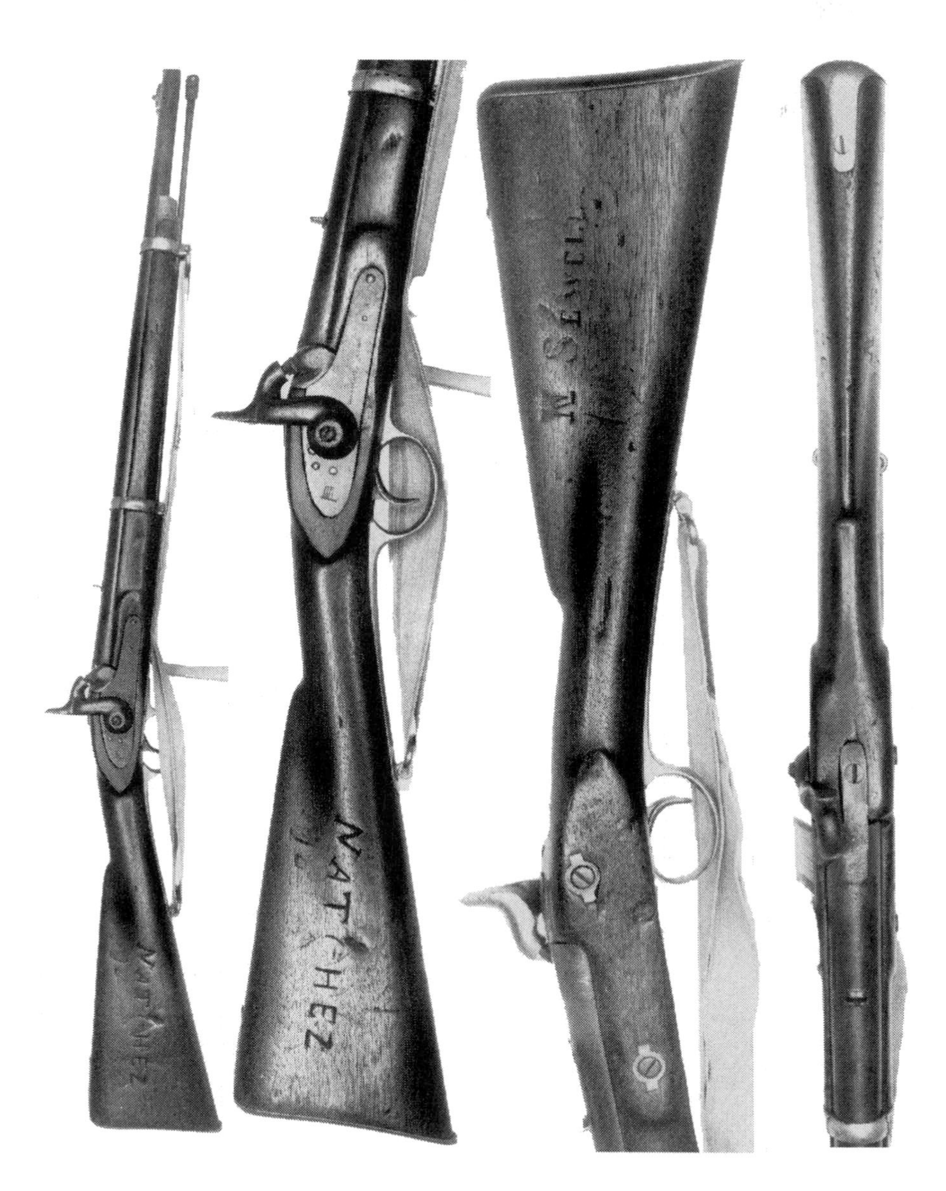

Cook carbine
Courtesy of Don Bryan

John Jacob Sheetz
maker of the rifle

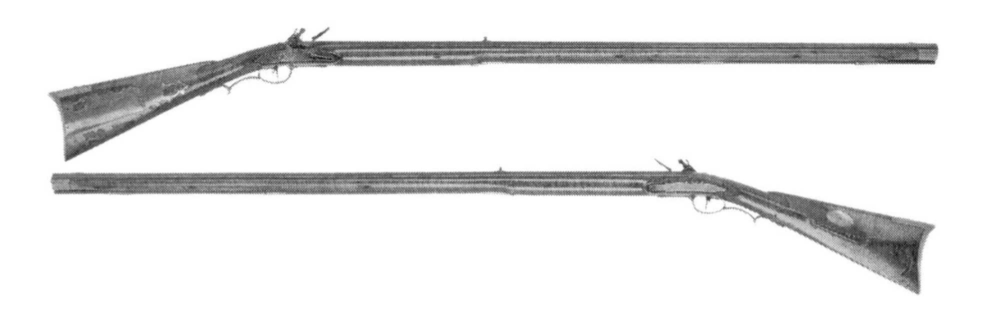

used by William Ross at the Battle of New Orleans
on 8 January 1814

Sheetz, John Jacob (1785-1860). gunsmith. Shepherdstown. [West] Virginia

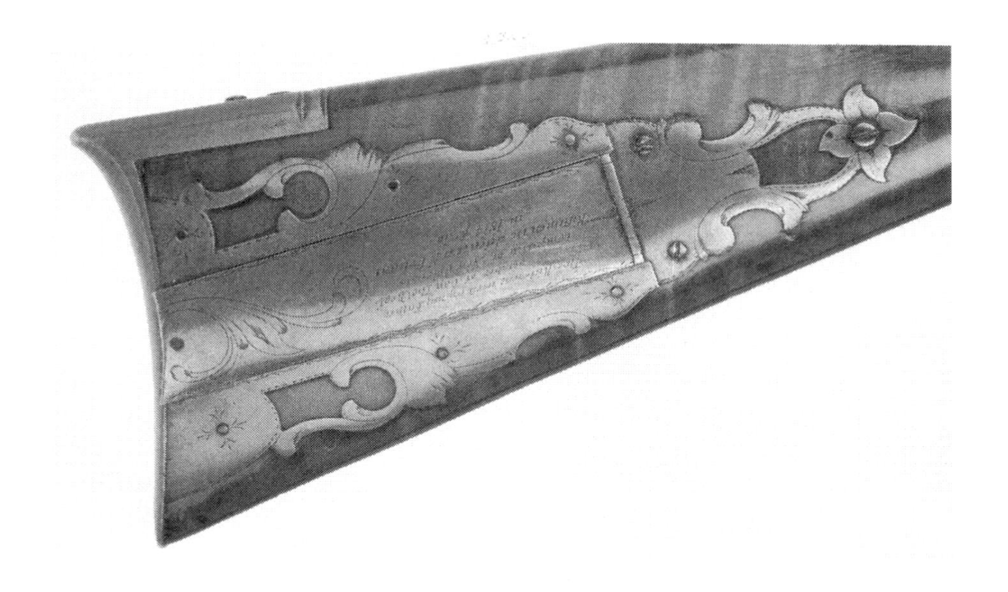

John Jacob Sheetz
"Battle of New Orleans" rifle

Marked Slocum
New Orleans marked gunlock

Close-up of Slocum, New Orleans flint-lock gunlock

Close-up of Cook & Brother gunlock
mounted on Enfield Pattern 1853 style Confederate rifle
1

Made in the USA
Columbia, SC
11 June 2018